TRANSITIONS

THE SPENCER SMITH STORY

Typeset by
Transition Sport

Front Cover Photograph
Delly Carr
SPORTSHOOT

Back Cover
Transition Sport

Printed and bound in Great Britain by
Cox and Wyman Ltd, Reading, Berks

TRANSITION SPORT

www.transitionsport.com

Dedication

**In memory of Bill Smith.
Larger than life and sadly missed by many.**

"I shared his last year with Bill and I saw him go through thirty seven visits for radiotherapy. I personally rushed him along with Barb to the hospital four times. I sat in a corridor at Charing Cross for twelve hours with him and we all saw him with the tubes and God knows what else in him, in hospital. Not once in this entire year with all that happened to him, did he ever whinge.
I am very proud to have known such a man."

Robert Burnell

Contents

Acknowledgements

In writing this book I would like to thank all of those who made it possible.

Bill Black for all his help, support and encouragement not just throughout the writing of this book but throughout my life and for helping me to achieve much more than I believed I was capable of or entitled to.

Robert Burnell for his open and heart felt accounts of the family, Spencer and himself, which gave me a true account of the emotions and traumas that the family had endured which at times had me laughing out loud and at others brought me close to tears when transcribing our interviews.

Stuart Coulson for his photographic memory and amazing ability to recall dates, times and places. I am still astonished to find that throughout my research that if Stuart said it was Tuesday at 2.35pm and the wind was south westerly, there seemed little doubt that he was right, top man.

Iain Hamilton, for his honesty and humour when relating to the numerous times that Spencer whooped him on the field, and his honest and frank interpretation of the feelings of both the British squad and the public when things on the field weren't so black and white.

Steve Freestone, for his London wit and tales of Spencer and Bill from the early days.

Rodolphe Von Berg for taking me at my word and trusting me sufficiently to give a full account of the trials and tribulations he had suffered at the hands of some of those who wield the power in the sport of triathlon, a true gentleman.

Ian Whittingham, for an insider view of the deals done at a business level, and an insight into some of the day to day activities of the sponsors.

Finally I would like to thank my partner Sibyl for putting up with my moods when the book was getting on top of me, tolerating me sitting at the computer for days and evenings on end and hardly saying a word to her when I became engrossed, and still supporting me and my endeavors irrespective of my sometimes obsessive nature.

DEFINITION - Transition
Oxford English Dictionary

'A change from one form or type to another, or the process by which this happens.'

DEFINITION - Transition
A Triathletes Guide

'A designated area where athletes are required to change from one discipline to another. Note. Nudity in the transition area is not permitted!!!'

PREFACE

There is little doubt that all of us have many people and events along the way that have an impact in our lives and those meetings in turn lead to transitions in our lives. Even sometimes things of which we are not aware can change our lives without us even being conscious of their existence or consequence. Other events can result in transitions that are so devastating and so manifest that they shake the very foundations on which we feel our lives are built.

This story of Spencer's life was not undertaken with the intention of showing what a great athlete he was and still is, all be that an undeniable fact. Instead it was undertaken to show how these transitions have occurred in the life of one of the most celebrated triathletes the world has ever known. Instead of referring only to the accounts of his life just through Spencer himself, this account also looks at his life through those people around him who saw his life unfold from the outside. Some of those people were extremely close to him and had a major impact on his life. Others were just bystanders or people who in the case of many an athlete, followed in his wake.

In addition, the nature of the events and other individuals who surrounded Spencer through those transitions are scrutinized in order to put his life within a contextual framework. In writing this book, the background research into the people in his life sometimes lead to a greater understanding of how they had come to be both involved in his life or the impact they had, and in those cases the book at times has retained detailed accounts of either the individuals or the events in question. In some cases however the book simply related to the feelings held by those who watched on, either in awe or in wonder.

'Transitions' is not only a book about winning or triathlon but also a book about life, about changes, about the ups and downs that make all of us individuals, about the choices that everyone has to make and the results and the consequence of those decisions. Whilst Spencer Smith is undoubtedly the central figure within the book, I have tried where possible to give a true and real account of the humour, sadness, accomplishments and failures that both he and those around him have endured.

Smith stretching out the field in Alanya 1993

TRANSITIONS ONE & TWO
The Early Days of Triathlon & From National to International

In the early 1970's millions of Americans were enveloped in the jogging craze, everybody was out there hitting the pavements, and in a country where it was not unusual for someone to drive ten yards to visit a neighbour, this was truly something quite extraordinary. But out in San Diego, which even then was the hard body center of the USA, some of the athletes had extreme ideas about keeping fit, and wanted to try something a little bit unusual. With an agenda on alternative and an American mentality that strived towards extremes in sport anything could happen in the so-called fitness boom and soon it did.

Whilst swimming and running events, were not an uncommon type of race, especially for running clubs that were based by the sea, these biathlons as they were called had not really captured the enthusiasm or the imagination of the runners. Instead these swim run events were seen more as a form of cross training that simply made a change from stomping the streets for hours on end, trudging the treadmill for what seemed like forever even if it wasn't, or constantly running in circles round an oval track. Even for the most committed runner there always appears a time in the season where the training is done out of commitment rather than enjoyment and a bit of swimming just added some variety where monotony could sometimes be the biggest hurdle.

In addition to the swimming and running, cycling was also a pretty common pastime among the fitness fanatics although cycle racing in the States would have to wait a further few years until Greg Lemond won the 1986 Tour de France before it would get the recognition it deserved as a sport. Even then many Americans would ask,.. The Tour de what?.... In a country that was obsessed with baseball and the NFL.

But in 1974, a group of Californians who some have been led to say, perhaps a little unfairly, were not good enough at swimming, running or cycling as individual disciplines to stick to one or the other, concocted a new sport. Despite some historical arguments to the contrary some more informed onlookers and insiders now led us to believe, perhaps rather than inabilities to perform at the top level at one event, it was most likely just a bizarre and warped opinion of what activities it would be nice to do on a Sunday when the sane and mentally hinged would be reading their papers, drinking their tea and eating their Weetabix, that led to the evolution of triathlon.

Not knowing that what they were doing was going to have a profound effect on sporting history a number of arguably misguided individuals from the San Diego Track Club, noting primarily Jack Johnstone and Don Shanahan conceived of a race, that combined three rather than the customary two events into one. Their race, a race that would have initially been two separate events, only came about as a result of the calendar chairman, suggesting that the two would be event organizers could combine their ideas so there wouldn't be too many 'weird' races on the schedule. Johnstone, having had the idea of a swim-run event and Shanahan having had the bright idea of a bike-run event. So this was how the first triathlon was originated, more by luck than by planning and more by error than by judgment. As a result of their meeting of minds, Johnstone and Shanahan would develop a race that would reduce swimmers to tears when they had to run, cyclists to panic when they found themselves all at sea without a big chainring in sight and all, even the most experienced and capable runners, to misery as their legs turned to jelly when attempted to completed their trial of tripledom, with legs of wood and sea water still stinging their eyes.

Promotion for the event according to common myth was a little bit erratic and perhaps not what we would expect today, with glossy brochures and online application via the internet but at this time Johnstone and Shanahan had to rely on a short advert in the September issue of the San Diego Track Club newsletter which read as follows:

RUN, CYCLE, SWIM: TRIATHLON SET FOR 25TH

The First Annual? Mission Bay Triathlon, a race consisting of segments of running, bicycle riding, and swimming, will start at the causeway to Fiesta Island at 5:45 P.M. September 25. The event will consist of 6 miles of running, (longest continuous stretch, 2.8 miles) 5 miles of bicycle riding, (all at once) and 500 yards of swimming (longest continuous stretch, 250 yards). Approximately 2 miles of running will be barefoot on grass and sand. Each participant must bring his own bicycle. Awards will be presented to the first five finishers.

For further details contact Don Shanahan or Jack Johnstone

It was a crazy event but then these were crazy times in America in 1974, Nixon had just become the first ever President to resign from office following the Watergate scandal, Mohammed Ali was about to regain his World Heavyweight title, and the American newspaper heiress Patty Hearst, who had been kidnapped earlier in the year by a revolutionary fraction was seen taking part in an armed raid.

It seems strange to consider now, that it was necessary to highlight the fact that competitors were expected to provide their own bikes but this after all was a new sport for everyone, with no apparent rules or at least only the broad outline of all start together and the first to cross the line is the winner. For a one dollar entry fee anybody could enter......so long as they had a bike.. Who knows perhaps Patty Hearst had been asked to bring her own gun.

To give an indication of how new the sport was, when trying to order the trophies. The people engraving the trophies called Johnstone and asked how to spell the word 'triathlon.' They were unable to find it in any dictionary and didn't want to make a mistake. It seemed at that point that the word must not exist, almost an evolutionary conundrum of which came first, the sport or the word, but fortunately for the sport, Johnstone was both literate and was not known to suffer from dyslexia or the world may have been forced to race something more akin to a trithlon or trathlon or some other weird and wonderful alternative.

Given the fact that neither Shanahan or Johnstone had ever put on a race before it was sure to be an interesting event, but their main concern prior to race day was ensuring they had sufficient entries to make the event viable. Whilst most of the club members were familiar with biathlons their major concern as promoters for this event was whether the inclusion of a bike leg might cut down on the entries received, a strange thought now, given the emergence of triathlon and corresponding decline in biathlon.

They needn't have worried. At 5:45 pm on race day forty six foolhardy but nonetheless enthusiastic contenders who had declared their interest and paid their dollar were permitted, if that is the right word to toe the line in anticipation. The number of entrants had somewhat surprised both Shanahan and Johnstone, leaving Johnstone to recall in his own words that numbers of competitors had, "significantly exceeded our expectations." So the race went ahead and during the event it would appear that if anyone had made a mistake it was not the engravers nor the promoters, but more likely some of the forty six entrants in being reckless enough to give it a go.

Despite the concerns initially voiced and much to the relief of athletes and promoters all seemed to go well in this inaugural triathlon, as the San Diego athletes swam, biked and ran, including interestingly, Johnstone who finished his own race in sixth place, and then helped with the officiating. And some time after the leaders had finished, well after dark, the, "last of the first triathletes," who had perhaps exceeded their own expectations, or not as the case may be, made their way across the inlet to the finish. The first triathlon had been swum, biked and run, and a new sport, all be it embryonic in form, was emerging.

Whilst the San Diego Track Club were racing their first triathlon in the far reaches of California, and the rest of the American public were practicing their John Travolta steps to Grease, about as far way from the sun and the sea and the sand as you could get, a young sixteen month old Spencer Smith, was tucked up in his cot in Hounslow on the outskirts of south west London. Some would say that young Smith had by default selected the much more preferable option, but little would his father Bill or his mother Barbara know, how intrinsically their lives would entwine with the world of triathlon and the city of San Diego as a result of their young son's future.

Spencer Smith was born on the 11th of May 1973, a year in which rail workers, civil servants, the Glasgow fire brigade, power workers and miners were all on strike. (More about Billy Smith later on this one.) The IRA were bombing central London, Picasso was drawing his last breath, Sunderland were beating Leeds in the FA Cup. (The first 2nd division side to win for 42 years.) Elizabeth Taylor was separating from Richard Burton. (For the first time…. I think.) Bruce Lee was kicking the bucket. Aborigines were granted the vote in Australia. The UK government was giving the go ahead for Channel Tunnel. (woops). Denis Healy was promising to tax the rich until, "the pips squeak." England were out of the World Cup. (Poland) The Arab Sheikhs were cutting the oil supplies and hiking the price by 100%. And in an attempt to take our minds off it all, Princess Anne and Captain Mark Phillips got married just before the whole of the UK industry was forced to go on a 3-day week as the miners continued their overtime ban.

Things generally around the time of, 'Smudger' Smith's (as he would eventually be nicknamed) birth, were not good in the UK, and having been born when the number one single was, tie a yellow ribbon round the old oak tree, it could be said that he could have been born in better times. On the bright side of life however, the average price of houses in London was just over £13,000 as compared to the £150,000 prospective buyers would have to fork out in 2001, Robert Redford and Paul Newman were staring in the blockbuster film, The Sting, and the cost of a pint was only twenty seven pence.

Born to Bill Smith a former professional footballer with Queens Park Rangers, (now a second hand car dealer) and his wife Barbara, Spencer was a big baby, but with a dad like Bill who stood six foot two with had hands like shovels, it was always unlikely that his genes would leave him wanting in stature.

Since 1973 was a time when Britain had achieved the unenviable reputation as the strike-happy epicentre of the universe, it was also a period when car sales were not at their peak despite the fact that a Ford Cortina (with obligatory furry dice) would cost about the same price as a moped at millennium prices. With the Cortina gaining the mantle of the king of the road, with an initial thirty five variations, ranging from the wheezy threadbare 1300 to the cosseting and zippy 2000GLX, complete with obligatory vinyl roof and trim. This was a time when literally millions of cardigan and flares-attired would be owners coveted such a gem and rushed eagerly part with their hard earned to own one, a number of them undoubtedly buying them from Spencer's dad Bill. But on the 11th of May, Bill would put the bonnet down for at least a few minutes because he had more urgent matters to deal with.

Robert Burnell, alias Bernie, who was Bill's closest and longest friend, recalled having visited Spencer's mum, Barb on the day that Spencer was born. "Bill said to me we've got to pop in and see Barb, she's dropped the nipper today." So big Bill Smith and his closest mate Bernie duly made their way into the entrance of West Middlesex Hospital where Billy recognized a friend Harry from the markets who was selling flowers outside. After making polite conversation and chatting about how difficult things were on the markets and Billy explaining that he was now a proud father, Billy thought it would be a good idea to get Barb some flowers.

Bernie recalled the story. "Billy said. Give us a nice bunch of that, that, that and that……. He said give us a tenner's worth, which in those days was a lot of money. So he's given him this great big bunch of flowers. Harry turned to Billy and said. 'That's a tenner Bill' to which Billy said. Remember that tenner you owe me Harry from two years ago and Harry went aaaagh. Done up like a kipper." Bernie laughed as he recalled the story. "Billy said that's handy, that's got that tenner back." It's a story that reflected the street wise and tough negotiating style of Billy Smith that would stand him in good stead in years to come when he would be negotiating over sponsorship deals, bike deals and racing contracts. Deals that would take place seventeen years later when little Smith junior would be swapping nappies for lycra and cribs for cycles.

Bernie and Billy had been the best of friends for some time and Bernie was used to Billy's ways, it had been something he had got used to on the first day that they had met some six years before Spencer was born. They had first met in 1968 When the Beatles were top of the charts with Hey Jude, the Americans were preparing to go to the moon and wine bars were just in the very early stages of popping up in the trendier parts of London. Their first meeting was in the Loose Reign Bar in Chelsea, which was one of the first wine bars in the area. Bernie came from Mortlake and he had a mate called Peter Mathews who told him he had a pal called Bill that was coming over from Hounslow.

"About an hour later this guy appeared in the door. It was packed this place. He filled the door, he had Rupert Bear check trousers on, he had another mismatched check jacket and he had the biggest hands in the world. And his face was beaming and he's gone. What's up! I've turned round and Peter's said to me 'that's my mate and I've gone, Fucking lose him quick! He looked like a clown at the door," recalled Bernie. The following morning after an all night party Bill offered Bernie a lift home in his Jag, and so started a life long friendship. On the way home, they stopped off for breakfast in café in Marble Arch. Billy always a consummate big eater, ordered a full English breakfast, but what Billy considered a full English breakfast and what the proprietor of the café considered a full English breakfast didn't seem to agree. According to Bill, a full English breakfast isn't exactly full or English without fried tomatoes, Billy asked the Indian owner if he could have fried tomatoes, but the owner looked a little confused by the request. Not to be put off, and never one to compromise, Billy then proceeded to go behind the counter and cook them himself, notably a practice that some restaurants now charge extra for as London vogue in the twenty first century moves from a help yourself to all you can eat, to a cook yourself all you can eat fashion conscious generation.

"I thought he's gotta be some kind of joker!" Recalled Bernie. But more entertained than embarrassed he continued to eat his breakfast and Billy soon rejoined him. "I said have you got a bird on the firm or anything. No he said. I'm married….. It's half past ten on a Sunday morning and I said but you've been with us all night at an all night party. He said yeah…. She won't reckon it too much." Whilst this story is not much related to triathlon, this also gives another insight into Billy Smith. Uncompromising, entertaining, always likely to go a little bit further than anyone expected.

Bernie and Bill hit it off almost immediately from then on. Like Spencer's dad, Bernie was a Londoner through and through, and had then as he has now, an immediately likeable, approachable and easygoing manner, caught up with a bit of mischief making and a bit of streetwise insight. At the same time Bernie was also not afraid to be outspoken, something of a personality trait that he shared with Bill that he has retained to this day, though if anyone could be more outspoken than Bill it was hard to imagine. If Spencer and Billy were hewn from the same rock then Bernie was certainly in the same quarry.

As the years moved on so Bill and Bernie became the closest of friends, and Bernie came to play an increasing part in the Smith family clan and eventually the management of Spencer's triathlon career. At the same time as the years moved on so Spencer would get older, and some would perhaps unfairly say that he also appeared to inherit his father's sense of fashion, that Bernie recalled so vividly.

So the story went, the naming of Smith junior was definitely a decision left in the hands of Barbara and in choosing a name for the wriggling infant his mother had chosen upon the name Spencer after American movie star Spencer Tracey. Spencer Tracy could challenge, charm, at the same time whilst inspiring audiences of all ages, so much so that Katharine Hepburn had once described him as, 'a people's star.' "His quality is clear and direct, ask a question-get an answer. No pause," she had once said of him. Perhaps that was what Barbara had also liked in Bill Smith's demeanor when she first met him. He was certainly a man of the people and direct and honest about both his views and feelings and now that was something she hoped that he would instill into their son…. And after all Spencer Tracy was spoken for so Billy Smith would have to do.

In naming the young Smith after her favourite actor who had made such movies as Fury, Captains Courageous, Boys Town, and Adam's Rib, movies that had made a permanent mark on Hollywood, the young Smith would have a lot to live up to. But in time the young Smith would make a permanent mark in another arena in the mean time he had some growing to do.

Whilst this insight into the naming of young Smith Junior, conjures up the high hopes Barbara had for their son, as always there is another side to the story and Bernie and Billy ever the jokers had another slant on the naming of Smith junior, which he and Bill had conjured up. "We always thought it was after Marks and Spencer," Bernie recalled. "She used to work in there, shop in there, everything, so we were sure it was Marks and Spencer, but it could well be. (The Tracy story)" Bernie roared at this one, which was obviously a long time joke between him and Bill.

Whilst Spencer was still in his nappies, news of the San Diego event emerged and increasingly more people became interested in this new sport but even then in the eyes of those who held true to their single discipline of running, and even in the opinion of the San Diego Track Club members, the triathletes were still seen as less than bona fide athletes. In a world where wearing the same trainers for fifteen years and a T-shirt that looked and smelt similar were signs of a seasoned and accomplished runner, the triathletes were just about as far removed as they could be. At least according to the runners. They were just a bunch of innovators caught in a new fad that would come and go as quickly as the space hopper or the pogo stick and to make it worse they were show offs, with their ostentatious bikes and dayglow lycra kit. And after all, they would never excel in running, or so it was said..... But a number of the triathletes clearly believed differently.

What with all the activities in San Diego, California was undoubtedly able to stake some claim to the founding of the sport, but for those who follow the sport of triathlon to its core, there is little doubt that in the heart of every fool who swims, bikes and runs to pass the time of day, there is in the present day a truth, and that truth is that Hawaii has become the real home to triathlon. With triathlon's Ironman roots clearly founded in Hawaii, the history of the extreme side of the sport is bound with tales of trials and tribulations which all stemmed from its initial long haul conception which is set to the backdrop of Hawaii. But on closer inspection it would appear that even the emergence of the Ironman even if only in terms of conception can claim to have its roots firmly planted in California.

would turn out, one of the competitors of the San Diego first hlon was a man called John Collins, who having enjoyed the event so much decided that he would expand upon its obvious potential and so it was that a US Navy Commander brought back the triathlon concept to Hawaii and in January of 1977 proposed what would become one of the most enduring and punishing sporting events in the world.

Following Collins's initial proposal in 1977 the official Ironman history started on February 18th, 1978, some four years after the first San Diego event, which as time moved on somehow began to pale by comparison.

It seemed somewhere between fitting and ironic that when the first Ironman was being staged in Hawaii, Warner Brothers were in the throws of launching the film Superman at the cinemas, since when US Navy Commander John Collins convinced the fifteen competitors, including himself, to wade into the ocean off Oahu there was little doubt that those who managed to finish the event were undoubtedly capable of superhuman feats.

On that fateful day, each of the entrants aimed to complete an event that would emulate the island's three toughest endurance races. But they would cover them in a single day! The Waikiki Rough Water Swim, the around Oahu Bike Ride and the Honolulu Marathon. The event, which had first been though up by Collins seemed ridiculous to many and few believed there would be any takers, but following weeks of planning and preparation, on that blustery February morning there was now no doubt that the event was actually going to take place and in doing so would start a new wave of extreme sport. The Ironman.

On the hand written instruction sheets that Collins distributed to the assembled athletes were the simple instructions: "Swim 2.4 miles, bike 112 miles, run 26.2 miles - brag the rest of your life!" He also told his inaugural field. "The gun will go off at 7.00am and the clock will keep running and whoever finishes first, we'll call the Ironman!" It all sounded so simple but nobody had any doubt that this would be one tough day.

Of the fifteen who started the race only twelve finished, but then that was still twelve more than many had expected to get round the course. The winner was twenty seven year old Gorden Haller, a former Naval officer and a seasoned and accomplished pentathlete, who crossed the line in eleven hours, forty six minutes and fifty eight seconds to beat former Navy SEAL John Dunbar into second place, whilst Collins himself came a creditable ninth. And it took some doing, without the sort of medical and support staff that are available today.

As triathlon and most notably Ironman gained in notoriety with the advent of the 1978 Hawaii race it was often claimed by those not party to its initial conception, that the race had been a result of a very foolish bet in a bar, but according to those who took part in both its planning and the competition nothing could be further from the truth. The Ironman had been a serious event from day one and according to Haller. "How could it not be serious?" With the event being held over such extreme distances: a 2.4-mile swim preceding a 112-mile cycle ride with a marathon to complete matters it seemed obvious to many that it was an event that had to be taken much more seriously than any other triathlon event in the world. Some would even say that the distances covered took any remaining fun out of the sport all together. If San Diego event seemed foolish then this Ironman event appeared complete and utter madness.

Whilst Ironman undoubtedly captured the imagination, it was the shorter distance triathlons that started to make a mass participation foothold in the 1980's but with it emerged evident resistance to the sport from some of the individual sports clubs who felt they were losing their identity and some of their most talented athletes. The interest for this innovative sport was too strong however to prevent the increased participation and its stature and reputation grew both in US and Europe where the triathlon scene continued to flourish, so much so that soon there was an abundance of events both in mainland Europe and in the States. The British scene was however a little slower to develop.

Whilst all this multi-sporting activity was going off in the US and Europe, climaxing with media footage of a young American college student by the name of Julie Moss, literally crawling the last hundred yards at Hawaii, as a result of fatigue and dehydration problems, only to be pipped at the post by Kathleen McCartney in the home straight, their British counterparts remained way behind the field and it would be 1982 before the Brits in the UK would even get a feel for the sport. But eventually they did and on Saturday 11th December 1982 the UK scene progressed when former Navy PE instructor and pentathlete Mike Ellis who had set up a local triathlon club, put on a race for a group of friends who were training for the Nice triathlon in France.

Nice at the time was an event of equal stature to that of Hawaii and despite the fact that the club, which Ellis had set up, was only small, (in fact a forerunner for Thames Valley Triathletes a club that is still in existence today) sufficient competitors were convinced into signing up and the race was staged in Reading where Ellis owned a health club. Whilst clearly not the first triathlon to be held in the UK it was however according to many, the starting point for the formalizing of the British Triathlon Association. (BTA)

Despite Britain's steady and somewhat belated beginnings with respect to the sport, it would only be a year later in 1983 that the first official BTA Championships were held at Kirton's Farm, once again near Reading when over two hundred wetsuit free bodies starting their 9am swim on a warm British summer day, and eventually a hundred and seventy three hardy souls finished the one mile swim, forty mile bike and thirteen mile run which the promotional literature described as, "short course."

The British media however paid little attention to this new sport in the UK, remaining then much as it does today focused on a small number of high profile professional sports like soccer, cricket and rugby, but the Times did at least cover the race all be it briefly with an article that they headlined 'is it a Spitz?, is it a Merckx? Is it a Zatopec?' At this time in fact the British media was much more concerned with the build up to the national elections which saw the Tory Party led by Margaret Thatcher get re-elected some four days after the race in the wake of the previous year's Falklands war and the ongoing IRA bombings in London, so there had been little room for triathlon on the front page but the swimmers bikers and runners continued resolutely with their campaign for recognition in the UK.

In Europe however things were a little more progressed in the sport and this was the same year that the triathlon guru, Mark Allen won his first Nice triathlon having only taken up the sport a few months earlier. By this time the Hawaii Ironman had been running for nine years with Dave Scott picking up his third title, and Hawaii was a name synonymous with the sport. Unfortunately the slogan, "Reading, home of British triathlon," didn't have the same ring to it and didn't conjure up an image that the British media were particularly enthused by.

As triathlon in Britain progressed slowly, so it continued to soar in the USA and Europe which brought as it always does the development of administration and organizations whose job it is to oversee the sport for the good of all. So in 1984 the European Triathlon Union or ETU was formed quickly setting up short, long and relay championships that would take place the following year.

In contrast the British calendar consisted of a mere twenty five events, and the sporting media perhaps justifiably took little notice of what was happening in Reading, Lincoln and Brighton but was instead transfixed by the Los Angeles Summer Olympics which saw an almost all out boycott by the eastern block countries, and the South African runner Zola Budd, racing under a British flag, sensationally tripping up America's golden girl Mary Decker in the 3,000 metres, whilst Sebastian Coe had brought athletics to the fore on a more positive note by winning gold in the 1500 metres just edging out Steve Cram.

By 1986 things had moved on in the UK and at least some sense came to the BTA who allowed wetsuits for the first time, recognizing the fact that safety issues and the dangers of hypothermia somewhat overshadowed the necessity to perpetuate the tough man image of the sport. Nevertheless their use was restricted to the sleeveless and short legged type, shorties as they have long been described in order to prevent athletes gaining a buoyancy advantage of a full suit.

These were undoubtedly hardy athletes in hardy times, but given that the sport had been born, developed and flourished in countries where the climate was significantly more appropriate to open water swimming, this change of rules seemed a fair compromise and showed a significantly more intelligent view, than had perhaps before been permitted by a tough group of extremists. Perhaps the fifty or so swimmers that had to be pulled from the hundred and twenty strong field at the previous year's Long Course Championships in Holme Pierrepont Nottingham had been a factor in the BTA recognizing the danger from hypothermia when swimming in the British waters, or perhaps they were just going soft! The viewpoints at the time it would appear were divided.

In terms of performance, if there was to be either a British male or female triathlon star at that time, then it had to be Glenn Cook who won both the British Long and Short Course Championships and Sarah Springman who did likewise in the female category. If they were stars however they received little recognition for their exploits outside of a very small and closeted triathlon community based primarily in the south of the country.

By 1987 the sport in Britain was expanding more solidly and the BTA membership had reached 1,700, with full wetsuits being permitted for the first time, strangely enough to come in line with both the ETU and American rules. The sport was gaining momentum with a much fuller calendar and an increasing number of more high profile media athletes entering and promoting the sport from other fields, such as ex Olympic swimmer Robin Brew who won the Grand Prix for the first time whilst Glenn Cook continued to dominate the long distance races winning the European Long Course. At this time however there was no sign of the young fresh blood that would eventually dominate the sport but a year later a young Londoner was to start to change all that.

Smith had started life as a swimmer but by the end of 1988 he had given it up. Having come third in the 400m and ninth in the 1500 metres at the National Championships Smith became both disillusioned and bored. To reach that standard Smith had been training over ten sessions a week putting in long distances but had not achieved what he wanted to. "I started swimming competitively at four years of age." Smith recalled. "When I was twelve I was in the pool at 5:30 to 7:30." Even then Smith was highly competitive. He admitted later that he was extremely disappointed in the outcome of all that training and didn't feel he could put in another year of the same kind of training. "When I was swimming over ten times a week with little of no recognition I just decided one day, I'd had enough."

The young Londoner had done a bit of running, primarily as part of his training for swimming, but just the odd three mile run here and there. Nothing serious, nothing structured. Prior to 1988 swimming was all he had focused on, but he wanted a change.

That change came about when he was introduced to the Thames Turbo Triathlon Club who were based at Hampton open air pool about four miles from his native Hounslow. The club had first been initiated by a certain Peter Moysey some three years earlier whose idea of training was to get a bunch of local elite athletes to swim in the Thames at Kingston, run three miles back to the pool and then go on a forty mile bike ride. The club would over a period of the next twelve years produce some of the finest triathlon talent that the world would ever see.

One of the other coaches at the club was Steve Freestone who recalled seeing Smith in the pool for the first time. "I was coaching another very good junior, a lad called Daren Chandler, and he used to tell me some times that this kid was doing, but like you do I thought this kid was spinning yarns. That was until I went down to the Kingfisher pool and this lad was virtually lapping Darren who was a very good swimmer and would be swimming sixty two for a hundred (meters) free. Spencer was swimming about fifty seven, or fifty eight seconds which at that age was pretty awesome."

There was little doubt that Smith's swimming strength was something that would hold him in good stead within the triathlon community in its early years since in the sport at this time you could become an accomplished triathlete by having one major strength and relying on it to pull you up the finishing order, but Smith was not one to only want to excel in one of the disciplines and was keen even then to improve on his running and biking.

Whilst Smith was starting to get involved in the sport throughout 1989 so the sport was starting to take itself seriously. Epitomized in its formative years by the Hawaii Ironman, the monstrous 140-mile endurance test, the events more acceptable distances saw the majority of races slimmed down after the International Triathlon Union was formed in 1989, with the standardized distances they settled on consisting of a 1.5km (0.94 mile) swim followed by a 40km (25 mile) cycle ride and rounded off with a 10km (6.25 mile) run. With these standard distances, the less crazy officials of the International Triathlon Union claimed they had tried to put some of the fun back into the sport, making it more accessible to a wider audience, which they inaugurated with the staging of the first official World Championships in Avignon, France, which saw New Zealander, Erin Baker, and the USA's Mark Allen taking the titles so emphasizing it truly was an international sport.

Despite the UK's slow beginnings, the men's runner-up in Avignon, was British athlete Glenn Cook, so the Union Jack showed itself from year one of the World Championships and if this was thought to be and indication of things to come, it would seem to be an accurate one as things would get even better for Great Britain over the next decade with British athletes Simon Lessing and Spencer Smith securing six titles between them in the eleven subsequent championships, a sure sign that despite its humble beginnings in the UK, the sport was to be firmly embraced by the British at the elite end of the scale.

In 1989 however, Smith was still only just learning what a bike was, whilst Lessing was just making his way out of South Africa in an attempt to avoid being conscripted into the National Service. Lessing had been born in Cape Town, South Africa on 12th February 1971 with Table Mountain and a regime of apartheid the backdrop to his formative years. With a mother who was a swimming coach Lessing had a good start but nevertheless was born into a country that continued to suffer from political turmoil. Only a year earlier in 1970 International Olympic Committee (IOC) had refused recognition of South Africa whose participation had been suspended since 1964, an act that would in time have a pronounced affect on the young South African's future.

Throughout the period that Lessing was growing up, the continued struggle and unrest of the black South African community had been heightened throughout the seventies culminating in some of the worst violence South Africa would see in 1976 when a hundred and seventy six people were killed during running battles between blacks and the police, violence that would be reinforced, when the black consciousness leader Steve Biko died in 1977 whilst in police detention with thousands attending his funeral.

Violence continued to plague Lessing's homeland and despite widespread political condemnation of apartheid, the South African government continued to be defiant of outside influence and political pressure and during the 1980's the struggle against apartheid in South Africa intensified tremendously resulting in an unprecedented number of anti-apartheid organizations springing up both in South Africa and in other countries throughout the world, with these groups initiating and coordinating many of the campaigns against the apartheid government. The South African Government responded to this opposition by introducing highly repressive measures, including schools and residential areas being segregated, whilst major efforts were made to indoctrinate white youth through school programmes like cadets.

Despite being brought up in such oppressive and volatile times, Lessing had as normal an upbringing as was possible in such a country and was a keen sportsman. Apart from his mother, his swim coach was one of the first adults to recognise Lessing's multi-sport talent, and with encouragement from the two of them, at the age of fifteen Lessing raced his first triathlon and progressed so quickly from there that by 1988 he was the South African Triathlon Champion and had been awarded national colours.

It should be said that whilst the majority of white South Africans made no effort to look beyond the lies and propaganda that was being fed to them, Lessing like many young educated South Africans was not happy living within the confines of the inherently unjust and unacceptable South African political climate, and with the apartheid state effectively eliminating any opportunity for international sporting competition as a result of the maintenance of its political agendas, Lessing felt he would have to leave his homeland if he was to achieve any form of international recognition.

Lessing had made sporting sacrifices for his beliefs even earlier in his career, which included pulling out in protest of a major athletics meet in 1987 when he was only sixteen, when a black pupil from a privately run church school was prevented from participating, and it was not unsurprising when a year later the opportunity to follow his own path in sport, proved stronger than his ties to his homeland. So it was that in November 1988 having completed high school, Lessing left his native South Africa to in part to escape the political regime and in part to avoid being conscripted into the South African National Service but more primarily, in order to fulfill his athletic dreams in Europe.

Since Lessing's mother had been born in England he was eligible for British Citizenship and headed to the UK in search of the opportunity to race. Bizarrely it would be a day before his nineteenth birthday, on February 11th 1990 some two years later that the first symbolic signs of the South African Government conceding to the demands of the rest of the world would manifest themselves when Nelson Mandela was released from prison after twenty seven years.

Meanwhile back in the UK the preparation for the National Championships were bearing down. Spencer hadn't raced any major races then, he'd raced at Hampton Pool and done a few biathlons and a few of the other low key races, but he wasn't really known on the circuit. But soon his face would be known a little better. The National Championships took place in 1989 at Holme Pierrepont, which was the first time Iain Hamilton ever saw Spencer Smith. It was a meeting not to be forgotten at least by the local Nottingham youth. "My first memories of Spence are really memories of his dad, I'd never met him before, I didn't know him from Adam," recalled Hamilton. "I had been doing triathlon for a year possibly two, and I didn't really know much about the competition because the junior scene wasn't really up and running. I was sixteen and I felt I was doing quite well because I was racing senior events and winning senior races. I hadn't heard about anybody from the south doing so well."

Whilst the National Junior title was up for grabs, because the number of athletes in that category was so small, the junior athletes found themselves racing in the same wave as some of the senior competitors, which meant some of them were four years older than

Hamilton, hence there was a degree of confusion out on the course as to who was in whose age group. "All the way through the race all you could hear from the spectator seating was this cockney voice going. Go on my son! Go on, Go on, Go on my son!" Recalled Hamilton. "And it was bloody annoying. In the end the race was won by Mathew Belfield and this cockney guy's lad, 'My son!' got second. I finished fifth overall and I was chuffed to bits. I thought I had won my category, which was the under seventeen category. I looked at all of them and they all had stubble. I looked at everyone and it was like. Yeah I've won it, I'm National Champion. I was chuffed to bits."

Hamilton was over the moon but his celebrations were soon to be short lived when he found that, 'My Son' was in the same age group. "It came to presentation and the guy that got second was my age, He could have had a full beard," laughed Hamilton. "It was Spencer. That was probably the only chance of me actually beating him in a race. After the race I heard that he had just packed in swimming to concentrate on triathlon, that was when he wasn't a brilliant biker and he wasn't a brilliant runner, but he was a little bit better than me at the time"

Considering the sport was still small in the UK at the time it was perhaps a little surprising that Hamilton had not raced Smith before, but Smith was the new kid on the block and they lived opposite ends of the country so Hamilton had never paid much heed to him before or during the race, but from then on would be paying him special attention. "Because Spencer was from the south I'd never come across him. You eye up your competition don't you and he wasn't somebody I was worried about, I was only interested in people who'd just reached puberty like me really. I never ever won a National Junior Champs because from then on I raced against Spencer in every one. They changed the rules a couple of years after so you couldn't win a junior award and a senior award, because Spencer would win the race overall so he'd get the senior and the junior."

It was about this time in 1990, that Billy Smith realized that he could support his boy better if he got involved in the promotion and sponsorship side of things. Ever the entrepreneur Smith senior set up a race in his local area. "It was like a novice race," recalled Freestone. "Bill was a second hand car salesman and everyone was trying to work out if he was trying to earn some extra wedge out of it." Freestone laughed. ... "Or whether he was doing it for the good of the sport"

As it turned out it Bill as ever had his fingers in a few pies and was doing it as a promotion for the health club. Spencer was using the gym at the Metropolitan Club for free and part of the deal was that Bill would organize two biathlon races involving a 400 metre swim and a 5km run, and an 800 metre swim and a 10km run. With both events starting at Hampton pool and ending up at the Metropolitan Club it was good business for the gym and an opportunity to promote the club to the swimmers, runners and triathletes who lived in the area and Spencer could continue using the gym for free. One of the things about Bill was if there was a deal to be done, he would do it.

Sponsorship wasn't a big thing in 1989 and 1990 and whilst Spencer was supported by Evans bike shop with some free kit, which was a sure fire improvement for the lad who at the start of his triathlon career knew nothing about bikes or position, and had to borrow an old Raleigh from friend. Even then the bike he was riding was not set up for triathlon or time trailing but instead had relaxed angles intended for comfort rather than speed. Coming from these humble and inexperienced beginnings, it would be a few years before Smith would get a thirst for and understanding of the importance of selecting the right equipment to perch his butt on.

Even though the sport was still pretty small in Britain, and at that time and you would have been forgiven for believing that most of the athletes would have known each other personally, the 1990 European Championships was actually the first time that Great Britain had a junior team and as there had only ever been two Junior Championships in the UK prior to this meeting, this was in fact the first chance that many of the squad had to meet up with each other.

So it was that the first mass meeting of the GB triathlon clan, took place at in the less than salubrious King's Cross bus station in June 1990, a few days out from the European Championship finals which were taking place in France at Mountlucon.

"Everyone was clambering along the bus to get a look at Spencer, because he'd just finished third at Swindon," recalled his then teammate Stuart Coulson. "A couple of weeks before the European Champs, Spencer had raced down at Swindon in an Olympic distance. He was only about seventeen but despite that he had come second to Glenn Cook, That was just a few years after Cook had got second at the World Championships in Avignon. Nobody was expecting Smith to achieve that. Everyone knew he was good, but Mathew Belfield was also good at the time. Spencer had taken a massive step forward. Coming second to Glenn Cook was like as good as coming top ten in the worlds as a senior at the time."

Matt Belfield had raced him the year before at the National Juniors in Nottingham but for many of the others like Stuart Coulson who was also in the GB squad who had a couple of years advantage on Smith, this was their first look at him. "I remember thinking that he was really big, and so was his dad," Coulson recollected. "He was always a different physique to everyone else, he was just huge. He was like one of those mid west farmer's kids who when you asked him to move his truck would lift it up and move it. He had huge, huge hands and I remember thinking if only I had hands like that. They were like paddles, no wonder he could swim."

Stuart Coulson's father, Peter Coulson was GB Team Manager at the time and Smith introduced himself. Coulson recalled him being exceptionally polite when he was introduced, "almost meek and mild. Not at all what you would expect." But when it came to the racing meek and mild was not a description you would have given Spencer when he was one of the three hundred juniors going to the lake for a two o'clock start. If his previous domestic performances were anything to go by, then Smith was not to disappoint when it came to International races.

Whilst in June of 1990 the French were leading way in banning British beef imports throughout Europe, the British contingency were by comparison exporting their best triathletes across the Channel in the hope of bringing home the bacon, and they were not to be disappointed.

"All the juniors were together so like we were seventeen racing against twenty year olds. There were three hundred people in this wave," recalled Hamilton who was also racing, "Spencer was starting to look like a professional athlete, where as the rest of us were only starting to get any sort of semblance of professionalism."

The swim was a tough fought battle and despite his general inexperience at this level and his relatively recent move to triathlon Spencer had lost none of his swimming abilities but it was Stephan Poulan and Francois Chabeaux of France who came out of the water together with Spencer just behind them.

In the early days of his transition to the sport, Smith would have got to the front on the swim and then endeavored to hold off his opponents but at a European level the competition was much more fierce, which meant Smith couldn't rely on such tactics. Nevertheless, working hard on the bike and the run Smith steadily pulled clear of the to French athletes and by the end of the race took the tape comfortably with none of the competition even within sight. "He like destroyed everyone," recalled Hamilton. "He was minutes and minutes and minutes and minutes in front. We were in the same race but I never saw him, honest I never saw him."

In his first ever international race Smith was the first youth by two or three minutes from the young Norman Stadler who would go on to take third in the Ironman Hawaii 2000 some ten years later, and had made a debut that had acted as a warning shot to not only the juniors, but also some of the senior athletes as well.

Whilst the young Smith was taking the glory at the European Junior Championships in a race over the same circuit, which was part of the French Grand Prix series a young South African by the name of Simon Lessing was also taking first prize in the male Senior Open Grand Prix race having not been selected for the British team in the European Championships.

The win at the Europeans showed that Smith had moved on even in the last month since the Swindon race, but there was still a lot of rough edges to Smith's performance and whilst he raced with more guts, determination and brute strength than many with much better technique out of the water could muster, standards were improving in the sport, and technique was sure to play an increasing part as the sport developed.

16th July 1990 National Junior Championships, UK

Three weeks after taking the European title Smith returned to home racing to stake his claim and retain the National Junior title at the National Watersports Centre in Nottingham the home of his first National Championship title a year previously. Still the strongest swimmer in the junior field, He led throughout the five hundred metre swim on the flat smooth lake but was caught on the nine mile bike circuit by Matt Belfield and Julian Bunn both of whom were exceptionally strong bikers.

It appeared however that they had worked too hard on the bike and Smith soon found himself regaining his lead throughout the final three mile run, beating Belfield by over half a minute. An important psychological battle as well as race had been won by Smith who despite getting on well with both of the other athletes was determined to let neither of them have the better of him either on or off the field of play, after all it was a small community and he would be facing them again continually throughout the rest of the season. If psychologically demoralizing for the juniors it must have been even worse for many of the seniors as his status within the senior rankings also continued to impress, with him consistently beating athletes five and ten years his senior.

If his ability to outperform the majority of the seniors was open to question then some three weeks later on 6th August at the Senior National Championships at Emberton Park the newly crowned European and National Junior Champion had the chance to silence any doubters when he took on the seniors and proved his pedigree against Britain's best. Despite a strong field from all over the country Smith had hoped to take home a second gold and whilst on this occasion he didn't top the podium he once again impressed with his performance when he placed second behind Robin Brew beating the 1989 National Senior Champion Rick Kiddle to a silver medal. Not a bad result at all for a seventeen year old kid!

In the one and a half kilometre swim Chris Humpage had exited the water first in just under seventeen minutes followed closely by Brew and Smith. Whilst Brew and Smith had been taken off course by a swim marshal, it didn't take to long before they regained the lead with Brew eventually pulling away on the bike, and leading all the way on the run to finish. But Smith whilst accepting of his second place always wanted to be first. He had dug in and beaten many of the top seniors and that counted for a lot but he wanted a senior title for himself.

For the first time but not for the last, he found his face on the front cover of 220 Magazine, a specialist triathlon magazine in Britain. It was the beginning of his recognition for many in the UK it was apparent that Smith whilst remaining a junior had well and truly made his mark on the seniors.

20th August 1990 National Sprint Championships, UK

On a wet and windy Sunday in Wakefield Smith got his second opportunity to go for a senior title but this time over the sprint distance. Once again however the youngster from London was to be foiled by the older athletes as honours were taken by Glenn Cook, Richard Hobson and Mark Marabini respectively.

"His bike had always been the really weak thing," recalled Coulson, but over a few months Smith had worked harder than ever on his training and by the time he got to the end of the season the improvements made to his racing were significant. "He'd certainly gone from pretty shit in April, relatively speaking, to being good in the middle of May, and being very good at the end of June to being bloody good in August." Coulson laughed, "it was just demoralizing for the juniors."

But despite all the training that Smith had been putting in it had not been enough to put him ahead of the older elite athletes even though it had greatly improved his performance. Many put Smith's improvement down to what could be called a 'swimmers mentality of work ethic' but there was still something missing. The tenacity with which he focused on his training was unquestionable, but it would be a couple more months before he would find someone who would build on that tenacity with a more methodical and scientific approach to his training.

Whilst the cover of magazines was nice a TV appearance was even more exciting for a sport that was still exceptionally young in Britain, and the Portsmouth triathlon had secured television coverage on BBC Grandstand, which was a big coup for the sport in the UK. With all the publicity surrounding the event all the names were there and Smith was determined that this would be where he would break through the elite ranks whilst the rest of the Smith family always present at his races, waited to see their boy perform for the cameras.

A proven strong swimmer there was never any doubt that Smith would be in the lead group on the swim and exiting the cold sea in front of a huge crowd Smith found himself in fourth place within feet of the leading seniors, Rob Barrel, Robin Brew and Chris Humpage, so far it was going to plan as he headed into transition but within a few yards on the bike Smith looked horrified as the tell tale whir of sluggish rubber on tarmac and accompanying wheel wobble told Smith he was out of the race. He had punctured. "My first ever puncture and it had to be on telly," complained Smith later. His frustration was manifest. Already a showman, his opportunity for a star performance in front of a huge crowd and one of the biggest television audiences the sport had ever had in Britain and he had barely got through the first discipline.

At this point in his career not one to be to concerned with his nutrition he was sitting eating chips on the side of the road before most of the rest of the field had even got on their bikes, his family and his chips having to act as consolation. Whilst clearly disappointed, Smith knew however there were bigger fish to fry as the last event in the 1990 calendar was to be the World Championships in Orlando Florida. Only a few weeks away in September.

15th September 1990 World Championships, Orlando, USA

At this race though Smith met with Lessing for the first time formally, they would not be racing each other. At nineteen years old Lessing would be the youngest competitor racing in the men's elite field, whilst seventeen year old Smith would be racing in the juniors.

For Lessing, racing in only the second ever World Championships and his first, the prizes were eventually to be denied him by the ever present Australian elites who dominated the elite race. Whilst Lessing was only just behind the leaders on the swim, he was unable to bridge the gap on either the bike or the run, eventually finishing in seventh place behind the antipodean trio of Greg Welch, who crossed the line in 1hr 51 min 37 sec, Brad Bevan in 1:52.40 and Foster in a time of 1:52.47. At nineteen the young South African racing under the British flag should not have been too disappointed with a time of 1 hour 53 minutes and 49 seconds he had certainly not disgraced himself.

The junior race in fitting with the junior title, was held in the Walt Disney Park grounds much to the amusement of many of the spectators, with a start area consisting of a pen around ten metres square in which all the competitors were held like prisoners before the swim. There was deathly silence thirty seconds before the start as the nerves started to set in amongst the juniors in what was undoubtedly the most important race that any of them would start at least in this season. Then suddenly, out of the silence boomed an unmistakable London voice. "Go on my son... sock it to them!"

It was a trait that Bill Smith would always be recognized for in subsequent years, wherever and whenever Spencer was racing. All the Brits were laughing, and even a most of the competitors allowed themselves a chuckle, all except one. "Spencer didn't seem to have noticed, he was so focused," recalled his teammate Coulson. "I don't know where he got his focus from." And then the hooter went and they disappeared in a thrash or white water.

Despite the focus and the support from his dad, the 1990 Worlds would not provide Smith with an individual medal any more than it had done Lessing, and whilst his eighth place overall would have been considered excellent by many, he wanted more. Instead, this season the British junior lad from south London would have to be satisfied with a silver medal in the Junior Team category. At least he could go home with something.

At this time the World Championships was a non drafting format, which would only change some few years later, nonetheless drafting was still an issue within the sport and in real terms was akin to cheating. Even at this time Smith hated drafting. Whilst Smith did not claim to incur any drafting problems in his World Championships, he later referred to the senior race as, "a joke." The problem he felt was the number of competitors in the race, which if not directly encouraging drafting, did little to help the situation.

Many agreed that this was a problem within the sport and struggled to find solutions to the problem. The solution to the problem that would eventually materialize through the ITU some years later would not however be the solution that many had hoped for and would change the face of triathlon racing, at least at elite level, forever.

Despite the serious side to the trip, the World Championships in Orlando was not all racing and gave the youngsters a chance to travel and have a bit of a holiday at the same time and the City of Orlando was built for fun. As a treat, the GB juniors went to the Wet and Wild themepark a couple of days after the race and whilst one may have thought they would have had enough of racing, triathletes being triathletes, they were soon having races in the wave pool.

Bill Smith, always good for a bit of fun would get everybody together and, "start it all off," as Coulson recalled, and to this day his then teammate still has in his possession a photograph that told a lot about the competitive streak in Spencer. In the photograph you could see the laughter and smiles all over the faces of the junior squad, and in the background a young Matt Belfield grinning, contrastingly however in the front is a young Spencer Smith with a look of resolve that showed his determination to get to the far wall first. "Even in the free time Spencer wanted to come first," recalled Coulson. "Such a will to win."

Unfortunately the competition between the youngsters was not always confined to the psyches of the individual kids themselves, and whilst they all mixed quite amiably, family and coaches inevitably played a major part. "He (Spencer) got on quite well with Mathew

Belfield but I think Mathew was always quite intimidated by him. Mathew was always psyched out by Bill." Coulson recollected. "Mathew had a really braggy coach, the guy just kind of used to try and wind up Julian Bunn, so in a way Spencer used to have Mathew in his pocket and Mathew had Julian Bunn in his pocket."

Inevitably where there are talented children there are also parents or coaches behind them who also feel it is their job to improve the chances of their siblings when in competition. At some points and in some cases, the parents can inevitably lose sight of what is acceptable and what is not. "They were all very, very talented," Coulson reflected, "but Spencer was the most strong mentally and had the best guy looking after him."

It was an expensive trip for the Smith family and Bill had in his inimitable manner had been looking for ways to finance it. And Bill being Bill he found it. Ever the opportunist, he found a cheap shop selling white Levi's, which were all the trend back in Britain so he bought fifty pairs, put them in Spencer's bike bag, and went back to the UK where he sold them at a pretty good profit. You could almost hear him saying, "That will pay for the trip my son," as he packed them away in his Orlando hotel room.

Spencer and his dad Bill. Inseparable.

Smith 1st, Lessing 2nd and Cook 3rd, Euro Champs Lommel 1992

TRANSITION THREE AND FOUR
Then There Were Four & From Water to Wheel

Spencer had left school just months before the World Championships and on returning to the UK had planned go to college where he intended to continue his education with a view to studying physical education and business studies, a mix that would offer him the opportunity to develop academically whilst at the same time allow him to study something which he was really interested in, but little did he know how and a chance meeting with his future coach Bill Black would put him on to greater things than just academic achievement.

Bill Black first came into contact with Spencer Smith when he enrolled at Richmond Upon Thames College for A' level Sport Studies in September 1990, a course which Black coordinated. Black had only spoken to Smith on the phone about his application to start at the college when his ears "pricked up." Smith had stated his first sport was triathlon and Black was intrigued, as in his words, "we didn't get many of those."

By way of checking out his seriousness about the sport Black asked what he had done that day in the way of training to which Smith replied that he'd done three and a half thousand metres in the pool, had just come back from a one and a half hour ride and would be going out for a run later. Black nonetheless was still a little skeptical at the claims and not immediately convinced by the alleged training sessions made by Smith. According to Black. "In those days I thought that was quite something, if you believed it. But then kids would tell you they play for Chelsea and when you'd give them a ball they couldn't kick their way out of a paper bag. So you just had to take it all with a pinch of salt." Eventually however Black agreed to take the youngster on the programme and had invited him to start the course in September and now here he was, all be it a bit late.

As if to prove a point about his ability Smith was eventually two weeks late enrolling at the college with the excuse that he had been at the Junior World Championships in Florida. It was a better excuse than many Black had received over the years but the lateness due to triathlon was a precedent that Black and the rest of the teaching staff would have to live with over the next couple of years. Training would always come first.

At this time Black had been racing triathlons himself for about three years, all be it at a participatory ad hoc level rather than a serious one, and when Smith eventually reported to his office, Black just out of interest asked him about his programme and about his coach. He was surprised to find that the young sixteen year old didn't have a coach at that time and was just writing his own programmes. Again simply out of interest Black asked him to bring in his training schedule so he might take a look.

Black recollected. "The next day he brought me in a postage stamp, with writing in all different directions." Black considered the programme a bit of a joke but was not surprised having seen many an equivalent type training plan purporting to be a schedule for athletes ranging from novices to elite across a range of sports.

Having been a successful National Coach for a number of years all be it in volleyball, Black considered what he saw before him studiously and given his paternal and supportive nature coupled with his interest in the sport and educative approach to tutoring felt it his duty to put things right and help Smith to develop a methodical and organised approach to his training. Black told the young Smith that they needed to get his training sorted out and ever the lecturer told him it would also help him with his studies. Smith at this time, though clearly more concerned with the former point agreed to Black helping him plan his training, hoping undoubtedly that it would make an impact on his racing.

Little was Black or Smith to know how this meeting and this offer of support would change both his and Spencer Smith's life forever. Whilst Smith was willing to accept the offer of support made to him straight away, Black didn't feel it appropriate to take over the youngster's training without the proper authority and told Smith to go home and have a chat with his mum and dad before making any decisions. At that time Black knew Bill Smith, Spencer's father, from the Metropolitan Health Club that was situated next to the college and even played squash with him. Bill Smith was such a well known character that it was hard to believe that anyone at the Metropolitan Health Club would not know the loveable wheeler and dealer, though linking him to this slightly podgy but clearly talented triathlete was not so obvious.

Eventually the deal was done Bill and Barbara agreed to Bill Black taking on the mantle of coach and Spencer had his first triathlon coach. Black would probably be the first to admit that he was no expert on the technicalities of swimming, running or biking at the time and as such it was a baptism of fire, but with a degree in sport science and a good knowledge of all aspects of anatomy and physiology, Black made use of his science background and used it to develop his own blueprint on triathlon training.

Even now some would undoubtedly consider Black to be one of the most highly accomplished trainers in the sport, much of the swim coaching at the time was left to Spencer's original coach at Thames Turbo. Black's role at this time was to develop the programme in line with Spencer's needs rather than work on stroke technique or the technical development of running or biking skills but in time Black would become an expert in all three disciplines.

Bill Black didn't consider himself a triathlon coach at the time, he just employed coaching techniques, but being highly analytical in his approach, Black decided straight away that the main areas of improvement needed to be on his biking and his running. In terms of biking, Spencer's normal training programme at that time involved somewhere between eighty and ninety miles per week but within the year Smith saw his training move up to anything around three hundred and fifty miles in a hard week under Black's watchful eye. Black's argument for this massive increase in biking was that Smith had to, "put the years of cycling into his legs."

"When we first analysed it in those days, we simply worked out the proportions of the time spent on each of the three disciplines and the transitions. The most time is spent on the bike so it stands to reason that if you want to save a minute on your race time, the bike's the easiest place to save that minute." At the time Smith was riding a standard road frame with normal frame dimensions and it was considered acceptable by Bill Black who after all had little knowledge in terms of triathlon specific theory, which was at the time in its infancy. But in time it would become apparent that Smith ended up perched on the tip of his saddle and so a greater focus would be given to his position.

Black also tried to work on weights with Spencer, but he wasn't particularly keen despite his strength and solid build so that idea was thrown out pretty quickly. As was doing speed work on the track, which Smith evidently hated and continues to hate to this day and replaces treadmill work in favour of the oval tartan track.

About the same time as Spencer was starting college, his dad managed to secure a sponsorship deal with Nike for the forthcoming season. Billy Smith always knew when he was onto a good thing, and had an ability to turn an opportunity into a profit. Having sorted out the deal, Bill was told to just go up to the Sunderland factory and get what he needed. Not a comment those who knew Billy well would have made.

By this comment, the Nike management had intended on Bill driving up with Spencer to pick up a couple of tracksuits some racing kit, and sufficient trainers to last him a season's racing and training. Bill however had other ideas. So legend has it, Bill turned up a few days later with a transit van he had hired for the trip, and proceeded to load it with sufficient kit and trainers to field an army of triathletes. With the van full to bursting Bill thanked the somewhat startled staff at the factory and headed home. Whether much of the kit was sold on the market back in London or where the kit eventually went to has never quite been established. Enough said, Spencer, Bill and his team of supporters looked very smart the following season, all decked out in their Nike kit.

With a winter programme planned out Spencer went to it with his usual commitment and enthusiasm which saw almost instant results in his ability both on the bike and in the running which demonstrated that what ever Black was doing to Spencer's training it was definitely working, a point that was highlighted by Stuart Coulson who recalled the training camp held at Crystal Palace in January a mere three months after Black had taken over. "I saw a different Spencer Smith at Crystal Palace, his body had changed again he was getting slimmer." Apart from getting slimmer Smith was also getting faster.

"We did four times a mile with a four hundred recovery on an icy track. I was leading a pack including Glenn Cook, Richard Hobson, and Robin Brew," recalled Coulson. "I was doing miles in 5.05. Spencer was twenty seconds ahead of me. I was thinking Christ there's no way I can run that fast." For a seventeen year old that was a pretty special sort of time. "He was good at the end of 1990, very, very good but he just jumped a huge level that winter."

When you consider that this was out of season, they had already done six kilometres of swimming that morning and that Smith was only seventeen years of age giving away at least two years to his closest rival, his times and his ability to outperform the rest of the squad become even more astonishing. It was then that many of the squad realised that nobody domestically apart from Simon Lessing was going to be able to compete with him, although many would have to try and dispel that thought in competition.

Whilst many would say that Smith was a pretty accomplished athlete before he even met Bill Black with a European Junior Championship under his belt at sixteen years old in 1990, the improvements made when Black got involved were undeniable and dramatic.

When Black was asked how Spencer's improvements seemed to come so rapidly his explanation was plain and simple. His criticism of Smith's original training programme prior to his involvement was harsh but undoubtedly true. "It wasn't scientific training, it wasn't structured, it wasn't built on a system, it was haphazard, but then again in those days very few of the athletes had the information or the expertise around to do that anyway, so we were probably the first to have personal coaching."

Apart from the coaching side even in the early years with the pressures of competition and training Black also sometimes found himself in the role of the calming influence when things got pressured between Spencer and his father. "I used to occasionally step in between the two of them when we were in the hotel room if they were having an up and downer. I'd either take Billy out for a drink, or I'd take Spencer out to train. Or we'd even put Spencer to bed and Billy would take me out for a drink. It was a good little team in that it took the pressure off the pair of them with me coming in." In addition to the three men in the team Black also confirmed that, Spencer's mother also played a major role in stabilising and supporting the efforts. "Barbara did a lot behind the scenes and without her it would have been more of a strain," recalled Black. "She did more than many people realised."

The top guys at the time were Robin Brew, Glenn Cook and Richard Hobson and they didn't have their own coaches for the triathlon. Whilst Archie Brew who is undoubtedly one of the best swim coaches in Britain may have coached Robin in swimming, often other parts of his training would be left for Robin to organize which at times can be difficult for an athlete to analyse. This was much the same sort of support for most of the best triathletes at the time.

Despite 8th place at the Worlds, on describing Smith when he first started to be coached by Black, many would be surprised to hear the description given to his talents, which according to Black were less than precocious. "Well he could swim, but he couldn't bike or run. Swimming was easily his top sport because he was a four hundred metre swimmer anyway. On the bike he just mashed the big gears but on the run he was maybe, forty (minutes) for 10km." On top of that Black rather unflatteringly described his build as stocky with a layer of puppy fat. This description was at least perhaps a little less harsh than a description given by Iain Hamilton who recalled with a smile being beaten in one of the youth races by, "a little fat cockney bastard dressed in black." Hamilton smiled as he said this knowing that Smith would probably smile too if he ever read it. Over the next few years Hamilton would continue racing alongside, or as he now states "behind" the fat lad for a number of years as a youth, constantly recalling images of his first competition against Smith.

Looking back, Smith is the first to admit that he was perhaps a little on the solid side, weighing in at about 190-195 lbs at sixteen years old he was bigger than most kids his age and was definitely a lot bigger than most triathletes he would come up against. "I was just a normal kid, I used to eat shit, like McDonalds and everything." He admits now.

On the outside he was your usual kid who liked wearing his trendy Nike running stuff and had his ears pierced as was the fashion at the time. Even then he was always very conscious of his appearance and preferred to be a bit different, even to the point that in 1990 Coulson recalled that everyone was wearing Oakley iridium shades including Spencer who had a pair too, but not wanting to wear the same as all the others he had swapped them with another one of the team for a pair that were two years old. On the outside the young Smith wanted to be different and he was, but it was not just his outward appearance that was different, on the inside too he was different, with a somewhat better than normal engine and a commitment and determination that would take him to greater heights than the rest of his teammates and classmates.

Putting the miles into his protégés legs was something Black took seriously, and Spencer started the season off with a few road races to get the legs turning. For a lad who had only taken up cycling two years previous, a third and a seventh place in some local events wasn't a bad start. Black's sessions were not only about improving athletic performance but were also about educating Spencer as to why he was doing things, and what benefits he was trying to gain from them. Black believed that an educated athlete would gain more from every session, both physiologically and psychologically and stressed the importance of this throughout Smith's training programme. Smith and Black would sit down and discuss every training session and every race.

19th May 1991 Bath Triathlon, UK

The first major race Black prepared him for was Bath 1991 although he had started the season with two wins at Reading, one at Ringwood near the New Forest and one at another small event in Putteridge, Bath however was a different league. With a short 400m swim over, the transition area was crowded but Smith and Chris Humpage who had left the water were the first to shoot through transition closely followed by Richard Hobson alias "Captain Quads," Jonathon Ashby and Kiwi, Scott Balance. Two minutes into the ride the pack hit Bathwick Hill, a testing climb that would end up testing Smith's patience as well as his strength. Leading the field Smith's chain came away from his chainring and as he struggled to replace the chain he lost valuable time to the rest of the field. Eventually with his chain in tact Smith made his way back through the field, but the time he'd lost and the efforts he'd put in on chasing down the lead group was too much for the youngster and at the end of the final run section despite a valiant effort he had to be satisfied with a third place behind Ashby and Hobson who had maintained a comfortable lead. First lesson learnt that season, irrespective of the capability of your body, a simple technical failure on your bike can cost you the race.

26th May 1991 Swindon Triathlon, UK

A week after Bath he raced again at Swindon which was the first major race he actually won under Black's guidance, beating Robin Brew into second place. The 1.5km swim start for the elite men was at 10:20am and as was expected Brew led out the swim but Smith was only conceding two seconds to the Olympic swimmer by the time they were exiting the water with Smith holding 18:37. Into transition Smith faced his second technical failure in two weeks as he struggled to get his wetsuit off, finding that the zip cord was a little to short for him to reach comfortably. Black ever the philosopher and always one to take the positive out of any situation would later state that this was a good learning point for Spencer emphasizing that every race was a learning opportunity. Smith would not make the same mistake again. In the end the zip problem made little difference to the transition times and saw Smith exit the transition closely behind Brew.

A 57:33 and 57:28 bike leg saw Brew only holding a seven second lead going into the second transition, leaving it all down to the 10km run to decide the placings, which with the improvements made by Smith over the past months meant he was the clear favourite to get to the line first. As expected once into the run Smith that took control of the race but the race was far from over with Brew digging in deep, and whilst the gap between the two went up and down Smith eventually surged ahead coming home to take the honours, all be it by little more than fourteen seconds but a 34:26 run split was enough to win it.

In article that covered the race in Triathlete magazine entitled 'Stormtrooper Smith,' Martin Higginson referred to the race as, "the event in which Spencer Smith came of age," and went on to predict that, "Europe and the world may have to prepare this season for Smith's entry to the big time events. They may have a nasty shock coming to them." A prediction that time would show was well justified.

Having only just really formed the team Bill Black and Bill Smith were overjoyed at the result, and as Spencer ran past with a quarter of a mile to go, and a comfortable lead over Brew and Glenn Cook, Billy Smith ran over to Black, picked him up and gave him a big kiss. "He picked me up like a rag doll and span me round half a dozen times, he was so proud of Spencer that day. All he wanted to do was share that joy." Black later recalled.

After that win, the perspective and expectations of the team had changed. Now only winning was good enough for the young Smith and, "from then on if we didn't come first we asked the question why?" Recalled Black. Whilst Bill Black worked on the coaching, Spencer's father sorted out everything else. "Bill was the Mr. Fix it and he always did," recalled Black. "All Spencer had to do was sleep, eat, train and race."

Black was still working at the college but was also a consultant to the gymnasium, which was set up in the Metropolitan Health Club, overlooking the Harlequins rugby ground and directly next door to the college. One of the best-equipped facilities in the area at that time it was regularly frequented by some talented athletes, which primarily came from rugby and rowing, but it also enticed a few faces from the professional cycling fraternity. One former Olympic cyclist in particular was a regular trainer in the gym as well as the bar, and both Bill Black and Bill Smith knew him pretty well on personal terms. His name was Mick Bennett. Whilst Bennett had now retired from professional cycling following a car accident, which had not only ended his career but killed his long term girlfriend, he was still extremely involved in the sport. A director of Sport for Television, he now made his living from staging major televised national and international cycling events for television and was the Technical Director for the Kellogg's Tour of Britain, The Nissan International Classic in Ireland and all the Channel 4 City Center Cycling that frequented the televisions. On top of that he also was the Manager for the Eveready Marlborough Professional Cycling team, which among others, included the former double World pursuit Champion Tony Doyle.

As a favour to the two Bills, Mick arranged for Spencer to go out on a training ride with Tony so that he could give him a few tips. Young Spencer whose favorite cyclist at the time was Greg Lemond (the 1986 American Tour de France winner) was chuffed to bits to get the invitation and took up the offer. Smith kept up with Doyle for the ride but as Smith was the first to acknowledge, when interviewed later, he couldn't be sure how hard Doyle was pushing. Nevertheless Doyle invited him to go out with him again which suggested that he couldn't have been too bad in the presence of one of the British legends in cycling.

Doyle's career had been one of the most successful of all the professional British track cyclists in the history of the sport, but unfortunately for Doyle this was at a time when the British media were more keenly interested in road racing.

Having won the World Pursuit Championships in 1980 and 1986, coming second in 1985 and in 1988, Doyle was one of the most highly respected track cyclists in the world and would have become a triple World Champion in 1988 had the tainted accomplishment of a silver medal not been as a result of a terrible catastrophic administrative and preparatory sequence of events outside of Doyle's control, without which would have undoubtedly seen him beat his Polish counterpart, having consistently bettered his time in every round up until the final race.

Unfortunately for Doyle it would not be until the emergence of Graeme Obree and Chris Boardman that the British media would take serious notice of the track, but irrespective of the lack of media interest in the UK, Doyle was still one of the best riders on the professional circuit, consistently picking up major wins in the European and World Six day circuit and as such Smith was lucky to have such an opportunity. Doyle would however perhaps view this opportunity differently believing it himself to be lucky to still be out there riding given the sequence of events that had taken place a year previous.

On Sunday 12th November 1989 at eleven thirty in the evening, Doyle's career and nearly his life came to an end during a six day track meet in the Olympiahalle in Munich. It was the fourth night of the Munich Six day racing and the second of the two Madison sessions, in which pairs of cyclists hammer the track at top speed and then throw their partner into the fray to maintain the speed and momentum of the race, thereby protecting their lead and attempting to take laps out of the opposing teams.

Doyle had just begun to attack and was accelerating round the banking into the straight when without warning, the Russian cyclist Marat Ganeev switched up the banking to his right decelerating rapidly. With no brakes on a fixed wheel track bike Doyle had nowhere to go and ploughed straight into the Russian almost stopping dead with the impact. Before he even hit the track it was clear the accident was serious and as he slid down the inclined track falling headfirst into the trackside chairs he hit his head on the concrete floor and immediately lost consciousness. It was obvious to all concerned that of the six riders who had fallen in the crash, Doyle's condition was by far the worst.

If the crash wasn't enough the incompetence of the first aid staff at the track compounded the problems when after putting the unconscious Doyle on a stretcher, they dropped him down a further flight of concrete stairs as they tried to carry him down the exit tunnel. As the crowd sat paralysed by the chaos, they eventually started to boo the medics who increasingly flustered proceeded to lift Doyle who remained unconscious by his shoulder which was visibly broken and then carry him out of the velodrome on the stretcher into the freezing sub zero Munich night air without giving due consideration to the fact that covering him up with a blanket in an attempt to conserve some of the heat in his sweaty motionless body may have been a sensible option.

As the officials exited the velodrome so yet another catastrophe occurred in that whilst they were exiting one set of doors, the ambulance was searching for them at another entrance. Leaving Doyle to freeze with still no blanket they went in search of the ambulance and eventually transported Doyle to Bogenhausen Hospital.

For several days it was uncertain whether Doyle was likely to survive the accident that had resulted in severe bruising to the brain and the threatened danger of hemorrhaging. On top of the damage to his head, Doyle was also suffering from a scapula that was broken in five places a broken radius in his right arm, severe bruising and lacerations and a lung infection. Unable to breath unaided Doyle was on a ventilator, and was under constant surveillance by the medical staff. It was eight days before his condition stabilised and he showed any degree of regaining consciousness and even then it had only been an opening of his eyes for a split second but it was at least progress.

Whilst the management team at Sport for Television, which included his close friends Mick Bennett and Alan Rushton tried to hush up the incident for fear it would affect the negotiations that were being undertaken with Doyle's sponsors at that time, Doyle began to recover slowly and he was brought back to the UK by air ambulance to RAF Northholt where he was rushed immediately to intensive care in Charing Cross. It took nearly two months before Doyle started to regain his memory and then only a bit at a time. As Doyle lay in a Charing Cross hospital bed in a darkened room unable to recognize people that he knew so well, with the weight falling off his previously toned and healthy body, there grew an increasing despondency that he would never ride again and would not recover fully, but at least he was alive!

Then suddenly over a couple of days just before Christmas, Doyle's condition improved, significant portions of his memory returned, and his speech that has been indecipherably slurred seemed to improve. His posture changed from being slumped despondent and helpless, to being almost back to the same old Tony, all be it a little bit laboured.

On the 23rd December Doyle discharged himself and went home to his wife Anne, but had to return to a rehabilitation center in Godalming on the 27th and would remain there for almost two months coming home periodically for weekends. He made it clear to the staff at the center that he planned to get back on the bike though it was clear that many were unsure if this was something he would accomplish, but

Doyle was determined to prove them wrong and by February he was back on his bike leaving grounds of the rehabilitation center for an hour long ride with his wife Anne trailing him in the car just in case. The next day he went out riding in Windsor Great Park with Mick Bennett covering around thirty miles, setting a pace that Bennett had not expected and wished he himself had trained for.

In the end Doyle's return to racing took place some months later in Portsmouth at a criterium, which was part of the Scottish Provident League. An inner city race with tightly packed bunches and sharp twists and turns, encompassing all out sprints both into and out of the corners, it perhaps wasn't the best choice but he finished it, which in itself was an accomplishment given the ferocity at which such races were contested in the UK by the British professionals.

In the months following his return to full time racing, Doyle got back into the six day racing and eventually retuned to Munich the home of that fateful crash. And what's more. He won it.

This insight into Tony Doyle emphasizes the single mindedness required to be a champion, and for Smith to be invited to ride with someone who could engender and demonstrate such tenacity must have been of great benefit to the young eighteen year old. Smith was clearly fortunate that he was surrounded by excellence, an excellence that encouraged him to set his sights higher and place his aspirations above many of the other athletes that surrounded him.

Winning is a selfish business and it can't be otherwise, but there is another side to Doyle which hinges on his tremendous capacity for building around him a network of friends, to whom he has been invariably loyal and generous to. That too was something that young Smith had begun to develop with both his family and Bill Black. Nevertheless, whilst Doyle was always a gentleman, he always took his training seriously and the likelihood of inviting Smith back out had he not been up to the tempo would have been extremely unlikely. But he did, so there was little doubt he saw something in the young Londoner, which was some respect from one of the best professional cyclists that the UK had ever produced.

23rd June 1991 Royal Windsor Triathlon, UK

The first ever Royal Windsor Triathlon gave Smith a chance to shine a little closer to home. Only ten miles from his native Hounslow, this event would continue to be one of Smith's favorite events over the next few years and gain great respect as one of the major and best supported events on the British calendar, despite its shambolic and rather humble beginnings.

When the gun went off, more than twenty of the elite field were not ready and mayhem ensued. Some of the late starters rushed along the bank to the starting point and plunged into the water, whilst others of them dived in from the bank, joining the leading swimmers, much to the surprise of some and the amusement of others. Whilst the shortening the swim would only have gained a few yards and saved a few breaths for those who took the short cut the following confusion surrounding the appropriate swim buoy to turn at, added insult to injury for Smith who was leading the race.

The race map that had been issued to the athletes prior to the event clearly showed that swimmers should turn at the first buoy, which Smith duly did. However in the race briefing immediately prior to the event the organizers had informed the athletes that it would in fact be the second buoy. Smith had not heard the change in the briefing and as a result took a small detour around the offending marker heading off in the wrong direction. With the error brought to his attention by both screams from the shore and a visible lack of swimmers in his wake, Smith quickly re routed his swim back on course and as a result of his strength in the swim managed to recover sufficiently to exit the water in the lead followed closely by Matt Belfield and a third Junior Laurence Nelson, whilst the leading seniors in the field exited the water a matter of seconds later in the form of Glenn Cook and Chris Humpage.

Out on the bike Cook and Smith fronted the field as they headed through the picturesque Windsor Great Park, with the police motorbike leading the way. Some of those further back in the field however struggled to find there way round a course that was poorly signposted and in one section led through a narrow potholed alleyway. Even the police motorbike didn't attempt to escort the leaders on this section and instead took a detour and met them on the other side. Smith eventually made it back to T2, having covered the 37km section in a time of 53:28 with a thirty six second lead over Cook, and a significant lead on the rest of the slightly diminished field.

Unfortunately Robin Brew and Richard 'Captain Quads' Hobson who had just returned from Portugal had both picked up a nasty stomach bug, and whilst Brew had elected not to race, Hobson had decided to give it a go and see how it went. Hobson however was clearly under par on the bike discipline, which was normally his strength and as he entered the transition area, he sprinted past the few athletes in front of him at a speed that would have given Smith a good run for his money. Fortunately for Smith, and perhaps the crowd, instead of heading out on the run, Hobson diverted his course, headed straight to the toilets and did not emerge for some minutes. The Portuguese bug coupled with a swim in the Thames was clearly not a good combination, and Hobson retired from the race. One down and just a few more to go for Smith.

Whilst Hobson was out, Cook and Belfield who were just behind had definitely not given up the race and continued to try to pull back the time on Smith but to no avail. Smith's running had improved considerably over the season and he eventually made it home with time to look around and soak up the atmosphere. With a run split of 33:24 Smith had succeeded in achieving a personal best for the 10k and the fastest swim, bike and run time. Spencer was overjoyed, as was the rest of the family and Bill Black received another kiss from Bill Smith. His boy had done it.

Cook eventually came in one minute and forty five seconds down on Smith with Dave Bellingham who would later take on the role of Chair at the BTA in 2001, crossing the line third only to find he had received a five minute penalty which demoted him to 13th spot.

The race referee had issued a five minute penalty to all the athletes who admitted that they had taken the short cut on the swim. Unfortunately for young Matt Belfield he was only one of the few with the guts to own up and paid the price for his honesty. That penalty put Ken Maclaren third, who despite being in the wrong place at the start of the race had run back to the correct starting place and fought his was back through the swim, covering the correct swim distance.

When asked after the race about the improvement in his performance over the season the so called 'wonder boy' put his improvement down to Bill Black's training. "The difference between this year and last is Bill," said Smith. Overjoyed with the win, the young Londoner pinned down his progress to two things that Black had been working with him on, the first thing was training schedules and the second thing was race preparation.

Smith admitted that the previous season he hadn't even really known what schedules were let alone what they did, but now under Black's watchful eye he was doing a lot more quality work, where as previously he had just been "putting the miles in." Smith's strength had always originally been in the swim, a fact that he himself acknowledged stating, "I like open water, the harder the better for me. As far as I'm concerned there isn't a hard enough swim." But now his biking, running and thinking, were making him a much more rounded athlete.

In terms of race preparation Smith was much more organized and knowledgeable about courses before he ever raced on them despite the mishap on the swim. Before a race Black would study the courses and go through them with his young prodigy, maps were drawn and profiles were produced that would highlight the contours of the course in terms of climbs and descents. Danger spots would be picked out, or areas where it was considered a good place to attack. From originally just racing the race at his own pace the young Smith had now started to consider tactics as a further weapon to his armory.

Smith would ride the course at least a couple of times before any race just to iron out any worries or queries in his mind, and come the race Black and Smith senior would arrange with Spencer to position themselves at strategic points around the course to give him splits and encourage him. A strong powerfully built lad Smith preferred the flat bike courses where he could grind out the big gears. "Pushing the big gear along is what I like," professed the seventeen year old after racing Windsor. And though modern scientific argument suggested that this was not the most efficient way of racing on the bike, it seemed to be working for Smith and would remain a style that it would take more than a decade to get him out of the habit of.

1991 continued to be a good year for Smith in terms of his performances with wins in Holland and Ironbridge, and for the first time he beat Lessing in a head to head at the National Championships in Wakefield, having only just returned from winning the 16-18 age category European Junior Championships in Losheim, Germany whilst Lessing won the 18-20 age category at the same event, a sure sign of things to come. With the Europeans over he then went on to pick up a further two wins at Bath and Portsmouth, bringing his total wins for the season to thirteen.

But even in 1991 the young Smith seemed pretty clear about his intentions. Smith saw his future in America, both racing and living.

Other ambitions included the Atlanta Olympics to be held in 1996. At the time triathlon was not an Olympic sport but was pushing hard to be accepted by the International Olympic Committee with the ITU profiling the sport heavily both throughout Europe and the States. Come the Atlanta Games, Smith would be twenty three and potentially near the peak of his capabilities a point that clearly excited the British contingency, but despite all efforts by the governing bodies, unfortunately for Smith, the sport of triathlon would not be successful in its bid to be included in the Atlanta Games and it would take a further four years until triathlon would be the opening event for the Sydney 2000 games, some nine years later.

Even at eighteen Smith had his sights on being number one in the world over the 'short distance' (1500 metre swim, 40km bike and 10km run). At the same time he was not beyond discussing the longer distance races such as Ironman. "I don't intend to move to another distance until I've conquered this one." Smith had said. "By that I mean everyone knows who I am and I'm number one in the event like Mark Allen." This was some statement from a youngster who had only cut his teeth in the sport a few years earlier. Mark Allen was Spencer's hero in triathlon terms, much the same as he was to the majority of the triathlon population and for Smith to consider himself in relation to one of the gods of triathlon showed the confidence the youngster had.

Looking back on the 1991 season, it would appear that on linking up with Black there was a simple yet fundamental change of philosophy. Initially when achievements had not been what Smith wanted he would look forward in terms of better result next time and would train harder without analyzing his training. In essence he would only look forward. Now Smith would learn to also look backwards and try to establish what had gone wrong in his training. For the first time Smith was starting to evaluate his performance against the programme.

He even had his own manager at the time, which was exceedingly rare in triathlon, and whilst it was his father Bill who was his manager, the young Smith could be sure that everything that was being done was unquestionably being undertaken with Spencer's best interests as the focal concern. Whilst Bill Smith was involved in the day to day administration of Spencer's life which included arranging the transport and 'doing the deals with sponsors, promoters and the like.' Bill Black's job was to write his programme, coach him and educate him. Meanwhile Spencer's mother Barbara had what a few onlookers would describe as the toughest role of the lot. Her job was to look after the lot of them. Feed them clothe them and keep it all together.

His dad had tied up sponsorship in 1991 with Evans bike chain of stores, Nike for clothing and Gatorade who provided all the drink Spencer needed. At that time there was no money involved, but then the sport was young and its profile still pretty limited for most sponsors. Money was not the focus. Winning was.

When asked about his relationship with Spencer's father Bill, Bill Black initially defined their relationship in terms of Spencer. "I think you've got to realize that when it's your son, you'll do anything for him, and anyone who can help him is obviously on your side. And in those days I was just doing it as a hobby. I wasn't getting paid anything. It was just a challenge for me. When he won at Swindon, Billy just picked me up like a rag doll, swung me round like you do with a little kid, and kissed me god knows how many times. He was so pleased. I didn't realize at the time but that was what Spencer raced for. Spencer's motivation was to make his dad happy. And obviously try and be the best. Not to be beaten. When Spencer made his dad happy that made Spencer happy and that was the main motivation. The bottom line. It wasn't the money, it wasn't so much the titles, it was to keep his dad happy."

Whilst Bill would do his best to psyche out anyone who challenged his boy, he also did his bit to help and encourage the other kids in the squad and as Stuart Coulson remembers it, it wasn't just cheering that Smith senior would do. "He wouldn't just shout go on Stu, he would shout proper motivation from a hundred metres away till you'd run another hundred metres down the road. For a good forty five seconds you'd get shouted at to punch your arms and to concentrate and to use the shade, stuff that reminded you how to race. I remember thinking that's what Spencer gets all the time, no wonder he's good. Bill was a major factor behind those performances."

It was undoubtedly a family thing, and whilst Bill may have been the most vociferous of the family, Spencer's mother, Barbara was no less an integral part of the success bestowed on the family. She would make sure everything was prepared for him at home, kit food, while his dad would make sure his bike was ok, would wake him up, make sure his sessions were laid out, get him to swimming. Nobody else was like that Stuart Coulson was at university, Julian Bunn was a postman, the closest to that sort of commitment to the sport was Matt Belfield who was trying to make the grade by focusing on training whilst trying to make ends meet on the dole, but clearly without the sort of support that Smith had. Spencer on the other hand was doing it properly, like a true professional a fact that he could put down fairly and squarely to his mother and father.

13th October 1991 Junior World Championships, Australia

Smith had performed well enough to secure National and European titles but now he had the chance to excel on the world stage, with the Junior World Championships being staged in Australia. Given the sort of support he had been given and the new professional approach he had, he certainly looked the part.

"He was always immaculately turned out, he was always smart, he was always trendy. I think Mathew Belfield got psyched out by that, I certainly did," recalled Coulson. "We had a team meeting a few days before the races, Spencer was there and Simon was there. He must have bathed himself in baby oil. There was just no fat, his legs were just chunks of muscle. Every year his build just got more intimidating and daunting."

There was little doubt that psychology played an important part in Smith's achievement but the intensity with which he trained meant that the competition had good reason to fear him. "You like to think it probably just happened because you like to think that nobody could train as hard as you, but I remember swimming with him for a week, and he would run to swimming, do a five kilometre swim set, run home, and that wasn't even his main run set. I thought my god."

Coulson's memories of the early days with the Smiths indicated the differences in the personalities within the clan. "Bill was always showy and in your face, where as Spencer certainly in the first two years or so was very quiet, and meek and mild... but equally flashy in dress sense. He was always immaculately turned out, he must have been a sponsors dream."

And a sponsor's dream he was. Spencer was well supported by sponsors because he was good for it, he always had so many photos in the magazines. Around this time, when he raced his kit resembled a billboard because he had so many logos plastered over his vest. It was the trend at the time partially because sponsors would only offer small deals hence the need for athletes to secure an abundance of small sponsors to make it financially viable and partially because the early 90's were about flash, the louder and the flashier the kit the better.

This was the beginning of the yuppie period in Britain where it was important to be flash even in sport. Outside of sport however the media was more concerned with the Gulf War and 'Stormin' Norman, the return of hostages John McCarthy and Terry Waite after being held in Beirut by their kidnappers since 1986 and 87, the assassination of the Prime Minster of India Rajiv Gandhi, and the statement by basketball star 'Magic' Johnson confirming that he was HIV positive.

Whilst the rest of the world was concerned with such issues, the Australian public, a population that takes its sport very seriously and had some of the best triathletes in the world, were 'getting out there' to celebrate the arrival of the triathletes who had come from all over the globe to challenge for the world titles. Smith had accomplished a lot in the season and his chances at least of medalling were considered pretty good especially having won the Junior Europeans just a few months earlier. This year however no amount of encouragement or coaching was going to make a difference to Spencer's performance on the day. Coulson recalled. "Spencer had a shit bike and a shit run, even I nearly caught him."

It was a long way to travel to have a bad day and both Billy and Spencer knew that was exactly what it was. "Even though Spencer was having a shit race, Bill was still in the most remote part of the course supporting all six junior Brits," recollected Coulson, "even though he focused on Spencer he still had time for us."

Whilst Billy, Spencer and the rest of the team knew it was a bad day, Bill Black was sitting at home eight thousand miles away waiting for the phone call that Barbara always made after every race that Black couldn't attend. It was an ongoing game that Barbara would ring Bill who was increasingly becoming part of the family and tell him that Spencer hadn't done very well, Black would play along as Barbara would recall how badly the days events had gone until she would eventually crack up laughing and admit that Spencer had won or come in the top places, between fits of laughter and cheers and claims of got ya!!

On this occasion the outcome was not the same. Black recalled the conversation he had that night. "On this occasion she said, he didn't do very well Billy, I said alright yeah, yeah, yeah, what? Did he come fourth?, No, no he came twentieth. Oh yeah I said. She said no seriously

Billy and this sort of thing went on for a while, and then eventually she said. 'Billy, this is for real.' Well I was just devastated."

The meticulous coach that Black was, he got all his files out and spread them across the floor and went through all his preparation notes for the last three months to see if he'd made a mistake somewhere. Try as he might he couldn't see it.

It wasn't until he came back and compared the training programme that he had set Spencer to do and the figures, which outlined what Smith had actually done it, the problem had become apparent. Smith had massively over trained doing far more than Black had set him in the preparation schedule. It was a tough lesson to learn for the youngster. More is not always better.

1st September 1991 Portsmouth International Triathlon, UK

Having returned to the UK in September clearly disappointed with the final outcome in Australia, Smith's subsequent return to racing was to be at Portsmouth, a venue that also had hosted a previously unsuccessful venture for him, and having punctured only 200 yards into the start of the bike section in 1990 Smith wanted to make amends to the disappointment resulting from that kind of setback.

On the theme of learning from every event Bill Black and Smith Senior had set Spencer the task of working on quick puncture repair practice and such was the commitment of Smith junior that he had practiced the changeover of inner tubes and inflation of the new tyre so many times that it had almost made his hands bleed. Practice however makes perfect and more importantly practice makes quick and so now Smith was able to repair and replace a front wheel in less than one minute and do the same on a rear wheel in two. As it happens it wasn't required on this occasion but nonetheless it indicated the type of areas, and type of practices, that had changed since Black had come on board.

Robin Brew set the pace over the swim section emerging from the Solent only two seconds short of twenty minutes, whilst Smith had tailed Brew for much of the swim and was out on the bike only twelve seconds down as the former Olympic swimmer. Smith however began to uncharacteristically falter on the bike, which in turn allowed Belgium international Diddier Volckaert to retrieve the two and a half minutes that he had lost to Smith and Brew on the swim, eventually passing Smith just as they entered T2. Out on the run however it was

Brew who began to suffer as Volckaert and a recovered looking Smith passed him at a speed that signaled he would have no choice but to leave them to fight it out for first place honours.

Having run shoulder to shoulder for the majority of the ten kilometer course and with only a matter of yards left on the run Smith kicked hard, his strength and power enabling him to edge out the Belgium and take first prize.

Unusually Smith and Black admitted that he did not practice much short sprint work but relied on his strength to pull him through in such circumstances, a principle which seemed to have been proven by the win. Black had found it difficult if not near impossible to get Smith to train on the track, or undertake specific speed work, especially over the shorter 400m and 800m distances. Instead many of Smith's quality session tended to be set on the treadmill, an unusual training technique but nonetheless one that clearly worked for Smith. Strength however was not the only factor in this equation as Smith also seemed capable of digging deeper mentally in the final stages of a race than many of his compatriots and challengers, a fact that Black was acutely aware of, and so it was that another win was notched up by the team.

Whilst there was undoubtedly a lot of pressure on Spencer to perform from both Black and his father Bill it appeared that the balance was right. "I'm enjoying things at the moment, but as soon as I stop doing that, I'll stop." He said. This was a clear indication that despite all the hours of training, the early morning swim sessions, the intensely painful run sets and the long arduous rides, the passion for the sport was still there. If he was missing out on anything in his youth it didn't appear to be fazing him.

When questioned about the things he may be missing out on, he referred to the places he had been, the things he had seen as a result of his accomplishments. Whilst many of his college peers were in the Cabbage Patch pub just half a mile from the college, Smith was often miles away out training on the bike, but to Smith the rewards for his efforts were overwhelming. He loved what he was doing.

A review of the season showed the massive changes that had taken a hold of Spencer's life. Thanks to his dad's efforts, the sponsorship was more supportive than before all be it not one that brought great financial reward, but given that, the young Smith was a realist and recognized that money was a problem because triathlon was an expensive sport. His family were so supportive however that he was largely sheltered from any such concerns at least at an immediate level, he was however bright enough to recognise the potential long term difficulties of trying to support himself as a professional athlete.

"I don't think that in this country it is possible to be a professional triathlete yet." Spencer had said in interview. He however believed that if he continued to prove himself over the next couple of years that he may be able to start to ask for "real money," rather than just product, which a vast array of manufacturers were willing to offer him.

He was still doing ok at college with his studies and the possibility a full time professional career in triathlon was still a year away if he was to complete his course, which he was determined to do. Nonetheless a year was not long in the life of an athlete and he was not ignorant of the fact that plans would have to be put in place over the next twelve months if he was to achieve what he wanted, neither was he unaware of the unquestionable and never ending support of his mum and dad in his quest for the top. At a time when many youngsters do everything they can to get away from their parents in an attempt to avoid their 'interference' Smith welcomed the support of his family, recognizing that without their efforts he would not have achieved half of what he had.

In addition to the family support that had always been there he now had an extended member of the family in the guise of Bill Black whose coaching had added to the support network that surrounded him and had made enormous improvements in his performance as a result of it. The future looked good for the young Smith and he knew it.

If the future looked good then the present wasn't too bad either, with his life in triathlon affording him the opportunity to travel all over the world, and in October 1991 Smith took up the opportunity to see Hawaii Ironman for the first time, meeting for the first time his hero Mark Allen who had won Hawaii in both 1989 and 1990 had retuned to win it again for the third time on the trot. A picture of Allen and Smith was shown in the a few months later in 220 Magazine with Allen 'the grip' looking as cool as you can and Smith unfortunately looking a victim of fashion wearing possibly the worst pair of Hawaiian shorts that you could imagine.

Smith was immediately taken with Hawaii Ironman, the long distance culture and the fact that you had to be really strong to win Ironman, which was a Spencer thing, but he still had plenty of hurdles to leap before any real plans to undertake such a race could be even considered.

Black had been working hard to improve Smith's biking through the winter training period and had decided in consultation with Spencer and Bill to put him in for some early for duathlons. "We did it deliberately because people said he was just a swimmer." Black later admitted. It was partly done just for the purpose of training, but in the end Smith achieved more in the duathlon than had been expected of him and than even he had intended when he first set out.

15th March 1992 National Duathlon Championships, UK

Following on from his travels to Australia and Hawaii, and his continued training through the winter period, by contrast Smith's return to racing in 1992 took place in less exotic surroundings when Burnham on Sea played host to the National Duathlon Championships. An event that in previous years had produced disappointingly small fields, 1992 however proved to be a little different when the race would bring out the strongest field for some time with even Glenn Cook returning from winter training in San Diego.

On a bitterly cold and windy day where only the most foolish, brave or brazen, ran in trunks and a vest, Smith set the pace from the gun averaging five minute miles over the first four and a bit run and gained himself a thirty five second advantage over his closest rivals. Decked out in luminous pink and yellow kit, which unfortunately was the height of fashion in the early nineties, Smith surged on the bike into cross winds and head winds that left the weaker bikers struggling to even stay upright. With a good lead off the bike he continued with a run from the front that never really looked as though he could be seriously challenged for the title.

At the time Smith was getting a lot of support from Nick Reardon and his wife Heidi who ran the Evans bike shop in Wandsworth, they had been one of the first real sponsors to help him out and in return on this occasion they got a full colour spread in 220 magazine with Smith decked out in his dayglow Evans shorts, arms aloft and arm warmers steadfastly glued to them.

Whilst Smith had continued off the front and taken the honours, Cook by contrast had somehow managed to get himself caught up in a flock of sheep that meandered onto the road and cost him considerable time and considerable embarrassment. But it was a story that races were made of and the talk in the dressing rooms remained in the main about how Smith had come came to take his first National title of the season. In a duathlon!! That was not a bad performance for a swimmer.

As if to prove that the win was not a fluke, an entry into the European Duathlon Championships in Madrid less than a month later also saw him pick up another win and another European title. It was becoming increasingly clear that the so-called swimmer who had learnt to bike and run, was no longer just a fish. He could also win it on the bike.

10th May 1992 Fairford Duathlon, UK

Whilst the European title was undoubtedly an amazing achievement, Spencer's most memorable duathlon at this time was at Fairford against the then Duathlon World Champion Matt Brick, and Black recalled it with some pleasure. According to those who had attended a lecture given by Matt Brick the night before, Brick had stated that anybody that gets into T2 with a minute, shouldn't lose the race with only a five kilometer run left. If such rules of thumb were deemed as the gospel to the attendees, this was one thumb that was to be well and truly bitten off. Black's version of the race was recounted like this. "On race day Spencer did a very good first run, and beat everybody back to T1, having got through transition and got on his bike Spencer had only done a few laps before Brick caught up with him and put distance between them in no time at all."

Black recalled." I just told Spencer to take his foot of the gas and go steady and see what he'd got left for the run." Some would have felt this a dangerous tactic, but Black was confident of Smith's running. At T2 Brick came in well over a minute ahead of Smith, but Smith had saved that little bit more and was taking time out of Brick with every step he took. As the small but highly partisan crowd watched, Smith clawed back the time on the run to take not only the finishing tape, and the first prize, but a valuable scalp as well.

"We put that win down to not going to the lecture the night before. We didn't know you weren't supposed to win if you were down by a minute at T2," laughed Black. "It proved he was a good duathlete, and even now he can still run a sub 31 minute 10k if he wants. In transitions he was very, very fast. He was a naturally fast transitioner, where as most people didn't pay any attention to it in those days, they do now.

But in those days he could gain a minute."

With an increasing number of wins under his belt, Smith's profile was undoubtedly greater than any of the other triathletes on the British circuit and despite the fact that triathlon remained small in terms of media coverage in general, by 1992 sponsorship had increased to include included Brookes and a few other minor sponsors. The triathlon media which was serving a very niche market was full of photographs of the young Londoner which meant negotiation for his father became easier and sponsors quicker to sign and Bill was quick to tie up any opportunities that arose and would make things easier for his boy and the family in general. If the sponsorship was looking sweet then the results were looking sweeter.

31st May 1992 Swindon Triathlon 220 series, UK

A qualifier for the Europeans, the fourth race on Spencer's calendar was Swindon. As the qualifying race for Lommel, the outcome was vital for all the Brits who hoped to make it to Belgium and as a result the field was full of the usual suspects including Lessing, Smith, Cook and Brew. This was the year that Smith and Lessing found themselves racing head to head, more than any subsequent years a spectacle that many now would be willing to pay dearly to watch and in 1992 this was the first of the many.

Lessing and Smith swam together exiting the water in 17:07 and 17:08 respectively with Robin Brew leading it out by a hare's breadth, with Cook and Belfield close on their tails at twenty seconds down. As Brew quickly faded after the swim and Cook struggled to keep the pace, only Belfield had the strength on the bike to pull back to the two leaders.

Having caught them Belfield amazingly continued to ride straight past them, perhaps partially acknowledging that without a good lead on the bike he was destined not to win, and having fully committed himself Belfield made it to T2 with seconds to spare before both Lessing and Smith who was riding his newly acquired Softride bike screeched into the dismount line.

Belfield was a powerful biker with the ability to push big gears and grind out times that many of the field could not hope to achieve. But having put in so much work on the bike was sure to cost young Belfield and shortly into the beginning of the run he was caught and dropped only to fade more as the ten kilometres progressed. Whilst Cook rapidly gained on Belfield there was little question that the chasers remained too far behind to affect the first two placings and it became apparent to the watching spectators that it would be left to Smith and Lessing to slog it out for the win over the three lap course.

Having stayed together for the first two laps, with half a lap to go Lessing kicked in his inimitably smooth manner and put sufficient time into Smith to secure the win. A year older and a year stronger Lessing had taken first blood.

Stuart Coulson recalled the scene. "Spencer's supporters which included some of his father's mates, were all decked out in their Gatorade tracksuits and Simon seemed a bit spooked by them." Coulson recollected hearing one of them say. "He'll not do that again," referring to Lessing dropping Spencer, a comment that could at the time have been interpreted as a veiled threat given the stature and demeanor of the guys saying it, but such is the imagery associated with having a big chest and a strong London accent.

In truth whilst Lessing may have perceived the comments as threatening, what was most likely meant by that comment but is now too far back to establish was that Spencer wouldn't let him do it again! With their undeniable faith in Bill's beloved boy and his ability to learn from his mistakes, those closest to the Smith clan believed Spencer capable of anything when he set his mind to it. Bill was a tough man. Spencer was a tough lad and they were sure that he would be back to win another day.

On returning home Smith was miffed over being beaten by Lessing. He didn't like being beaten by anyone but as Bill's closest friend Bernie recalled despite the whole family's disappointment he wouldn't get much support for his grievances. Bill didn't want Spencer put on a pedal stall, and being the way Bernie was, i.e. very similar to Bill he was never likely to do that.

"Spencer was not moaning but clearly a bit upset at Lessing who had kept on tapping his feet during the swim, which was putting him off his stroke and generally just annoying him." Bernie remembers the outcome of that conversation. "I said well do it to him then you prat, if they're the rules that the boys are playing you've got to play the same, so do it back…. I said right there's another rule now….Barbara used to go to Marks and Spencer and buy gold chocolate biscuits, Spencer loved them and no sooner they were in the cupboard than they would be gone." And Bernie knew it.

"I said you can only have them you little bastard when you win! So if you come second or third there's no gold" and that was every race. "He'd come back and I'd say how did you do and he'd say first and I'd say gold, if he didn't I'd say to Barb. Not one gold biscuit, he gets them old shit penguins!!"

It wasn't as if Spencer needed chocolate as a motivation to win, but every little helps. The only question you would have to ask is what on earth would he have had to eat if he had come out of the top three. Thankfully for Spencer it was something that in 1992 he would never have to find out.

Even at that stage, Bill was confident in the ability of his son to compete with the best, Bernie had not really followed the racing, having a family of his own to focus on, but Billy confided in him that he thought that Spencer had the makings of a champion. Bernie remembered the conversation. "Bill said. He's good my boy, I think he's gonna be World Champion, in fact I'm pretty certain he will be. I said he's that good then, and he's come from you! Leave it out!" They'd both laughed but Bill was serious. "He said he was gonna be World Champion," recalled Bernie, "and not only was he, but he did it the next year."

Smith continued his 1992 season with a late burst of events in June taking first in Hull on the 14th and a week later winning the Royal Windsor Triathlon 220 series and taking gold at Nuemen a further week down the line. But around this time Smith had other issues to contend with, having to focus on his college work with his finals spread out in June.

In the middle of June Smith would conclude his studies at Richmond College, which meant some decisions would have to be made as to his future. It had been a difficult balance for Black to make between coach and tutor. He was aware of the possibilities and opportunities that Spencer had as an athlete but was always concerned about the negative affect that the demands of training were having on Spencer's studies. The difficulties he faced had been compounded by a number of the other staff at the college, who whilst wanting to be supportive of Smith's commitment to his sport, were increasingly concerned that his future plans were based on dreams and obsession rather than the practicalities of a solid future and a stable career.

When asked by one of the other tutors at the college what he wanted to do as a career when he completed his studies Smith had informed the lecturer that he wanted to be a professional triathlete. Whilst trying to be supportive of the young lad, it was difficult for the tutor to condone or support the idea of such a risky venture or comprehend the likeliness of him achieving his dream. In fact the said tutor had approached Black in a meeting later and discussed her concerns and admonished the idea of this young man making a living out of swimming, biking and running in a rather flippant manner. It even became a bit of a staff room joke (all be it not malicious) among some members of the academic team. With this background of unsuppressed disbelief, Black and Smith had found the ear bashings a continual part of college life.

In essence, whilst the staff at the college had all wished him luck in his sporting exploits, few believed he could make a living from it, but then they weren't close enough to know the possibilities. In subsequent meetings a few years later after Spencer was a full time professional, the aforementioned tutor approached Black and conceded that they had all been wrong about the young Smith. Being sporting herself and coaching a number of sports at the college, she was really pleased that Smith had achieved what he had set out to do, and was more than happy that she had been wrong. She just hadn't realized at the time that being a professional triathlete was a viable option for the young lad from Hounslow.

Smith eventually came out of Richmond College with a 'B' grade in his Physical Education A'level, but had dropped his business studies course, more through lack of motivation and commitment than capability. Despite not always the most committed academic, all be it that according to his lecturers, he was a capable student, a 'B' grade at advanced level was a good achievement given the lack of time he dedicated to his studies, but Smith would probably be the first to admit that part of the reason for his success in the exams could be due to the fact that the gods looked kindly on him when he sat his finals paper. Smith could not believe his luck when the second physical education paper he sat was placed in front of him. The exam related to three sports questions. One on swimming, one on biking and one on running.

Black recalled. "Everyone in the exam hall looked at me as if I had set the paper because I was an A' level examiner, but the questions had been set two years earlier, which was before I had even met Spencer. He came out grinning from ear to ear when I saw him."

With the exams over, Smith now had to concentrate on the next big race. The European Championships in Belgium and at a time that the French lorry drivers were bringing chaos to the roads in Europe, Smith was keen to do his part to help out.

5th July 1992 The European Championships Lommel, Belgium

Spencer came out the water in 19:07 with only Lessing and Michael Adamec the only other two athletes to break under the twenty-minute barrier. With Lessing only fifteen seconds down and the knowledge that Adamec had no great pace when it came to the run section, Smith decided to push it on the bike, just to get away from Lessing.

Whilst a good cyclist in triathlon terms and certainly one of the best that Britain had to offer, there could some argument that Smith was not the best cyclist in the European field and at that time, and nor was Lessing, in fact at that time many would still consider Glenn Cook to be the best of the Brits at turning the big ring. Despite that Smith was keen to lead from the front an continued to head the field increasing his lead on Lessing, but Cook, Remy Ramteau, Thomas Hellriegel, and Diddier Volckaert were determined to bring Smith back and were working sufficiently hard on the bike, to pull back more than one and a half minutes on him, eventually leaving Smith finishing the bike a mere ten or so seconds ahead of Cook and Hellriegel who had by this time overtaken Lessing.

Smith's split of 56:53 on the bike was only the 12th fastest recorded time out of a field of twenty three, a far cry from the power man on the bike that in years to come he would be renowned for. Nonetheless, it was now all a matter of whether Smith could hold on for the run. Lessing was undoubtedly one of the strongest runners in the field but with a thirty seven second deficit to Smith as he left the transition Smith was determined that he would not be caught.

Lessing however had other plans and pursued the leaders relentlessly running his way back through the field, overtaking Hellriegel and the tiring Cook, but even to Lessing as the race progressed it became obvious that Smith was not weakening and would hold on for the gold. As Smith crossed the line, Lessing came to the realization that he would have to satisfy himself with a silver medal, whilst Cook would stake his claim on the bronze to make it a British one, two, three. In the end a mere twenty eight seconds separated Smith and Lessing, whilst Cook lost out to Lessing by only ten seconds. All in all it was a good day for the Brits.

For many this type of lead from the front type race was best suited and synonymous to Spencer's type of racing. Coulson felt this was a turning point for Spencer. "That was when his 'racing on his own' type of mentality came about, a mentality that he used that to great affect over the next few years. Once he was out on his own he wouldn't get caught. He wasn't the best runner, he was a very good runner, but he wasn't the best, so he had to get out on his own. In ninety he was swimming really well, in ninety one he was swimming and cycling really, really well in ninety two he was swimming cycling and running really well, so he'd improved in stages but at a phenomenal rate."

Between the European Championships win and the forthcoming World Junior Championships Smith put in a couple of races just to keep himself sharp, but two DNF's didn't bode well for the Worlds and a 16th at Embrum a month before the finals following a bout of the flu did nothing to instill confidence that he was going to perform to his full potential.

Bill Black's coaching had made a significant impovement to Smith.

TRANSITIONS FIVE & SIX
From International to World & Moving On

12th September 1992 World Junior Championships, Canada

Bill Black didn't go out to Huntsville in Canada for the Junior World Championships due to work commitments. Most of the travelling they did then was in Europe and was over the weekends so Black was able travel over to keep an eye on the racing side of the event as well as the training, but Canada was long haul and other obligations meant he would have to wait back in the UK to hear news.

"We prepared well for that, and he kept to the programme." Black recalled. "Obviously we didn't send him out three weeks before." An expensive lesson learnt the previous year when they sent him out too early to Australia for the Worlds and Smith trained himself into the ground over the course and despite being expected to romp home with the gold finished a disappointing 20th well out of the medals on a course that had begun to bore him to death

Black now admitted some mistakes had been made and was quick to adjust Smith's preparation. It became obvious that three weeks was too long, too early to arrive at a competition and given that Smith travelled well and acclimatized well it was concluded that just a few days would suffice.

Whilst he continued to emphasize the importance of knowing the course, he now believed that it was too easy to lose the sense of aggression sometimes required in racing if the terrain became too familiar. Black the consummate professional has always been a stickler for knowing the course prior to even getting to the venue an had spent hours going over maps in an attempt to match training to the demands of specific races.

In those days races didn't provide race profiles so Black improvised the best he could by planning out the course route on a map and using an Ordnance Survey map to work out the hills and descents using the contours to estimate the elevations. In addition to the race route Black would also work out the quickest routes to cut across or get round the bike and run routes so he could keep an eye on proceedings as the race progressed.

If Smith was there to win, so was Lessing, but on this occasion they would be racing different events, since Smith would be racing the juniors whilst Lessing would be racing the seniors. Whilst there was some obvious rivalry between the two athletes, feelings between the two weren't bad at this time though they would soon deteriorate over the next few years. Lessing got himself psyched up for his own race by listening to the radio, which had the commentary of the junior race.

The Junior team at the time comprised of Smith, Mathew Belfield, Richard Allen, Iain Hamilton, Lawrence Nelson and Martin Haggert but the expectations laid heavily on Smith's shoulders, and just to add to the pressure, the start was delayed by a couple of hours because of fog which left the organizers with concerns over the safety in the water. If you couldn't see them you couldn't be sure they were safe. "That was really bad," recalled Hamilton. "You couldn't see any more than forty metres in front of you because it was so foggy and everyone was getting quite tense. If you swam in the wrong direction you could still be swimming now. So I guess they were right to delay it."

At the time of course not everyone felt the same. Nerves played an important part in the race and according to Hamilton, the stress was telling on both father and son. "There was a lot of pressure on him. People knew that he was going to do well. Bill was massaging Spencer all the way through, he was chomping at the bit." Hamilton also recalled that Spencer and Mathew whilst not enemies, didn't see eye to eye at the time, believing they were probably still too close in terms of competition to be totally comfortable with each other. "Myself and Richard were no-ones, with not a great deal of pressure on us. It was easier for us."

Eventually the ok was given for the race to start and at the sound of the hooter the field swam self consciously into the fog, whilst onlookers peered out half in concern and half in expectation.

As the script would have it, it was the misty silhouette of Smith, which was the first to exit the water and the first onto the bike. "The bike was a ten mile out and back on one road and I knew where the leaders were because there was a helicopter above them and this helicopter was like miles away," recalled Hamilton. "I'm talking a good mile away and I though shit I'm in trouble here." Then Hamilton saw the helicopter coming back in the other direction. "Then Spencer went past, (in the other direction) and I was like, phew that's good, that makes me feel better, then there was this huge gap before the next rider went past. I mean I was in the top twenty and I was actually quite happy there, It was only ten miles into the bike and he had this huge gap, he had literally ripped the legs off everyone. He was a different class."

Smith had secured a solid lead on the bike and pretty well had it all tied up by the time he hit T2 barring disaster. "There was like daylight between Spencer and the rest of the field. In fact there was night and day between them," recalled Hamilton.

At 5km there was a run turnaround and Bill Smith and Pete Hamilton (Iain's father) were there as Spencer stormed past. It was obvious that Spencer had won it and Bill was already in celebratory mood. "By the time I got to the 5km point they had cracked open the beers already. In fact my dad was pissed," Hamilton laughed recalling the euphoria that he witnesses as he passed by them.

On the day, Hamilton finished fourteenth and helped to secure the silver team prize, but Smith had devastated the field to take first. Smith was Junior World Champion. It was time for the first British celebration at the Worlds in Canada.

By the time the race had concluded all the British supporters and especially the parents had already had a few celebratory drinks, courtesy of Bill Smith of course. All the juniors' parents were drinking and toasting the south London boy. Spencer after all had won and Bill was not one to allow such an event to go by without a real celebration. Always the first to the bar Bill kept the drinks flowing as long as people kept on wanting to drink. By the end of the celebrations Bill was a little worse for wear, having over indulged perhaps a bit more than a little and according to a number of onlookers Spencer wasn't really happy.

As the drinks continued to flow, by the time the presentations took place Bill was drunk and Spencer, despite having won the World Championship was clearly not in the mood to celebrate with his dad. To make matters worse, because Spencer and Bill in their normal manner weren't staying with the team, Bill had to drive back to their accommodation but was clearly incapable, or at least not safe to do so. Spencer couldn't drive, and Bill was too drunk to get behind the wheel. There was no choice but to wait and let Bill sober up.

Spencer got his gold medal, got his team medal, and he still had to wait a good few hours before Bill could drive. In defiance Spencer literally sat in the car with his bike packed ready to go home, for over an hour. It was Spencer's way of showing how pissed off he was. Bill had only wanted to celebrate the achievement of his son. Spencer had won his first World Championship from the young Aussie Cameron Brown who came second and British teammate Matt Belfield who came third but as is often the case the emotion overtook the situation and the celebrations had partially overshadowed the achievement. But given the closeness of Bill and Spencer, it wasn't for long and soon the team were back celebrating the win.

In the senior race Lessing had the opportunity to make it a double world victory for Great Britain if he could fend of his old adversaries, Muller Horner, Hellriegel and Rob Barrel and when Lessing exited the water after the 1500metre swim, in the top five with only a matter of seconds separating the top placings it looked like he was on target. His tactics on the bike however were in stark contrast to Smith's earlier race. Lessing was significantly slower than almost the rest of the field in turning over the gears, but he knew that as the strongest runner on the course he just had to make sure he got to the second transition without conceding too much to the leaders on the bike.

One by one the stronger riders caught him, and passed him, but none at sufficient speed to put any distance between themselves and Lessing to concern him unduly, so by the time they hit T2 whilst Gareth McCarthey had a lead of twenty five seconds over a chasing group of ten which included Lessing, his plan was still intact. McCarthey was no real threat to the runners in the group as his running was by far his weakest discipline, and as he was swallowed up by the field, so Lessing continued to make his presence known. Lessing at this point must have known that today was going to be his day as he stretched out the field eventually spitting out the back all of his would be challengers. Having split off from his nearest rivals some metres earlier Lessing eased up in the final yards to soak up the win and cross the line with a 31:53 run split that saw him finish twenty five seconds ahead of Rainer Muller-Horner and the flying Dutchman Rob Barrel whose run of 32:36 left him in third place.

The British celebrations throughout the trip were as you can imagine were orchestrated by Bill Smith. It had been a great World Championships for the British and Bill was keen to ensure they enjoyed their stay in Canada and to this point Bill had chosen to hire a car to give them the freedom to look around the surrounding area. However for Bill the temptation to see just that bit more than time would actually allow and poor timekeeping had resulted according to legend, with him left him in a quandary on the last day.

Given the need to catch a scheduled flight back to the UK and the problem of fitting in all the things they had planned. The option was to drop off the hire car at the appropriate spot, get the bus and then fly home or alternatively get an extra couple of hours sight seeing or something like that and then drive to the airport dump the car in one of the car parks. Unfortunately for the hire rental company, The temptation for sightseeing was too great and Bill took the second option dumping the car at the airport... On returning home to the UK Bill dropped in to see his mate Mick Bennett at Sport for Television studios and got him to fax a message to the car hire company apologising for dumping the car. "That was just Billy." Mick laughed. "Live for today."

The Bath triathlon was scheduled for two weeks after the Worlds, and the organizer was trying to get both Lessing and Smith to race it. It would have undoubtedly been a major draw and a good race but according to some parties it was believed that they had colluded to make sure that they didn't both go to that race. Rumours were rife with stories ranging from the fact that they didn't want to race each other, to the fact they weren't offered enough money and that neither felt the organizer deserved to have a race off between two World Champions.

In the end however neither of them raced, which was not only a pity for the promoters but also an opportunity missed to showcase themselves on prime time television, with the BBC televising the event. On the day, it was left to Rob Barrel, and Matt Belfield to take the top placings with British favorite Robin Brew a little further down the rankings. The viewing figures issued by the BBC shown on their Sunday afternoon Grandstand reached an unprecedented 4.1 million people tuning in to watch. In addition figures showed that the numbers actually increased over the fifty minute program which was in significant contrast to the London Marathon figures for that year which actually started with around 4.7 million viewers but eventually fell to 3.7 million by the time the program closed. But the rumour-mongers now started to see Lessing and Smith as bitter rivals and it was a belief that would perpetuate throughout the rest of their careers.

Having won the biggest race of the year, Spencer continued his season with a win at a significantly lower profile duathlon event in

Barnsley of all places and then finished with a final win in Alanya at the end of October and with the racing season ended as the winter training reared its cold and dark beckoning welcome Smith took a well earned rest, whilst Black started work on a programme for the following season which would of course include among others the World Championships which were to be staged in Germany at the end of August.

If the plans had already been drawn up, then in November those plans needed to be quickly reviewed when The ITU broke the news that they had withdrawn the contract from the German Triathlon Union for the ITU World Championships that had been set to take place in Germany in August of the following year. The official reason given was that the DTU had failed to submit a stage payment on time but rumours were rife that there were other reasons behind the ITU's unprecedented decision, especially when the funds were eventually lodged with the ITU treasury shortly after a further request form their administrators. Some believed that the poor organization and management of the World Duathlon Champs in Frankfurt earlier in the year had been partly to do with the withdrawal, whilst other cited failures in the organizers ability so present an acceptable course had been the major reason.

Whatever the real reason it seemed clear that the 1993 World Triathlon Championships would not be going to Germany, and so another venue would have to be found. The question however was where? A question that would soon see Manchester throw its hat in the ring.

If the ITU and the German Federation were having problems in terms of venues and politics, then that was not the only issue that the ITU were facing and in 1993 the ugly issue of drafting continued to raise its head only with increasing rapidity. Unlike cycling where drafting is an acceptable and inherent tactical part of the road racing scene, in triathlon it was a dirty word that was unlawful according to the rules of the sport and involved cheating at an unacceptable and basic level. Drafting was an activity on the bike that involved a rider using the slipstream of another rider to save them energy which could account for up to thirty percent of their effort and was a practice that would ultimately allow them to race faster than they would have been capable had they raced it without the draft.

It was however an issue that was increasingly hard to police with increased numbers of athletes racing and even when implemented was always likely to result in competitors complaining about decisions given against them. The continued frustration with ineffectual enforcement of the no drafting regulations laid down by the ITU had led some to advise that drafting be allowed but should be restricted to the ranks of the elite, a proposal that struck at the very heart of the sport whose traditions of individual efforts fueled solely by the efforts of one person, looked now like it could be lost to a sport that would revolve around team tactics rather than individual ability.

On top of the problems of enforcing strict and fair rules on all athletes equally, an added complication that gave weight to the draft legal format was the commercial sector, i.e. the television companies that felt that without draft legal races, then viewing figures would not be sufficient to sustain the programming and hence no TV. For the States and Australia this was a significant enough issue to result in the Pan American and Australian series to allow drafting. It was a simple issue of no drafting equaling no television resulting in no sponsors and hence no event. For many it was felt it was a fait accompli.

For athletes like Smith who excelled at the cycling discipline, this would put them at a significant disadvantage to those who were run specialists. The argument was simple. If they all rode round in a procession then it would simply end up as a running race with the fastest runner crossing the line first, a point that was felt to defeat the purpose of staging the first to disciplines in the first place. Acutely aware of the issue Smith was concerned at the possible implications of a change of rules by the federations but ultimately as the 1993 season started he had more immediate issues to concern himself with, most notably the early season races.

If concerns were playing on his mind they were certainly not obvious when Smith began his season in style on the 25th April winning the St Anthony's Tampa Bay Triathlon in the United States setting a course record of one hour and forty six minutes with a breakaway run separating him from the rest of the field. Smith over the last two seasons had started paying more attention to his bike position, following advice from Tony Doyle and Mick Bennett and by now he was riding a road bike with his seat pushed back in a cyclist roadie type set up and it seemed to be working for him.

It was a good start to a season following a winter training schedule set by Black and the season looked like it would only get better for the young Brit when few weeks later he would pick up another lucrative win in Singapore, but with Rennes just around the corner, which was sure to bring in a tough field of competitors, which would include Lessing, some felt that this would be his first major race, since winning the World Championships, and his performance there would be a better indicator of his form, especially as the Junior World Champion and the Senior World Champion would be racing head to head.

16th May 1993 Rennes Triathlon, France

So with a significant pressure on him to perform a week after his twentieth birthday, Smith continued his season with the race in Rennes, but some days it is better not to get out of bed and the race at Rennes was to prove one of those days for him even right from the off when a lack of concentration at the start of the race meant that Smith was not even facing the right way when the starting gun was fired. Caught in the mêlée of flailing arms Smith eventually recouped his composure and made his way through the field coming out of the water alongside Lessing, but it was not to be his day.

Normally quick through transition, Smith faltered this time with a zip that just wouldn't budge, eventually leaving him no choice but to literally rip his wetsuit off and charge out of transition in search of Lessing. Even at this point luck was not on his side and a collision with Czech athlete Tomas Kocar cost him yet more time, and the run faired little better so much so that in the end it was too much time, fifty three seconds too much, which was what would have been needed to catch and overtake Lessing before he crossed the line.

With the result a clear disappointment to Smith it would not be long before he would get back to his winning ways, but there was further good news for the young Brit, Manchester having bid to take over the World Championships from Germany had been successful and so Smith would be defending his title, all be it that he would be moving up to senior level, on home territory.

23rd May 1993 National Championships, Swindon, UK

With the World Championships scheduled to be held in Manchester in August there was an increasing urgency among British triathletes to qualify this year in particular. For some especially the age group athletes, it was the only way they could afford to race at the World Championships especially when they were so often held in the States or some other far flung reaches of the world and for others it was likely to be a rare opportunity if not their only opportunity to race in the World Championships on home soil in front of a home crowd.

The first opportunity to qualify for the Worlds was the BTA National Olympic distance Championships, which were to be held at Coate Water Country Park in Swindon. The turnout was sure to be good and for the first time the British media were beginning to take an active interest in the sport because of the Manchester bid, but first there was a race to be run.

For those who thought the race was a formality for Smith they were not far wrong. Smith won his second national title to once again prove his dominance of at least the UK circuit crossing the line over three and a half minutes quicker than his nearest rival. Though it would not be true to say he had it sewn up after he exited the water, after all anything can happen in a race over the full Olympic distance. But having punished himself and wiped out the majority of the field over the first 1500 metres it appeared there were only a few others who could stay anywhere near him. One of the few that did was Matt Belfield with the other challenges, all be they limited coming from Robin Brew, Duncan Rolley and Mark Stenning, the majority of the rest of the field remaining a minute and a half down. Whilst Belfield managed to draw level by the end of the bike by making up a thirty second deficit. Belfield eventually blew up on the run losing eight minutes to Smith and dropping down to seventh place overall.

As if to prove that the rules apply to everyone, race officials added a two minute penalty to Smith finishing time taking it up to 1:58:59 which was still a minute and a half quicker on paper than his nearest rival.

Whilst Smith's win was to some degree to be expected, the women's elite race was won up by Helen Cawthorne, who at thirty one had been in the sport some time but had not won a national title before. Cawthorne had exited the swim in eleventh place but had steadily moved through the field and took the lead in the second lap of the run where she put in the fastest run split to come home in 2:18:27. Interestingly the Junior race over the same course was taken by Richard Allen in 2:06:44. An athlete who would later be contesting a place in the GB Squad for 2000 Sydney Olympics.

Whilst the non-sport media at least turned out to watch for many of them what was their first triathlon, it appeared that they were more bemused by the sport than in awe of it. It is sometimes difficult for those who participate in the sport to fully appreciate how difficult a sport it is to comprehend for the uninitiated.

Upon watching the event Simon Barnes of the Times was led to write "The event a 1.5 kilometer swim followed, at once by a forty kilometer bike ride, followed at once by a ten kilometer run requires the skills you don't meet every day. High among these is the ability to remove a pair of rubber trousers at high speed. Seeing these highly trained, highly charged athletes fighting to wrench their wetsuits free from there ankles is one of the most rewarding sights in the sport." He went on to lament the sufferings of the triathlete stating. "The race is continuous. That means you must cycle and run in your clammy wet bathers, which is not the most attractive aspect of the sport. But it's all worth it for the shades." (Sunglasses) Which he referred to as absolutely 'de rigeur.' In closing Barnes's final remarks at least acknowledged the sporting nature of triathlon when he stated. " But I suppose the point is that there are serious athletes lurking behind them. Spencer Smith, shades, baseball cap, pony-tail won the men's event and Helen Cawthorne, shades, no hat cropped hair won the women's. Lots of futuristic androgeny."

Despite references to wet knickers the sport was at least receiving some mainstream media attention for pretty much the first time in the UK since 1982 when the times had published their brief Spitz article covering the BTA championships at Kirton's Farm.

It was just around this time when the sponsorship opportunities really started to pick up for Smith and it was a time when even the cycling fraternity was taking an interest in the sport. Perhaps the sponsorship opportunities arose through the increase in media attention or perhaps simply because triathlon was becoming considered more acceptable to the die hard one discipline athletes, either way it was to serve to the benefit of Smith.

Ian Whittingham and Jason Taylor were partners in Sigma Sport, which they had set up in 1991. Primarily from a cycling background they soon found themselves involved in triathlon for the first time, a relationship which would expand over the next few years. Their first contact with Spencer was in 1993 when the Milk Race came to within a stones throw of their shop and started in the near by town of Thames

Ditton. Spencer a keen cycling fan had gone down to watch the depart of some of the top amateur cycling teams in the world with both his father and a few other members of the professional cycling fraternity who he had got to know through Tony Doyle and Mick Bennett. "We met Bill and Spencer at the start who were introduced by Tony Doyle who we were quite friendly with at the time, because he was importing Assos clothing into the country," recalled Whittingham. "After the race I invited them back to the shop had a chat and a coffee. By the end of it we'd agreed a small sponsorship package in the form of some money, to have our name on his bike and helmet for the rest of that year which encompassed the Manchester World Championships."

On reflection the deal hadn't taken long to do. With Bill's street-wise approach for negotiating, business deals were sorted quickly whilst the deal was still hot off the press and focused in the minds of the sponsor. Let it go cold and you would lose the sale. Having said that Bill was also shrewd and wasn't one to renege, deals were fair and everyone was a winner.

"That was the way Bill worked," recalled Whittingham. "There was some business to be done, we saw an opportunity and it was done and we were pleased with it." The deal was a thousand pounds, a small amount for Spencer who at the time was still contracted to ride a Specialized bike. But still a grand was a grand."At the time we were new to this, it was a lot of money for us, we were struggling along, business was tough to get things rolling, so it was a lot of money, but we thought he was a pretty amazing guy. It was great to be involved."

While the money was coming in unfortunately for Smith the podium gold slipped from his grasp for the second time that season as he headed to the European Championships which staged on the 4th July in Echternach Luxembourg was not to be Smith's favourite race.

Once again going head to head with Lessing, Smith had got disqualified from the race whilst Lessing went on to win the race by twenty three seconds from the German duo, Hellriegel and Muller-Horner. Smith had been penalised once for drafting at the beginning of the race and on the second occasion that the draftbuster challenged him for drafting Smith got an immediate DQ for telling the official where to go, a habit that would come back to haunt him again in subsequent races.

A non drafting race, the gap between riders was supposed to be kept at ten metres to stop them gaining the benefit of catching the draft off the rider in front and Smith was adamant he had been outside of that distance and had been racing legitimately throughout the race. For the other members in the British squad it wasn't such a big deal, with Lessing winning and Robin Brew taking seventh the team could go home happy, but for Smith it was the worst thing he had faced. An accusation of drafting that he hated and blemish on an otherwise almost perfect season to date.

The relationship between Lessing and Smith clearly deteriorated more by the time the 1993 Senior Europeans were taking place and Spencer getting disqualified and Simon winning that was the worst possible scenario for both Spencer and his father. "Bill went ballistic, saying that was it, they were finished with triathlon and that they would move to cycling," recalled Coulson, whose father was the GB team manager at the time.

The threat that whilst this time was said in anger, and was soon dispelled by a long talk between Bill Smith and Peter Coulson, would however be a threat that some years later would come to fruition.

15th August 1993 Strand Triathlon, Helsinki, Finland

Lessing could not have hoped for better preparation for the defense of his world senior title when with only a week to go he won the Strand Triathlon in Helsinki, Finland. More importantly in some ways he finished ahead of Smith who many believed to be his closest rival. All be it only by seventeen seconds, the win was many believed a psychological advantage that could stand him in good stead. Whilst the race was only over a sprint distance and perhaps was used more to put some speed in their legs than to test out form, nevertheless, the psychological games were all part of the preparation, all part of the strengthening and the weakening of the opponents, and Smith's strength of mind would have to hold firm as would his confidence if he was to beat Lessing in Manchester.

Smith hated losing and held firmly in his psyche a quote that summed up his approach to racing something that had become something of a saying within the team that had now developed around him. "It doesn't matter whether you win or lose. It only matters if I win or lose." USA's Mike Pig took third but he didn't matter either Smith knew in his heart of hearts that the World Championships in Manchester would be between him and Lessing.

The speed with which the Manchester event had to be put together was always going to be of concern, but within the spectrum of issues that resulted from the preparation time available, one of the major topics that would come under close scrutiny would inevitably be the course itself.

The problems of having a course, which began in Bolton and ended in Albert Square, Manchester were always going to be evident. Sport for Television who had taken on the organization of the event had their background developed in professional cycle racing and most definitely not in triathlon. Normal triathlon courses start and end in the same place and involve only one transition area unlike bike races, where especially in tours it is not uncommon to start and finish a race in completely different venues. Everybody in triathlon tried to convince the organisers of the event that it was how it should be but as promoters of the event and the holders of the purse strings Sport for TV were determined to hold onto all the councils that made a financial contribution to the event and Manchester City Council were determined to show off their city in a bid to secure the Olympics.

Manchester's initial reasons for taking on the World Triathlon Championships at such short notice were clearly tied to their attempts to secure the Olympics. Based in the north west of England, whilst Manchester remained an important regional city in Great Britain it has lost some of the extraordinary vitality and unique influence that made it such a phenomenon of the Industrial Revolution. Manchester was continually trailing behind London in the race for recognition, and had been attempting to reinvent and rejuvenate itself through a number of high profile events, among which was its highly publicised bid to host the Olympic games.

Whilst historically Manchester could justifiably claim to be the first of the new generation of huge industrial cities, a city prototype if you like for the industrial era, not only in the UK, but in the western world its profile was now beginning to suffer following the demise of the manufacturing industry. Its transition from a market town with a population of 10,000 in 1717 saw it grow rapidly through the development and success of its textiles industry, so much so that by the 1850's it had a population of some 300,000 inhabitants spilling out of its satellite suburbs and by 1911 that population had grown to some 2,350,000 with a ring of satellite cotton manufacturing towns such as Bolton, Oldham and Rochdale expanding the urban development and the prosperity in the area.

Manchester at that time was indisputably Britain's second city, a manufacturing dynamo, and strangely enough it was Manchester's climate that made it such an excellent location for the textile industry. In simple terms, it was wet. Whilst the generous climatologist may describe the city as mild, moist, and misty, the less poetic may call it damp, dank and dreary. On the positive side, Manchester's temperate climate is without extremes with mild winters and cool summers. On the negative side, its rainfall is legendary.

The reason for the abundance of rainfall is simple geography. The winds in Manchester prevail from the west and south and bring with them frequent rain derived from the almost constant succession of Atlantic weather systems. These conditions mean that whilst annual rainfall is not notably high by the standards of western Britain it occurs on no less than half of the days in an average year. i.e. fifty percent of the time it is raining in Manchester.

Whilst at first glance this would appear to offer no major benefit to the region, it was these very climatic conditions that would prove to be a major advantage to those working in the textile industry. Since the atmosphere in Manchester was always damp, this meant that the cottons being used retained their moisture whether being stored or being woven. This dampness made the cotton more pliable and less prone to snap during weaving, thereby speeding up the weaving process and producing better quality cloths. This believe it or not was one of the major reasons for the success and emergence of Manchester as the second city in the early 1900's. Unfortunately it was also likely to be one of the major contributing factors towards the failure of its Olympic bid.

If the rain wasn't enough, then the lack of sunshine was also probably a major factor in reducing the likely success of the bid. The wet Atlantic air banked against the Pennine slopes to the east of the city produces extreme cloudiness and on about 70 percent of the days of the year, the afternoon sky is at least half covered by cloud. Manchester was definitely not the sunshine city and it was bidding against the likes of Sydney, Australia.

Manchester's golden age had hung on precariously by the thread of the cotton that it weaved but as the 20th century evolved Manchester's textile trade faced a dramatic decline in its fortunes as a result of technological obsolescence and foreign competition. The reasons for the decline in Manchester's significance are not hard to grasp. It almost seemed preordained that the city that was the first to experience the industrial revolution would also be the first to suffer as a result of the post-industrial decline. The ravages of de-industrialisation were catastrophic and the legacy of that decline could still be seen to some degree in the city's surrounding districts, where abandoned mills and warehouses, grand red-brick structures with broken windows and collapsing roofs on the banks of decaying, neglected canals made up the majority of the skyline.

By the early 1980s Manchester was left with an ugly central business and shopping district, surrounded by industrial dereliction, giving way to a series of inner-city public housing projects, which announced their desperation in the Moss Side riots of 1981. In the modern era Manchester struggled with its constant second city status as it continued to be overshadowed by London where at least the sun shined now and then.

If Manchester was to aspire again to the heights it had once reached it was going to have to do it on the foundations of something far removed from manufacturing, and in its attempts to reinvent itself, Manchester focused on bids to host major events both sporting, business and cultural which ranged from attempts to secure themselves as the chosen venue for the new European Central Bank, Britain's new national stadium, and most notably an attempt to host the Olympics.

Even when the bid for the Olympics was being made Manchester could certainly not be perceived as an ideal place to host one of the most prestigious sporting events in the world. The scars left over from the decimation of their industry base were still clearly evident, and its high unemployment and deep rooted social problems were manifest. Nevertheless the council were determined to try to host them and staging the World Triathlon Championships and making a good show of it was sure to do them some good.

22nd August 1993 World Championships, Manchester, UK

Given that the race was to be held in Britain it gave both Bill Black and Spencer the opportunity to really get to know the course. Spencer went up to the course in Manchester on a number of occasions to test it out with the intention of getting to determine appropriate gearing for various parts of the course and more notably refrain from using his breaks on the course by gauging and practicing contours of the road. The first fifteen kilometres of the bike section were exceedingly technical with numerous bends and hills and if he could avoid using his breaks he could save a lot of energy as well as gain some time on his rivals. Come race day he really knew the course well.

If the weather was expected to have an impact on the race, its impact on Lessing's race was nearly catastrophic. It nearly cost him a start. Lessing was using a system on his bike called the Mavic Zapp System. It was battery operated gear system, which meant you didn't have cables on the bike. It was the newest technology, top of the range, and highly innovative but it had one major potential design flaw. It relied on batteries. It rained heavily the night beforethe race, it was Manchester after all, and everything was damp and his battery was gone, the whole system had fused. No battery for Lessing meant no gears on the bike, and these were batteries specific to the Mavic products.

Now whilst the most organized of athletes would ensure they had the odd spare pair of goggle or even bike shoes with them, it had not occurred to Lessing to bring a spare battery for the system, and so on the morning of the event when he realised what had happened all panic ensued.

Iain Hamilton recalled. "We were staying a long way away from the race venue, a place in Bolton, a place called the Last Drop Inn. It was at least twenty five to thirty minutes away by car, and bearing in mind it was the World Championships, they had shut all the roads and there was virtually no way you could get back to the hotel to pick up a spare battery. Everyone was buzzing and panicking. The next thing I knew was that Bill Smith was coming back in with a relieved looking Simon."

Rumour had it that Bill had driven all the way back to the hotel in his usual devil may care driving style, picked up Spencer's spare bike and removed the battery from the Specialized bike computer driven all the way back and given it to Simon. But the truth was much more interesting and related more closely to the preparation that Bill Black had put in to Spencer's pre race timetable.

There was a strange irony that it would be Bill Smith who would come to the rescue of his son's closest adversary. Had Smith senior not gone to the trouble to solve Lessing's problem it would have potentially meant that Lessing would be out of the race, thereby improving

Spencer's chances of victory considerably. But those who knew the Smiths knew better. "I don't think Bill ever wanted Spencer to win that way and I don't think Spencer ever would have wanted to win that way. Any day of the week he would rather Lessing raced. If he loses to him then he lost but if he beat him then he beat him fair." Said Hamilton later when relating the incident. "As much as he didn't like losing if Lessing wasn't there then he couldn't beat him and that may have been viewed as a hollow victory."

Lessing and Smith by this time were manifestly not close friends. Very different personalities with very different backgrounds they were too polarized to become friends. "They were rivals, they were proper rivals and they never pretended to like each other, and a lot of the time when you were in the same teams as those two it was difficult because you knew that the two best athletes who the press were looking at didn't like each other," recalled Hamilton. "Spencer was always confident, he was never cocky, he was always confident and that was probably the difference between Simon and Spence." Given the rivalry between the two athletes, this was not a race where many felt they could honestly hedge their bets. They either wanted Spencer to win or the wanted Lessing.

"The weather was shit." Hamilton recalled. "Typical Manchester, it was dull, it was wet. It was horrible." Now that was coming from an athlete who was based in Nottingham, so when that perspective was then translated and projected onto the feelings of those athletes who had come from sunnier climates such as Australia, Mexico and Brazil, those feelings were clearly magnified.

With the majority of the athletes having to get up at around five in the morning and catch the bus to the swim start, it was not the brightest of mornings in terms of either mood or weather and added to that it was bitterly cold. Black however had made alternative arrangements for the Smiths. Black had spent hours deliberating over maps for the last few days prior to the race but this time not in order to assess the bike course but instead in an attempt to try and avoid it. Black worked out a course that would circumnavigate the road closures implemented by the police, and in doing so he established that by using the back roads and going the long way round to the race start, they could allow Spencer an extra hour in bed and keep him out of the wind and the rain, whilst the other athletes would have to shiver under the makeshift tarpaulin that had been put up at the last minute but inadequately protected them from the elements.

On the morning of the race the hotel was empty of competitors by the time Smith was up and eating his breakfast. The plan was to get Spencer to the start just in time to give him a warm up on his spare bike before they had to get into the water, and thanks to the planning put in by Black and the driving put in by his father, the plan worked perfectly.

Black recalled. "When we got there most of the athletes had been standing around shivering for an hour." He grinned as he summoned up the memory in a way that said the plan was coming together. It had been whilst Spencer was warming up that the news of Lessing's bike was bought to the attention of Bill Smith and quick as a flash Bill came up with the solution suggesting they tried the battery out of the bike computer on Spencer's spare bike. Much to the relief of Lessing, they tried it and it worked, but the stress had clearly got to him.

Using Rivington Reservoir near Bolton as the venue for the swim the murky water looked uninviting and even though his was a race that had one of the world's classiest fields none of the field looked particularly pleased to be getting their feet wet. As the hooter went an array of wetsuited figures with yellow swim caps surged forward into the water and headed out on the 1.5km swim. Greg Welch took an early lead with Brad Bevan and Benjamin Bright, as the defending Senior World Champion Lessing wearing number one kept a close eye on things with the Junior World Champion Smith alongside him.

Exiting the water Robin Brew came up first in 18:00 dead with Kevin Richards and Yves Cordier of France on his shoulder, whilst Smith and Lessing exited four and five seconds later with the pack in their wake. With a long run to the transition area along a carpeted track, Black had briefed Smith before the race to run as hard as he could. He knew valuable time could be lost on the run to transition with only the very focused able to sprint the full distance and was keen to see Smith at the front of the pack from the beginning of the bike section.

Despite Smith's surge, Lessing was first to come out of the bike racking area just a metre or so in front of Smith but then Lessing made his second mistake of the day the first being the bike problem. On the green carpet just before the mount line prior to officially exiting T1 he started to mount his bike. Smith ran past Lessing and then looked back screaming at Lessing, No! Officials quickly pointed out the mount line to Lessing who immediately dismounted and proceeded having to run the bike to the mount line where he had now lost his short advantage over Smith.

Feet on top of his shoes which were already attached to his bike Smith lurched forward to lead the race, picking up speed quickly prior to slipping his feet into his shoes in a matter of a few hundred yards. Desperately seeking a rhythm on the bike Smith held the lead for the first part of the race but by merely a few yards, until eventually the lead was wrestled from him by Brad Bevan of Australia and Hamish Carter of New Zealand but it looked like none of them were sufficiently strong in the early part of the course to take control of the race. Whilst the three immediate leaders swapped places, Benjamin Bright remained in contention and Lessing seemed happy at least at first to retain his position in the top five.

As the bike leg continued so Smith continued to put pressure on the leading five, upping the pace on the hills and pounding the big gears until the group started to fracture. Eventually the young south Londoner started to pull away significantly with only Hamish Carter able to stay close enough for the TV camera crews to show more than just Smith in the lead. As the gap expanded so Smith continued to pile on the pressure, more and more until he had expanded the gap on the chasers to the point that eventually none of the chasers had him in their sights by the time he made it into Manchester and T2. If his plan had been to lead out the bike and hold it on the run, it looked like the plan was working.

Racking his bike as he entered the racking area, immediately outside of the transition box, Smith then ran barefoot into T2 along the red carpet and upon entering T2 flicked his silver Specialized helmet from his head and rushed towards the station where his running shoes were placed. The issue of the removal of his helmet before he reached his individually identified transition point would later be something that raised questions over some technical rules, which ultimately could have resulted in a time penalty or even worse a DQ, but at the time Smith was too focused on the run ahead to be aware of any such possibilities.

Smith's time at T2 was clocked at 1:19:13 Carter followed just under a minute later 1:19:51 with Bevan 1:20:52 and Lessing riding in on his ill fated but fortunate Look bike in 1:21:00. So if Lessing was to catch Smith he had to recoup nearly two minutes, which even by Lessing's standards would be some achievement.

Despite the lead he had, anyone who thought Smith would be permitted relax on the run didn't know Lessing's capabilities, and

Smith knew the race was far from over and that he had to give it all he'd got if he was to be sure. Iain Hamilton was standing with his father and Bill Smith about a mile into the run. Bill had managed to circumnavigate the road closures and get the car parked up in order to see Spencer leading the field out on the first part of the run. Hamilton who had raced earlier in the junior race recalled. "He came down the main road in front of the Arndale Centre which was probably about a mile into the run and it looked like he was crying. Not because of joy but because of the pain he was going through. He was trying so hard."

With five more miles to go on a run course that twisted and turned in the city streets of Manchester, Smith had the opportunity to see his challengers as the two lap course doubled back on itself. Lessing was running strong and soon challenged Carter for second spot, as the New Zealander who had worked so hard to try and stay with Smith on the bike eventually succumbed to Lessing's stride.

Hamilton recalled the feelings of a lot of the crowd that day when Smith came out of T2. "We knew Spencer was a good runner, but we were talking relative to Lessing who was doing a thirty one minute 10k. Spencer was probably doing a thirty two. He got off the bike at Manchester with a minute and twenty and so he knew he had to run bloody hard to win it because the person who came next was Lessing. We were one and two but the Brits weren't really shouting for Lessing, like they were for Spence, everyone that was there was shouting for Spencer, at that point Lessing was still seen by many as a guy that came to race for Great Britain because he couldn't run for South Africa."

There is little doubt that the crowd made a difference to Smith's performance and having worked so hard over the first five kilometres, by the end of the first lap Smith was now too far in the lead to be seriously concerned with Lessing and continued to race confidently now to the cheers of a predominantly British crowd. With a few hundred yards to go Smith even had time to pick up a Union Jack flag held out to him by a spectator and run with it arms aloft as he headed towards his second world title and his first senior world title. Just as Smith came to the line with arms aloft he looked to the sky and mouthed, Yes! Yes! The twenty year old Londoner had done it, he was World Champion.

If those few seconds were for reflection the next few seconds were sheer theatre as he crossed the line and ran straight into the arms of his mother and his gran, and was then was engulfed by a sea of his closest allies, a smiling Bill Black amongst them.

Whilst the celebrations ensued by the Smith family clan, further back down the road Lessing was clearly in line for second place and having run through the cheering crowds, despite being clearly disappointed even he even managed a smile as he crossed the line some one minute and forty seconds later. In stark contrast to Lessing, always one to celebrate, the effervescent Kiwi, Hamish Carter literally skipped across the line clearly ecstatic with his third place a mere twenty seven seconds behind Lessing.

"You can only dream of these sort of things and its just a dream come true." Said Smith later, but his dream had almost become a nightmare when the alleged infringement of the rules concerning the removal of his helmet in the transition area led to an enquiry which could have resulted in him forfeiting the title. Officials might well have disqualified Smith for throwing his helmet away in the transition area between the cycling and running stages rather than placing it in the box as it was believed the rules stated, but there were issues over exactly what the rules stipulated.

It appeared that a marshal, who had shouted instructions to Smith, reported the incident and, it looked possible that Smith would be disqualified. There was concern as one journalist later put it that "injustice might prevail." And at the time there appeared to be considerable confusion as to how the decision to not penalize Smith was made.

According to some, the jury of the International Triathlon Union met and dismissed the infringement on the grounds that no advantage was gained, according to others, the jury could not be summoned quickly enough and the referee, Didier Lehanoff, made the decision. According to others there was equal confusion about what the rule actually stated. There was little question that Smith had racked his bike appropriately prior to removing his helmet, and also no question that Smith was well inside the transition area when he took his helmet from his head. The only question that remained was whether it was a rule that he placed it in the basket provided by the organizers. And even then if that had been stipulated in the localized rules there would have still been controversy over whether this was an official requirement because there was no doubt that it was not a standard rule written into either the ITU or the BTA handbook. Whether Smith had actually infringed a rule and, if he had, what the penalty would or should be had in the end been left to the officials on the day to decide who decided in favour of no penalty.

Interestingly as with any decision made where the rules were open to interpretation, the final decision would have been undoubtedly influenced by the mood of the athletes, who were very pro Smith and wanted to see justice done. None of the competitors felt a penalty against Smith should be awarded. Most notable was the standpoint of Lessing who had both made it clear that he did not want to be awarded the world title on the basis of a technical disqualification and Carter who supported Lessing's stance. Both Carter and Lessing made it clear to the judges that they believed Smith to have won fairly on the day and neither would support any attempt to penalize him, and so it was that justice prevailed and honour among the competitors remained intact. The best athlete on the day had won.

Apart from the medal and a world title, which for many would probably be riches enough, Smith would also go home, richer in monetary terms having pocketed a cheque to the value of seven thousand pounds for first place.

Looking back on the race in hindsight the technical bike course from Bolton straight into Manchester probably suited Smith who was one of the best riders in the pack, and the elite race which had always been profiled as the major event had certainly not failed to deliver, especially for the British contingency, but many of those who raced in the age group events recalled that in Iain Hamilton's words, "the event planning itself was awful. I don't think it helped British Triathlon in some ways, at least from an organizational perspective more than a promotional one. Part of the problem was athletes were waiting for their kit to come back after the race. I don't think it was possible for the busses to get the kit back quick enough. Athletes were cold and shivering in the rain." There had undoubtedly been a compromise between practicality and promotion because the city needed to put something on that showed the centre of Manchester as a result of the Olympic bid and added to this, the short notice with which the event was staged following Germany's pulling out, meant some issues were never really solved. Coupled with this the Manchester weather had just made things worse but promotionally the event had been a success for Manchester.

Manchester could just about cope with staging the event with only three months to really prepare because it had an infrastructure that was used to major events and it was still a major city, which was close to a main airport and the abundance of hotels meant that it could accommodate all the athletes at short notice. But in the words of one cynic. "The local people were not happy really that they had all these road closures in order to benefit a load of skinny vest and pants wearing athletes running around their city." Hamilton purported that. "Perhaps the event had been put on for the wrong reasons." But in the end agreed that wrong reasons, right outcome was better than the other way round.

In the eyes of the British triathlon public, the event was a success. It had been won by a Brit, and that was for many, the most important thing about it. For the City Council investors however, it was only a part of the jigsaw, which would continue to be put together in terms of promotion and publicity for their ultimate aim. If it had fallen short, it was not publicly stated in the publicly generated by the city itself but the wider media and public were not always as positive.

Reflecting on the events of the day Bill Black said it was the proudest moment of his coaching career. The pinnacle of his achievement in triathlon was seeing Spencer cross the line, but in addition, it was Bill Smith's driving that Black recalled moist vividly that day, having rushed around the course giving Spencer his splits the traffic then began to get heavier as they headed towards the finish in the city center. "Patience wasn't Billy's middle name," recalled Black, "and it was only as we jumped our third set of red lights that I began to worry. It was at that point that I decided to keep my head below the dashboard, partly out of fear, partly out of embarrassment. I remember coming up for air, so to speak, only to find us travelling at a rapid rate of knots down the wrong side of a dual carriageway. When we arrived at the finish you could have wrung out my shirt. But it was worth it to see Spencer cross the line first and run into the arms of his two most ardent fans, his mum Barbara and his gran."

In terms of summing up the race, Coulson summed up the race and the feelings of Smith's British teammates and supporters. "He went to Manchester when he was twenty and he won it by taking two minutes off of everyone on the bike and then running scared for ten kilometres. It was brilliant!"

As the triathlon world moved on in search of another World Championship venue for 1994, the City of Manchester continued to look for opportunities to improve their bid. Often hindered by the sarcasm perpetuated by the rest of the country, which manifested itself in spoof articles claiming that special events would be held and changes to the Olympic programme would be undertaken in order to fit in with the Mancunian culture the City tried in vain to shake of its troubled image.

It was alleged that the opening ceremony would have to be kept as brief as possible due to the low boredom threshold of the average Mancunian and proposed that there should be no parade of athletes around the arena, because if they left their rooms at the village for more than two minutes, they would be stripped bare by the time they got back. In addition, bright sparks philosophized as to whether the Olympic flame should be ignited by a petrol bomb thrown by a native of the city wearing the traditional costume of shell suit and balaclava mask.

Closer to the sporting events, others suggested that changes could be made to the competitions themselves in order to improve the success rates of the locals with the Modern Pentathlon disciplines amended to include mugging, breaking and entering, joy-riding and arson and targets in the shooting arena should be adjusted from the traditional bulls eye type to a moving police van or a Post Office counter clerk as was traditional in Manchester. Whilst such musings may have been humorous to many it was unlikely that they did anything to help the Manchester bid any more than the weather had done at the World Championships.

In the end Manchester came a distant third behind Sydney and Beijing for the 2000 Olympics it had already failed in a bid for the 1996 Olympics, which had gone to Atlanta, and press reports suggested that Manchester having spent about £12 million on its bid was simply money wasted. Other more positive onlookers however felt it had at least been a worthwhile attempt to rejuvenate the stagnating city through sport and on a slightly more selfish level, for the British triathletes at least, it had bought some profile to their sport in a country that was still largely unaware of its existence.

If the rain had not put the nails in Manchester's Olympic bid coffin then that was clearly left to one of British sports most highly influential figures when after two failed bids for the Olympics this decade, Sebastian Coe, one of Britain's most famous modern Olympians, remarked that if the United Kingdom really wanted the Olympics, it should recognise that the only place that would be taken seriously internationally was London. This was a true stab in the heart for

Manchester and in the end, the City's consolation prize for not getting the Olympics was to win the bid to host the Commonwealth Games in 2002.

The evening celebrations started early for the GB squad. After a long season of training and racing they were ready to let their hair down and Manchester if nothing else was one of the best venues for a night out and Spencer, following in his father's footsteps who remained renowned for his dress sense planned to make a night of it. From the sponsors point of view Spencer was always immaculately turned out. He would wear exactly what he had to wear to keep the sponsors happy and Bill had always been extremely professional in that aspect of his management. Iain Hamilton recalled however that on this occasion things were a little different. "The only time when he wanted to wear his own clothes and he wasn't allowed to was when he got the medals at Manchester. The medal ceremony in Manchester was done in a nightclub. Manchester Madness! It was just a nightclub where everyone was dancing and the next minute they just turned the music off and handed out the World Championships medals." A situation that many felt was just a little bizarre.

"Spencer non racing was Spencer 'Jack the lad,' and dressed the part, but because the evening presentation was in the night club he was expected to wear his GB top. Spencer was not happy. All the team managers asked Spencer to wear the GB top. The answer came back a definite no!" In Spencer's mind it would appear that he was out clubbing not racing and like any youngster he wanted to look a bit cool rather than looking like some sideshow prize all dressed up in a Union Jack.

He was told he had no options he had to wear it but he remained resolute and defiant, he was not going to change. "Five minutes before the presentations were about to start he was still in his clubbing gear. Absolutely no way was he going to wear the GB tracksuit. I remember all the officials were going apeshit," recalled Hamilton. "Literally everyone from the ITU to the IOC bods who were there because of the Olympics, tried to get him to change his mind. No chance."

After Mick English, who was a good friend of Bill Smith, and someone who Spencer respected, had a word with him and still got nowhere, they soon realised that only person who had any chance of getting him to change his mind was going to be his dad. They found Bill at the bar unaware of all the commotion. A few words from his dad and Spencer did as he had been told, all be it begrudgingly. Spencer put his tracksuit top on, walked up, got his medal and walk away again and headed back to the dance floor to continue with the party, it was not after all every day you became World Champion.

Whilst the celebrations went on that evening, the controversy of the possible infringement of the rules was already being scripted in preparation to hit the morning papers, and the following day Andrew Longmore of the London Times in an article entitled, Confusion clouds British one-two, picked up on the issue claiming the event had, "produced its share of dummies." And he was not referring to the athletes. At a time when Manchester, was still a vying for the Olympic Games in 2000 the British media continued to lambaste the possibility of an event such as the Olympics coming to Manchester and continued to take any opportunity to destroy the credibility of British governing bodies of sport. It is strange but such was and often remains the way of the British press.

Assistant chief race marshal David Haskins responded to the criticism made in the Times, explaining the delay in the decision. In his letter to the editor of the Times, Haskins made his point clear. "As with any event involving almost 1,400 athletes covering 51.5 kilometres, it took a while to get the necessary people together, but the final decision was made in seconds." It would appear the logical conclusion to what for many had been a triumphant British World Championships.

With his medal safely stored, a week after the Worlds, Smith returned to racing when he headed out to the States again which was where he was able to find more high profile races and better prize money on show. Having put in an appearance at Chicago where he would put up a brave fight but have to accept second, a further two weeks later he raced his tenth race of the season in Muscoko where he returned to his winning ways which took his tally so far that season to seven wins, three seconds and a DQ.

With the Bath Triathlon held in the UK offering a showpiece of British talent, many had hoped that Smith would head back to the Britain and go head to head with Lessing but Smith had selected not to race citing an injured foot so Lessing if he was looking to take revenge would have to wait a little longer. Of course with the non appearance of Smith the rumours once again started to surface with some onlookers continuing to feel that the two athletes orchestrated their lack of head to head battles, either because they didn't want to see their status undervalued whilst some others felt it may have simply been a personal thing since there was little doubt that there was friction between the two camps. "I think they became too much of a threat to each other and I think Bill tried to increase the antagonism," admitted Coulson some time later. "I think Bill resented Simon being on the British Team because otherwise Spencer would have been the top dog"

Whilst there was undoubtedly some credibility to the story, in truth Bill Smith was not the only insider who was not comfortable with Lessing taking a place in the GB squad. Permitting athletes who were born in other countries and had little real contact with Great Britain had been a contentious issue for some time, not least among the athletes who may have made the squad but for the inclusions of the so called 'colonials' often accusing such athletes of abusing the joint nationality or heritage system.

In the case of the Lessing-Smith relationship however, it appeared to many, Stuart Coulson among them, to have its foundation in not only threats to the status of Spencer but also on the most human of elements, a simple personality clash. Given the up front and outspoken nature of Bill Smith there was never likely to be any bond between Lessing and Bill Smith. "Bill didn't have a problem with Hobson or Glenn, (Cook) Coulson stated, "but he did have with Simon, and Simon was a better runner. If it ever came down to the run Simon would always win. But I think it had more to do with the fact that they were also just so different."

Personalities aside Smith now had to focus on the end of the season, and whilst the triathlon season was practically over, having won the European Duathlon title the previous year, he was keen to try his luck at the Duathlon World Championships to see if he could be a double World Champion in the same year. The event that took place in Dallas, Texas was held just short of two months after Manchester on the 18th of October so his season had been considerably stretched and Smith admitted to being tired, but he was keen to do well in the run, bike run which consisted of a 5km run, 40km bike and a second 5km run and had prepared well for the race.

Despite it being a close run thing the gold medal eluded him leaving him to pick up a bronze behind winner Greg Welch who had been the 1991 triathlon World Champion and the Swiss born Urs Dellsperger who took second, whilst Matt Brick who had been champion for the past two years and Smith had so memorably beaten in Fairford a year earlier surprisingly and uncharacteristically failed to podium. Not satisfied at letting his season finish without a win, Smith stretched it out even further and a month later picked up his last win of the season in Bilbao to take his total wins of the season to eight, It had been an awesome season for the youngster and he clearly hadn't wanted it to end.

As would be expected Spencer having won the National Champs and then the World Champs was selected as the BTA's Triathlete of the year whilst Helen Cawthorne having won the Sprint, the Olympic and the Middle Distance Championships, took the female prize. On a world scale Smith also picked up the World Triathlete of the Year, and on 19th February in front of more than three hundred guests aboard the Queen Mary moored off the coast at Long Beach California Smith, dressed in a black tuxedo with green tie and hair tied into an immediately recognizable ponytail, picked up his trophy, thanked his sponsors and his friends and dedicated his award to his dad, "Without whose unwavering support he couldn't have achieved his stature in the sport"

At the end of the season, a season that had seen a young lad from Hounslow reach the top of his sport at only twenty years old, one quote from Spencer would sum up his feelings. "Now whenever I am introduced as the World Champion, I think yeah, that sounds good...." And now coupled with a World Championship gold medal he had received another award that demonstrated the respect of his peers manifestly presented on a trophy which read: 1985 Scott Molina, USA. 1986 Mark Allen, USA. 1987 Mark Allen, USA. 1988 Mike Pigg, USA. 1989 Mark Allen, USA. 1990 Mark Allen, USA. 1991 Mike Pigg, USA. 1992 Mark Allen, USA. Now it would read 1993 Spencer Smith, Great Britain. At last he could say he was up there with his heroes.

Apart from the trophy which clearly meant a lot to Smith, Mark Allen who received triathlete of the decade, added to the tribute that Smith had received and composed a speech that cited him as, "leading the new generation of athletes in renewing excitement in the sport." Praise indeed from one of Spencer's biggest heroes.

In contrast to the positive side of the sport, whilst the racing and the celebrations had continued to make the triathlon headlines in 1993, behind the scenes the usual political wars had dogged the sport. The Triathlon Pro Tour (TPT) which had changed its name to the Triathlon

World Tour (TWT) had ruffled the feathers of the International Triathlon Union claiming the Mrs. T's Chicago Triathlon held on the 21st August, to be the World Championships.

The ITU claiming the rights to the title World Championships as a result of the International Olympic Committee decree then went about "advising" a number of the high profile selected pros to stick to the ITU events or run the risk of being banned from all ITU events including the World Cup Series and the World Championships. Whilst the TWT made it clear that they believed all athletes to be free to select which ever races they wished, and that they would support them if they wished to challenge the threat of sanction that the ITU had proposed.

In the end the TWT agreed to return to their original name but the embers still smoldered in the political arena, and the fires of political struggle would erupt again as the warring fractions continued to try to use the athletes as pawns in their power games.

In 1994 Smith continued his habit of appearing at events looking somewhat like a walking advertising hoarding, Saucony Shoes, Ergomax creatin, Rider Sports wear, and a wetsuit made by Snugg, along with a range of other sponsors emblazoned his kit including the strangely named Fashion Fun Fanatic. Spencer was also used to model and promote the launch of the Speedo S2000 fabric which was part of the new GB race kit with a claimed "lowest coefficient factor in the world" tag attached to it was the talk of the swimming fraternity even if for most the UK triathletes the customary wetsuit worn over the top meant little advantage was really gained at least in the cold British waters. Quite how his other sponsors felt about Smith being used to promote it even if in a relatively subtle way didn't seem to be raised and the pages of 220 Magazine seemed to give more opportunity to see pictures of him racing than pictures of him standing hands on hips in a somewhat self conscious pose.

His relationship with Speedo was slowly building, and even though at the time he was only wearing their goggles when racing, when servicing the needs of the innovative apparently cash rich triathlon market, new product developments was a must for Speedo, and their investment in Spencer needed to show returns. So Smith also found himself working closely with Speedo's research and development department, in an attempt to develop better goggles for the long distance and the open water market.

Apart from the developments in the swim technology, Smith had spent the winter working on his big gear ambitions despite the protests from Bill Black who had been trying to develop a more efficient and less taxing spinning style to Smith's riding. Nevertheless, confident in the improvements in his strength Smith had selected to go for a bigger chainset with a 39/53 tooth chain ring and an 11/23 tooth sprocket. Coupled with this he had moved yet again to another bike, this time a rigid carbon Cyman frame and had upped his cranks from 172.5 mm to 175mm.

Intent on maintaining the power concept of racing Smith quipped. "I'm not saying I'll be using the eleven sprocket constantly but when I can I will." Having seen Chris Boardman set a new time trial record at the Olympics on the revolutionary Lotus bike, the British built carbon fibre Cyman frame which Smith now had in his possession must have felt like a move in the right direction, especially in defining a better aerodynamic position that he and Black had been trying to do for some time, but the frame was a disaster.

The frames cracked, the gears slipped and Smith went through an incredible thirteen bikes in only sixteen weeks. Eventually as the season started to get under way it became obvious that the Carbon Fibre frame would have to be dropped. Smith was just too powerful for it and having broken so many it seemed ludicrous to continue with trying to make the bike function properly and mechanical failures couldn't be risked in races, even if they could in training. So in Spencer's words it, "went out the window."

Ian Whittingham at Sigma, remembered the Cyman bike vividly. "Part of the deal was that we serviced and looked after Spencer's bikes at the time. I remember it was made by a formula one company and our poor mechanic spent many, many hours trying to make that pile of shit work. It was an awful bike, it was a totally flawed design."

Despite the problems with the bike the provision of mechanical services by Sigma and the flawed Cyman bike meant that Bill Smith was in the shop most weeks and would ultimately led to Bill Smith gaining an advantage as he always did. This time it would be an apprenticeship in bike mechanics. "He would turn up clutching a Magnum ice lolly for me and Jason, walk through the door and then make himself at home for the rest of the afternoon." As Billy watched over the Sigma boys working on the bikes he became more experienced in the mechanics of the bike. A role that he would increasingly take over in the Spencer Smith team but at this time he was happy to sit back and learn from those around him who had been in the sport longer.

In the end just as the season got under way Spencer and his dad Bill settled on a Belgium bike sponsor. The bike was more laid back than any of his previous bikes but as Smith pointed out in spite of that he still felt he could get his best power output out of that design, but as he was to find out as the season progressed, that assumption was wrong.

Apart from changing bikes, which in itself appeared to offer little concern to the Smiths, a move of residence was also on the cards for the family and in April, Smith and his family moved to San Diego where apart from the lifestyle that it afforded them, the climate was also arguably more beneficial to his training. There was never any question that the whole family would move. The reasons behind the move were obvious, the West Coast of the USA was a far cry from Hounslow and Twickenham and could offer improved facilities, all round terrain and better weather than west London with its traffic and its rain.

Smith was confident that the move would help him progress. With flat traffic free roads on the coast and plenty of hills if he headed inland and a climate that made training feel a little less like a punishment. Smith was obviously pleased to be making the move, but recognized he would miss a few friends. "Maybe I'll miss a few other things as well," Smith mused, "but the benefits outweigh the advantages." Obviously his move to the States would cause some difficulties with regard to training schedules and programs which had been put together by Bill Black for such a long time, but Smith confirmed that Black would continue to set his programs, which he would fax him across and they would continue to maintain contact over the phone.

According to Black in his assessment of Spencer's outlook and character he felt he would have no problem fitting in well in America. The whole Smith family had enough experience of the States to be able to identify the pros and cons of the move and the, "sporting, youthful, action packed and vibrant character," of Spencer that Black had commented on in the media, in many ways were characteristics that could be seen reflected in San Diego. In addition Black whimsically noted at one time that. "He was fast in the water, on the bike or running… but he hated walking." The final point being a characteristic also thought common to most Americans.

Whilst Black had commented on Smith's hatred of walking in jest, if the research undertaken by a researcher in the University of California some years later were to be believed the point that

Americans fail to walk was not just a common perception, but also a serious problem for the American health organizations. It seemed strange that in a country that had invented the Ironman and prior to that had established the jogging craze, that according to the research at the time, over eighty five percent of the population of America could be categorized as obese with an astounding thirty five percent categorized as totally sedentary. By this it meant that they literally walked nowhere. The research found that the average American walked on average less than seventy five miles a year, which whilst at first glance may be considered a reasonable distance for the average Jo as opposed to an Ironman triathlete who may clock up that sort of mileage in a week, a closer scrutiny of that figure becomes more concerning when you establish that that distance equates to just over 1.3 miles a week, which in daily terms results in an astoundingly sloth like three hundred and fifty yards. A distance that could easily be covered simply walking round the office in search of a pen that works.

It looked like Smith would fit right in if only on the walking front even if his running swimming and biking distances may have been a little out of line with the American average. In truth however San Diego had a thriving triathlon community with many of the world elite located there for much of the year, so Smith would not have any problem finding training partners.

Having sold up in London, the Smith's secured a condominium on a golf course and the whole Smith family headed west. "I'm really pleased they're coming." Smith had said, of his parents, as if there was any chance that his dad and mum would have been separated from him. Smith liked having the support of his family and duly admitted it, but was also conscious of their needs and had stated that. "The main thing is that we're all happy." On that score there didn't seem to be any complaints from either Bill or Barbara, who were clearly looking forward to the move as well. How long they would stay in San Diego was a matter of conjecture and they had placed no time limit on how long they would commit to the USA, but sufficient to "settle in" was an indicator that it would be for some time.

As a result of Spencer moving to San Diego, things would inevitably change on the sponsorship front and whilst Black remained his coach, Sigma were no longer his local bike shop and so the relationship terminated at least on a business level, with Nitro in San Diego becoming his local haunt where no doubt Bill would take up residence and entertain the troops much as he had done back in south west London.

Prior to the season Smith was confident he could build on his success but felt the improvements may now come a little steadier than had been the case over the past few years. "The better you get, the harder it is to make big jumps in standards." The two buzz words for Smith were stronger and experience, but it was hard to imagine how much stronger he wanted to be, already by far one of the biggest triathletes on the circuit.

Spring preparations saw Smith drop off the mileage that he had built up over the closed season and start to concentrate on shorter sharper quality sessions. Black had always been keen to ensure that Smith had sufficient recovery time in between racing and training and the recognition that Smith picked up speed through racing as the season developed was an important consideration in the structure of his training schedules. With a plan to do no more than thirteen or fourteen events in the season the future looked bright and sunny for Spencer and the rest of the Smith clan but things did not go according to plan.

The 1994 season didn't start well for Smith with an unfamiliar tenth place in Tampa at the end of April, a sure sign that something was not right. With his next race scheduled for late May, where he would be going head to head with Lessing and have to try to improve on the second spot he had got the year before there was little doubt some improvements would have to be made

21st May 1994 Rennes Triathlon, France

The Rennes triathlon had it all, sponsors, money, stars and spectators. The event in the heart of Brittany was the brainchild of a local restauranteur cum triathlete. With a chain of over one hundred restaurants he had enough political and business clout to ensure that the event was a huge success. With the money that Monsieur Le Duff was offering he was able to tie in both Lessing and Smith to the race, which cut no corners and promised much. It was the first time they would race head to head in 1994 and the triathlon press interest was acute, not least because of the French wine and food offered by way of the VIP hospitality.

Lessing had started his season well with two straight wins in the US and a second place to Aussie former World Champion Miles Stewart in the Bercy indoor triathlon in Paris. A somewhat chaotic spectacle that revolved around a swimming pool in the middle of a velodrome with a running track wedged between the two.

What the event lacked in organization, it certainly made up for in terms of spectacle in front of 7000 fans screaming to the sounds of rock music blasting over the PA system and it was an interesting if not high profile win. In addition to his continental jaunts Lessing had also managed to secure a tougher than expected first at the Reebok Duathlon only the week before and was clearly on good form.

Spencer on the other hand had had a poor start to his season. His uncharacteristic tenth at the Professional Tour race in St Anthony's in Florida on April 24th was his only serious outing so far, and if losing the event was not enough then losing it by a margin of nearly five and a half minutes over an Olympic distance was sure to have dented Smith's confidence.

With the race starting in the afternoon the athletes had been treated to a VIP lunch, but many had had to pace themselves Smith included despite the delicacies on offer. Normally Smith would have been one of the first to the buffet but on this occasion there were other races to win.

As it was when it came to the racing, Smith was first out of the water with Lessing on his heels and Aussie Ben Bright not far off the pace. Despite a good number of the French elite squad and a number of European based Aussies in the field, it was from then on a three horse race. Unusually for Smith he actually started to lose contact with Lessing and Bright on the bike, something that few had ever witnessed and evidence once again that all was not well with Smith. Fortunately however with the alleged support and perhaps somewhat illegal drafting that was possible behind the flotilla of press cars and motorbikes on the course Smith eventually clawed his way back up the leaders and then maintained his place in the group of three.

Bright perhaps psychologically as well as physically resigned himself to third before they even got off the bikes and even if they left the transition together it wasn't long before Lessing pulled easily away from Smith and Smith pulled away from Bright. Smith, never one to give up looked despondently up the road as Lessing continued to stride away, but Lessing on the other hand never looked back at him and was eventually well beyond his reach and well beyond his vision. So far in fact that by the time Lessing took the tape he had put two minutes into Smith who admitted he was gutted at coming second.

Of course, he had been second to Lessing in the same race the previous year and had then gone on to win the Worlds, but Smith was not one who liked to lose, not at any race and given the first couple of results, it appeared that whilst Smith's family and luggage had been safely transported to California his form had been lost in the move.

The following week prior to heading back to the States, Smith took up the opportunity to race in Europe again, but this time in it was in Holland. Still clearly under par in terms of performance he no doubt regained some of his confidence with a win but the race was not a major event with few of the major players lining up at the start and Smith remained concerned with the way he was performing, knowing that against stiffer competition he would not have found the win so easy.

5th June 1994 Mazda Orange County Triathlon, USA

Despite winning in Holland, after losing to Lessing at Rennes and the tenth spot in Tampa it was clearly not just the psychology that was affecting Smith's performance but also the physiology, and the Orange County Mazda race which he had headed back to the US for was yet another disappointment for him, and his supporters who saw him pull out in the run with a back strain and return to his dad Bill who dragged him away from the journalists, intent on getting his son onto the massage table so that he could get him a rub down. As Bill put it. "Now son, now." Not one for stretching, Spencer had always risked injury from a lack of flexibility coupled with pushing big gears, a habit he had yet to get rid of. In 1993 and 1994 Smith would push a gigantic 54/11 or 53/11 gearing ratio, whilst most other triathletes would at their most, ride a 52:12, and then only down hill with a tail wind. It was a habit that Bill Black had tried to get him out of for some time in an attempt to improve not just his biking but also his running but Smith had always fought against it.

From originally being considered a swimmer who could bike and run, Smith had now become a much more accomplished bike rider, undoubtedly one of the best on the circuit, if not the best, but he insisted on continuing to ride the big gears, Black had tried to adjust Smith's technique for some time, but in Black's words. "Without any success. We tried to move him out of the big gears, but he'd be pushing something at about 70 rpm."

"For those that saw him on Portsmouth Hill in ninety one, which is a 1 in 10 ascent, he was so over geared," Black recalled of a previous encounter, and it seemed that the lesson still had not been learnt, he still wanted to ride big gears, irrespective of the inefficiency and potential damage it was doing him.

At the time of the 1991 race, despite being aware of Smith's big gear tendencies, Black hadn't seen the over gearing because he was further down the course, but when it came to light on television. He recalled the response from one of his Bill's close friends who had been an Olympic medallist on the track. "He had the rag taken out of him by Mick Bennett, (then Manager to Tony Doyle the World Pursuit Champion) when he returned home." Black grinned savouring the moment. "But even given the ridicule he had endured he had stuck to his own way of riding." After all he had won the Portsmouth race anyway, and now two years later he was the current World Champion, and how much ridicule can you give a World Champion.

"Once he makes his mind up that's it," said Black. "You couldn't always be by his side either in the car or on the motorbike, you have to rely on the athlete to try and keep to what you set them." Black's approach was simple. "If you spin more you can run faster." Given that Black was now farther away from Spencer and had even less opportunity to keep an eye on him it was clear that he was at liberty to adjust his training to his own preferred style, and it appeared to be working against him. Black had continued to work on Smith's cadence since day one but it wouldn't be until some years later when Smith found himself in professional cycle racing that he would finally accept the need to improve his cadence. Until then it would appear that the Smith philosophy remained, 'bigger is better.'

On reflection Black felt that some courses, especially the flat out and back courses in Holland, lent themselves to riding a big gear, but felt the big gears ridden by Smith in these early years were more a reflection of Smith's attitude to training rather than Black's own training schedules. Undaunted Smith had continued to ride big gears and it appeared they may have been taking their toll. "Having big legs, massage is vital for me," admitted Smith at the time. With legs that bulged like a track sprinter or bodybuilder the only way Smith could displace the lactic acid from his legs after a strenuous workout was through massage and his dad Bill would ensure that he got a massage after every race and at least two or three times a week whether he was racing or training.

Shortly after Orange County, despite his liking for the big gears Smith admitted that he was considering dropping down to a 53 tooth chain ring and reducing his crank arms from 175mm to 173.5 in an attempt to help him speed up his pedal stroke. So it seemed perhaps that the idea was hitting home. In contrast however he also commented later in the season that he planned to undertake a committed strength programme once the season was over, so the power theme was still clearly reflected in his planning.

On reflection Smith acknowledged that his early training schedule had been too much. He had gone so well in 1993 that his motivation had gotten the better of him. He had got so excited about the way he had been performing that he wanted more of it and the only way he could see himself improving was more time spent at an ever increasing intensity. It took so much out of him that he admitted he was tired before the season even got underway. "Too much, too long."

Having moved to San Diego two things had happened. Firstly he was surrounded by athletes, cyclists, runners, triathletes and every day he would find a new training partner who always seemed to be on their toughest training day of the week. By the end of it Smith was fit, there was no doubt about that, but there was no speed left in his legs, he was in a condition more suited to Ironman races than the Olympic distances he was racing.

Secondly he had lost his routine. Swapping from the early morning swim sessions he was accustomed to and the treadmill sessions that Bill Black would so meticulously plan had meant his training patterns were shot almost the minute he unpacked his suitcase. Being away from Bill Black had made a difference, Bill had always been a strong controlling factor in Spencer's training. To top it all, despite living in San Diego, Smith had been travelling significantly more, including a considerable number of races in Europe which had messed with his routine even more. Smith would admit later. "My confidence was at an all time low."

Smith didn't race for the next month, instead trying to recover and get himself back on track both physically and mentally. But whilst Smith was recovering the European racing circuit continued with the European Championships scheduled for the 2nd July in Eichstatt.

As it happened Smith had confirmed earlier in the season that he would not be racing the European Championships instead deciding to concentrate on his preparation for what looked to be a heavy racing schedule in July and August. This perhaps said something about the value placed on a European title but given his performances it was probably not such a bad idea to avoid the races anyway and it was not just Smith who had felt the European Championships were not important enough to race. It had not been expected that Lessing would race either given that he was to be racing Nice the weekend before in the inaugural ITU Long Distance World Championships, but in the end whilst Smith wasn't there, Lessing was.

For Lessing the decision to race was made only two weeks before, having decided to pull out of Nice during the bike, when a tyre that had been specially prepared for him by his wheel sponsor Mavic, punctured early into the race. Not normally the end of a race for a classy professional like Lessing, on this occasion the punctured tub had been stuck on so well by the Mavic team that it refused to come off the rim in the cold wet conditions. As if having had to shred the tyre off the rim using a quick release skewer on his bike before he could fit the spare wasn't enough, to add further to his misery, of the two aerosol puncture canisters he had with him, one refused to work whilst the other sprayed foam all over the road. Eventually having borrowed a pump from a team mate and successfully pumped up his tyre, over seventeen minutes had passed, leading Lessing to decide that a warm bath rather than a cold race was a better option for the day. Hence Lessing was at Eichstatt.

In a race that Lessing dominated from start to finish little could be criticized in the way Lessing performed. He left the water joint first with Russian Aleksander Merzlov, who whilst a good swimmer was not expected to make any major impact on the race and was certainly little threat to Lessing, whose speed on the bike and run was significantly faster than the rest of the field. Having simply extended the lead to the point that it was almost unassailable by the time he reached the second transition Lessing headed out on the run and proceeded to expand his lead by a further fifty six seconds over the 10km course, crossing the line nearly two minutes ahead of Ralf Eggert and Muller-Horner who took second and third.

9th July 1994 Seefield Triathlon, Austria

Whilst Lessing's form was excellent, despite the rest, Smith's poor performances continued to dog him and Lessing appeared to be revelling in it. The week after the Europeans they raced head to head for the second time that season in the Protour Mountainman event in Austria. Lessing won again with Smith finishing a tortuous tenth. A tenth place obviously did little to renew his confidence. More rest, more recovery were needed, Smith was concerned, his family were concerned and Bill Black was concerned.

Black had seen it all before when he had set up the programme for Smith prior to the Junior World Champs in Australia, and young Smith had trained himself into the ground almost totally ignoring the schedule Black had written for him, but on that occasion Smith had returned to the UK where Black had been able to identify the problem and show him the error of his ways.

On this occasion Smith was not coming back. It was now up to Smith to work it out for himself, as Black could only guide and advise from afar.

24th July 1994 Strand Triathlon, Finland

Two weeks later in the Pro tour of Helsinki Lessing and Smith came head to head for the third time in the season, previously a rarity in itself it now appeared almost a weekly occurrence. But despite the fact that Smith exited the water ahead of the field, Lessing once again proved too fast for him on the run pushing him into second place despite Smith holding onto his a narrow advantage throughout the bike.

Mike Pigg, Smith and Lessing were all there or there abouts with little to separate them by the time they entered T2 and on the run they had shadowed each other closely. So closely in fact that according to onlookers Smith and Lessing began blocking each other when they were going for water and it was getting a bit physical.

Given the stature of Smith and the character of Lessing there was little doubt who would come of worse should it come to blows and so it appeared that with a kilometer to go Lessing decided to kick before tempers boiled over.

Undoubtedly the best runner on the circuit Lessing was able to kick hard leaving Smith in his wake. The psychological and the physical lines had clearly been drawn and on the face of it, it looked like 1994 was not going to be Smith's year. Over-training however was only one of the factors that Smith could put down to his lack of form.

In retrospect it appeared that Smith had also made the mistake of mixing racing in Europe with racing and training in the States and it had upset his routine and his training. The travelling had got to Smith and he was determined he would not make the same mistake in the future. With only a few months to the World Championships, Smith's training and racing schedule had to become a little more focused and he knew it.

21st August 1994 Mrs. T's Triathlon, Chicago, USA

Chicago was the third race in the Protour series, a high prestige race and a potential good earner for the Londoner. Having finished in second place the previous year and with prize money totaling $50,000 it would have been a good day to put in a top three performance but Smith's poor performance or bad luck, depending on how you viewed it surfaced again and saw him pull up after the bike complaining yet again that he had been pushing to big a gear.

Smith's DNF left Lessing to scoop first prize and his fourth win over Smith in four outings, with American and Australian double act Mike Pigg and Greg Welch picking up the other podium spots. Having also pulled out in the Orange County Tri earlier in the year suffering from a back pain, Smith seemed to be having a problem coming to terms even with his own advice of dropping down the gears let alone Black's.

With his left leg having been previously diagnosed as being slightly longer and stronger than his right, there was always a danger of over compensation which in the long term could affect posture and cause back problems if not resolved. It was not an uncommon problem among athletes, in fact World Track Champion, Tony Doyle who had mentored Smith for some in the early days had an identical problem, which he had overcome. But right now Smith had to get it sorted, because it was a problem that was definitely costing him wins and potentially costing him money.

Spencer would look back on the Chicago race as the low point of his season. "On the bike I had nothing," recalled Smith some time later. "I was off the back, I couldn't keep up with anyone. Mentally my confidence was being affected." Smith knew he had not been achieving the bike splits in the season, which he felt he was capable of. "The more I tried to keep up. The more my legs weren't fresh for the run." He said, and a look over his performances seemed to back up this view. Smith recalled that the other athletes were very supportive, most athletes have been there when the results just won't come, and its not a place that is easy to come back from so its rare for those racing to gloat over failure as much as the media sometimes do. Smith was appreciative of their backing.

Smith not willing to put over training and big gears down as the only reasons behind his poor performance had also felt that it could be his riding position or even the bike that was at fault and at the end of August 1994, Smith had a chance encounter with a family run shop in California, where the Allen's, a father and son team of bike builders offered Smith the opportunity to ride their SpeedFrame model.

With a 78 degree seat angle the bike was considerably steeper than the road bikes that he had become accustomed to but according to Smith the bike felt right from the moment he started pedaling with the balance problem of being positioned right over the bottom bracket dissipating the minute he was on the move. Convinced of the benefits Smith took up the offer and started riding the Allen SpeedFrame in the hope it would overcome some of his problems.

1st September 1994 The Big Bear Triathlon, Chicago, USA

The weekend after Chicago Smith selected to race the Big Bear Triathlon in Southern California where the turn around for his season started to take shape. "I had a fantastic race, I just did it for myself," recalled Smith. Whilst the field was strong it was not full of world-beaters, nonetheless Smith was ecstatic and rightly so given the performances he had put in earlier in the season.

Athletes often know when they're on song recognizing that It's not just about the time achieved, but about how they feel when they're out there, and Smith was feeling good. Picking up only his second win of the season Smith had broken a bad spell but more importantly he had broken the course record and regained some of his confidence.

His racing on the up he continued to race in the States picking up wins in the Malibu Triathlon in California a couple of weeks later and the Lighthouse Triathlon in St. Augustine, Florida at the beginning of October and with only one more race scheduled before the World Championships, where he would have to defend his title, he knew that he was coming back to form, It was just a matter of whether he could sustain it.

30th October 1994 ITU World Cup Triathlon, Ixtapa, Mexico

With the Worlds only a month away, racing this event in the seaside resort of Ixtapa, Mexico, was a big step for Smith even though he wouldn't know it and it was to be no easy ride. This was to be the first draft legal race that Smith would ever race a format that Smith was strongly against. Despite his reservations over the draft legal issue Smith now felt he was on good form and hoped to perform well, a point that he duly demonstrated from the start where his intentions to still race from the front irrespective of the drafting were obvious as he exited the water with a large group of and then tried to break away from the lead group on a tough bike course that saw some 25,000 wildly enthusiastic Mexican fans lining the route.

Despite the format and the top quality field Smith continued doggedly to try to get away on the bike on a number of occasions, nearly managing to do so twice, but eventually realizing the futility of his attempts in a bunch that refused to let an individual breakaway go, he eventually fell back into the pack and accepted the almost inevitability of being forced to slog it out over the run.

T2 was a not a crowded affair with Smith and a few of the front pack having managed to split the field, and upon exiting the racking area and heading out on the run Smith found himself running stride for stride and shoulder to shoulder with the young Australian Brad Bevan, and that was the way it stayed with neither facing a challenge from the rest of the field. With only the final three hundred metres to go they remained neck and neck but then Bevan started to pull clear.

With legs still tired from his previous attempts to break away on the bike Smith, found himself unable to stay with Bevan as the Aussie surged for the line and so it was that Smith would eventually find himself losing out to Bevan who took first place. Smith however was feeling good about his performance despite coming second. "It felt nice to be back where I used to be and should be," Smith thoughtfully added. "I train hard to stay there." There was little doubt that Smith was disappointed not to have won but his response was garnished with a sense of relief that his performances were starting to improve.

Whilst the good news for Smith in October related to the fact that his form was coming back, On a much wider scale there was further good news for the sport of triathlon as a whole when the story was broken in the media that triathlon was to be officially added to the

Sydney 2000 Olympic Games a mere six years after it first official World Championships had been held in Avignon. Les McDonald, the President of the ITU, who had been at the forefront of the campaign with the IOC said that, "triathletes had captured the imagination of the IOC members." Now it was the imagination of the athletes that were running wild. The Olympics was undoubtedly one of the biggest moves forward that the sport of triathlon had made, but six years and Sydney seemed a long way off and there were more immediate tasks at hand with less than four weeks to New Zealand.

With Spencer's form improving he continued to put in over twenty thousand metres of swimming, two hundred and fifty miles of cycling and around thirty miles of running into his weekly training schedule ranging from recovery sessions, to lung bursting all out keep going till you cry, lactic acid burning sets both on the treadmill, the turbo and on the road. Smith's aim was clear and definite, he was going to retain his title, he was going to win, but whilst Smith was preparing to win the World Championships in triathlon, the British media continued to ignore the sport and seemed more concerned with who was going to win the first British lottery

27th November 1994 World Championships, New Zealand.

An insight into the psychological games that Bill Smith could play with those who challenged his boy was highlighted when there was controversy over the allocation of numbers issued by the International Triathlon Union. Hamish Carter was the hometown favorite and it was being discussed as to whether he should be given number one for the race. In addition, Brad Bevan was the World Cup leader at the time and was also making a claim for the number.

If the ITU even contemplated the possibility of giving it to anyone else apart from Spencer, they soon changed their mind with the help of a little verbal persuasion from Bill. Spencer was the reigning Champion and Bill was adamant that Spencer would be wearing number one. To make his point clear, He had put a big notice up in the foyer of race HQ hotel. It read. "SPENCER SMITH IS NUMBER ONE."

Spencer's form may not have been good all season but Bill Smith would allow them to take nothing away from his boy. As would be expected with Bill on the case, Spencer eventually raced in number one. A psychological blow in favour of the Smith entourage even before the race had started.

Bill and Spencer were so close that they were often the subject of ridicule, perhaps sometimes out of jealousy or perhaps just because some people couldn't see what they had for what it was. Spencer when asked about his relationship put it in perspective for all to see "There's a strong thing between me and my dad. No matter what anyone writes or anyone says. I don't give a shit to be honest with you, and the more they write and the more they say, the stronger we get."

In the build up to the race Bill had done his best to keep his son in the media's interest whilst still protecting him from the pressure associated with being a defending champion, a difficult line to tread. Spencer himself had kept a pretty low profile leaving it to everyone else to speculate as to who would be on the rostrum at the end of the race. Even if they had won the first stage in the psychological war, there were clearly questions over the patchy performances that Smith had put in over what had become a very long season and Smith was aware that local support for New Zealander Hamish Carter who had got bronze in Manchester the year before was bound to be high. In addition a significant threat was also sure to come from Aussie Brad Bevan who had raced consistently throughout the season and had just come off a six race World Cup winning streak. Smith had reason to be concerned, especially as he had just lost to him a few weeks previous.

When race day emerged it was an overcast and gently breezy morning, which was much to the relief of both the promoters, and those competitors who had endured the gales a few days previous that had put an end to any pre race preparation in the windy city, and resulted in the abandonment of a yacht race in the harbour whilst calling upon the skills of the coastguard to rescue a number of sailors by helicopter.

As it was, at ten am in the morning, huddled together in a deep and choppy sea the race commenced with the best triathletes in the world departing with a flurry of arms and legs in water that was so cold it bit to the very core of even the hardiest of the field. Unperturbed by the waves, however, the young French athlete Benjamin Sanson went straight to the front to and continued to lead out the swim for the duration of the 1500 metres. A strong swimmer who was coached by his father, Sanson was determined to make an impact on the field and indeed in the swim he did. Having in his normal manner taken the mantle of lead swimmer from start to finish, the Frenchman exited the water alone some thirty three seconds in front of a pack that included

Smith and the ever present Brad Bevan .

His joy at the front of the race however was to be short lived as Smith having exited the first transition, hammered hard on the pedals and in a flurry of brute force and spit, and surged past Sanson into the lead with only a matter of metres covered on the road. Despite an excellent swim Sanson was no match for many of the race favourites and as had been predicted by the pundits eventually drifted back through the pack as he suffered on the bike and struggled valiantly on the run but finally finished in a time more than five and a half minutes down on the leaders.

Whilst the remainder of the pack pushed headlong into the wind, Smith in his usual manner punched out the big gears on his SpeedFrame and headed along the long flat section of motorway that made up the first 10km of the bike course. By the time Smith hit the first hill at 13km he had nearly forty seconds advantage, and was racing where he liked to be, off the front! Smith dug deep determined to put some yet more distance between himself and the Aussie, Bevan who he knew had a good run and still turning over a massive 54:11 gear he continued to grind away.

It was now up to the others to chase harder but no one seemed willing or able to respond. Hamish Carter who would normally have been one of the workhorses on the bike had punctured at 5km and was out of the running and no one was willing to commit with a punishing 10km run race still left after T2.

By the time Smith hit the second transition he had a lead of 1:44, which by the end of the day would show Smith's bike split to be the fastest over the course by some thirty seconds. Putting that sort of gap between the chasers and the leader was a dying art, and perhaps nobody had expected it, but now they would have no choice but to respond. If Bevan was to catch him he would have to do something both immediately and spectacular, but whilst there was little doubt that Bevan was a good runner and was capable of pulling back time on Smith, the question was how much time.

Smith continued to push whilst Bevan continued to reel back the time but as the kilometres passed so Bevan was to realize that the gap Smith had secured at the end of the bike was simply too big for him to bridge, the chase was futile and the race was lost. Contrastingly, by the last mile Smith knew it was won and even had the opportunity to ease up, and soak up the atmosphere. With the Union Jacks waving, Smith crossed the line to take gold for the second year in a row. "You want to savour every moment you can," said Smith in reference to his steady last mile, and as if an afterthought commented. "These things don't come every year." Of course for Smith it appeared they did.

Despite a concerted effort by Bevan who ran an awesome run split to bring it back to forty five seconds at the tape, Smith had managed to secure his second World Championship title. In third place Eggert who had claimed in the swim. "I drowned, I swallowed water and I was beaten up," ran strongly to take third having obviously recovered from his ordeal, but the focus once again was on the young lad who originated from Hounslow.

When asked after the race why he felt the others let him go on the bike, he questioned if that was really what they had done. "No disrespect to the others," he said quite honestly, "but they couldn't stay with me." Smith was not one for excuses and saw it as what he did that mattered and in his mind the others just didn't have what it took on that breezy day in Wellington. Smith didn't say it was easy, it hadn't been. "I was just grovelling out there! Everyone was grovelling! I just grovelled the fastest," he said. Smith however believed that the pack mentality had to some degree helped him tactically. He believed that whilst a lot of athletes were capable of riding off the front, the new mentality that was emerging was just to be in the lead pack on the bike and therefore they never gave themselves the chance to test their abilities to the full. Smith on the other hand always performed his best when he was off the front and alone. First Manchester, now Wellington.

Whilst Smith had been grovelling in the elite male category a young Aussie by the name of Ben Bright blew the Junior field apart. This was a young Aussie that Smith was greatly impressed with and knew he would have to keep his eye on, but another thing he was having to keep his eye on was the politics in the sport, that was starting to twist and turn in relation to the drafting format. Whilst Smith was happy to talk about his racing he was less happy to get involved with the politics that surrounded the ITU. When asked to comment he was quick to move away from the subject. "I don't want to get politically involved." He said, "It makes it very awkward for me." Whilst Smith was not foolish enough to say he would never race in drafting events he didn't agree with drafting being allowed in major championships like the Worlds. He believed that the ITU had not put enough thought or effort into overcoming the drafting problem and were just taking the easy way out rather than following the correct line.

Little was Smith to know, but this would be the last non-drafting World Championships, and he would eventually boycott the 1995 Worlds and thereby lose the opportunity to make it three in a row. Perhaps the comment about it not happening every year was something of a self fulfilling prophecy with the recognition by the newly crowned World Champion that the acceptance of drafting by the ITU was to become an inevitable factor in the way the sport was run.

On a more positive note, whilst Smith was collecting his second senior gold medal, another young Brit by the name of Richard Allen was collecting his second silver Junior World Championship medal in seven days having led the team to second place and having won silver at the Junior World Duathlon Championships a week earlier in Tasmania, this too was an athlete that Smith would have to keep his eye on, but for now Britain had something to celebrate and Bill Smith was once again buying the beers.

Smith runs to a European Duathlon Title. Madrid 1992

TRANSITIONS SEVEN & EIGHT
Wins and Boycotts & The Short and Long of It

In March and April 1995 whilst the world press were relaying the news of the Oklahoma bombing, the release of nerve gas in the Tokyo subway by members of the Japanese Am Shinrikyo cult movement and the Queen's first visit to South Africa since 1947. Under the title of "Not another Bike!" the British triathlon press in the guise of 220 Magazine showed a caption of Smith with yes, his new bike! The text underneath read. Yes. It's true. Spencer Smith has another steed for the next hour – day – week – month – season – year – decade – millennium…..(Tick preference)

Smith's habitual swapping of bikes had become almost as much a topic as conversation as his fashion sense, but the SpeedFrame was eventually replaced by an aluminum frame with 26 inch wheels and a 78 degree seat tube angle almost identically set up to the SpeedFrame he had been previously riding. It may have seemed foolish to swap bikes having had such a problem in 1994 but given that the set up hadn't changed Smith had little concern when it came to his position on the bike and in the end it came down to finance. Unfortunately the Allen's were just a small set up and could not afford to continue to sponsor Spencer now that he had secured his second World Championship title, but fortunately Quintana Roo could.

Keen to promote the fact that Smith had signed up to them, QR launched a series of adverts with Smith standing alongside his new steed with the strap line. They say it's the man not the machine. Underneath the copy said. Tell that to Spencer Smith. Thirteen machines broke underneath him last year. Other machines he tried just couldn't get him in the right position. Spencer knows why so many triathletes chose the machine made by the company who invented it all……Quintana Roo: Inventors of the triathlon bicycle.

Whilst perhaps stretching the truth, there was little doubt that despite his previous tendency to go to extremes in changing his position on the bike he at last seemed satisfied with his set up, it must however be said that riding this new Quintana Roo bike with 650 wheels and a forward seat post he did appear almost perched on top of the bike which looked a little small for him, like he'd borrowed it from his kid sister, but perched or not, Smith continued to improve his biking.

Whilst Spencer was never one to brag about either his performance or his capabilities he was always self assured and confident in his ability, especially when it came to the bike, and in March of 1995 Smith was to be set a challenge that he couldn't turn down. It would appear that while Spencer, his dad Bill and German Ironman triathlete and renowned bike specialist, Jurgen Zack were having a couple of quiet drinks discussing the pros and cons the do's and don'ts and can's and can'ts of the of the cycling world when the subject of Palamo Hill came up. Palamo Hill was known as a killer by all that had ridden over it or raced over it, a real dead leg lung buster of a hill, which Tour de France climb specialists such as Andy Hampsten has been known to climb in fifty five minutes. Covering twelve miles in total, the hill rises over 4000 feet and is one of the hills that the local cyclists and Ironman triathletes to the San Diego area scale once in a while on the long rides, and all of them dread.

As the conversation got more competitive Spencer and Zack then challenged each other to a race. Zack was Germany's number one triathlete at the time, a thirty year old powerhouse from Vallendar, near Koblenz, who had been competing in Ironman since 1989 taking seventh spot at his first attempt, and had placed in the top ten on four other occasions. Despite this, Zack hadn't really got a great deal of media attention until he set a new bike course record in 1993 of 4:27:42 and now had a reputation among Ironman competitors of being able to dictate the pace of the race because of what was now termed the "Zack attack," so in any case Zack would always be considered a fearsome cyclist.

A hundred dollars each into the pot and the winner takes all agreed both riders. It seemed a reasonable bet by most peoples standards, but not one to do things by half Spencer's dad Bill felt a hundred dollars to be a paltry wager and got them to up it. Neither of them wanting to lose face the wager was eventually raised to a thousand dollars each. Cash!

A week later after a 'gentle' two hour ride to the bottom of the hill, the money was handed over to an independent observer and they set off up the Palamo Hill side by side with Bill looking on with a grin as wide as the Grand Canyon. As they pushed onwards and upwards, Spencer looked increasingly comfortable on his new Quintanna Roo bike and eventually pulled away from Zack as they ascended the twisting turning climb. As the climb pushed through the clouds Zack started to falter and was only left with the hope that the thinner air up the climb would put stop to young Smith's pace, but alas for Zack's pocket it was not to be and Smith Junior crossed the top of the climb just a few seconds short of sixty minutes with his German counterpart just fifty seconds down whilst Billy duly picked up the winnings. If there were two lessons that Zack should have learnt from this they were one: Never gamble with Bill Smith and two: Never bet against his son either. Spencer went home a thousand dollars better off, with Bill no doubt thinking to himself. 'Not a bad pay-day for an hour's work.'

With Smith's early Stateside, Australian and Continental form mirroring his performance against Zack, the beginning of the season went well with early season wins in March and April, at both Alabama and his home town of San Diego and then again in Australia, finally picking up his fourth win in Flanders on the ETU circuit. With these confidence boosting wins behind him, so it was Smith was scheduled to race a number of ETU races and with his early form looking so good many thought he looked set to pick up yet another European title if his form held, but in the end the ETU Series races were not to be Spencer's favorites in 1995.

With events held in a number of European cities Smith had been keen to show off his World Champion stripes across Europe but following some highly controversial and somewhat dubious decisions by ETU officials he felt the undue scrutiny under which he was placed by some officials was just not worth the effort.

The Zundert race had caused controversy throughout the peleton when Smith and Thomas Kocar both got DQ'd for drafting, a practice that seemed to be evident in most of the ETU races, and whilst he drew little consolation from it, with both himself and Kocar out Smith acknowledged after the race that, at least it was a Brit in the guise of Robin Brew who took the glory.

If the controversy started in Zundert then there was no let up in Geel, where Smith was two footed whilst riding in a pack of eight or more riders. Strangely, Smith was the only one penalized, and close to tears after the race, Smith clearly felt he was being deliberately picked out by the officials. Once he had been two footed he was as good as out of the race as the speeding bunch continued to gain ground drafting off each other like a time trial team on the Tour de France. Smith had been especially keen to do well for his new sponsor Xenia but after a short while running he dropped out clearly dejected and upset at what appeared to be special treatment.

In between the two races Smith had returned to Rennes in the mean time to win the elusive race which Lessing had beaten him at in the past two years but despite a further win at Middlekirk Smith confirmed the ETU series was no longer part of his plans that season saying "That's it, I'm not racing any more ETU series." With that said, Smith was as good as his word and with only the ETU official blemishes on an otherwise perfect season, Smith returned to the UK to race near his home town and continue with what looked to be the start of an awesome season, which ignoring the ETU disqualification and the following penalty that had led him to drop out had seen him post six wins on the trot.

11th June 1995 Royal Windsor Triathlon, UK

Windsor was Smith's first race in the UK since the Worlds in Manchester in 1993, with the move to San Diego and a heavy European and American calendar preventing his earlier return, but now Smith returned to the UK like the prodigal son welcomed with open arms by his own people and in top form Smith looked lean and confident as he approached the start.

As expected Smith lead out the swim and went out on his own with a twenty second lead on Olympic swimmer Paul Brew (brother of Robin Brew) who would fade quickly on the bike, but more importantly a minute plus lead on Steve Burton and the young Richard Allen who had just picked up the silver medal at the Junior Worlds, and Iain Hamilton who had dug in deep to stay with the leaders. Iain Hamilton recalled the day's racing. "At the time Steve Burton was going well, Richard Allen was going well, I'd had a good winter. The three of us got together and said if there's any way were going to catch Spencer were going to have to work together. There was no way we would catch him working individually."

This was a race in which drafting was not allowed, but as is often the case winning takes precedence over honesty. "We made a pact." Hamilton admitted some six years later. "Spencer was heading out of transition as we were heading in to it. When we set off on the bikes we went for it." At the turn around point twenty kilometres into the bike Spencer saw them all working together trying to close him down and whilst some athletes with the odds stacked against them would have decided to drop back into the pack and share the ride, it was not in Spencer's nature to ease up and instead, more determined than ever he pushed even harder on the pedals, heaving round a big gear.

"For the next ten miles or so he must have taken another thirty seconds out of us. Three of us were working together and we still couldn't catch him," Hamilton admitted. Looking back Hamilton laughs at what happened though at the time he would have undoubtedly denied the collusion since drafting was a serious issue as it is today in the age-group ranks and in Ironman where it is still not permitted. It had to be admitted that the Windsor race in 1995 had some serious problems with drafting, some cases of which were unavoidable because of the large number of athletes all on the road at the same time due to a miscalculation in terms of the amount of time needed to clear the course for the next wave of age-groupers to go, but notably Hamilton acknowledges now that he probably deserved a penalty of being two footed for drafting, even if he and others were not so willing to admit their tactics on the day.

Even with the group behind drafting, Smith still managed to get off the bike well ahead of Allen and Burton having put a further minute and thirty and minute and forty seconds into them respectively. Whilst Hamilton lost more time on the bike and never got back in contention. As Smith crossed the line in 1:47:34 the crowd screamed like banshees welcoming home their long lost son. It would be a further three and a half minutes before Allen would take second place and a further minute and a half before Burton would cross the line for bronze whilst Hamilton took seventh with a lesson learnt and duly acknowledged in how good Smith really was as he secured his seventh successive win of the season.

A week later Smith picked up his eighth win at Kapello, followed by a ninth win in Hasselt and then a tenth win in Belgium. He was undoubtedly having the best run of his career, he was on fire and it looked like it nothing could go wrong, but then in July 1995 the news broke. Following a board meeting in Cancun, the ITU Executive had decided to allow drafting at the World Championships in Mexico later that year. It was the news that Smith had dreaded and had he been able to swap the thousand pounds he had won of Zack earlier in the year to reverse the decision he would surely have done so. Smith's greatest advantage had for some time now been his strength on the bike, with the change of rules, it now meant that advantage was gone. It was clearly no longer a matter of being the best in all three disciplines. To many it had stopped being a, "pure race" and could now be sullied by team tactics. Smith' greatest disappointment was that the BTA hadn't even voted. "At this moment I am saying I will be going, but I am not happy with the situation." He told the press after the announcement. "It has always been an individual thing. Every World Championship I have won, I have got away on the ride. It is going to be difficult for me to get away."

Smith was obviously worried about the implications of such a move by the ITU but right now he had more immediate concerns and had to regain his focus with respect to the forthcoming European Championships which were due to take place in at the end of the month.

30th July 1995 European Championships, Stockholm, Sweden

The tragic death of a young fifteen year old Estonain boy who was racing in the youth category completely overshadowed the whole championships. Despite being held on closed roads, Karl Pallas was piled sideways into a car that had come to a closed road and stopped side on in the middle of the road. In a youth race that had an innumerable number of potential safety problems involving misdirection and crashes, the death brought home to the collective and assembled triathletes the dangers that are inherent in such a pastime. Given the circumstances, the ETU executive board met and decided to cancel the following days racing, but following a team managers meeting where new and prolonged safety assurances were given both the promoters and the police, it was voted that the racing should continue and so the following day in a somewhat somber atmosphere the men's elite race took place.

In a swim that was undoubtedly a little short, Smith exited the water first in a time of 15:55 with a small group containing both Luc Van Lierde and Muller-Horner just twenty seconds down. With similar transition times of around one minute they left T1 within yards of each other, but within eight kilometres Smith had opened up a forty five second lead on a chasing group of five and by ten kilometres he was up to a minute. But as the chasing pack swelled to ten and became more "organized" so they managed to claw back the time and by the time they hit thirty two kilometres he was back in the bunch with both the frustration and the anger showing on his face having ridden for so long out on his own, only to be chased down by a pack that had clearly been drafting. Given that the race under ETU rules did not permit drafting, Smith was right to be angry and almost quit the race in protest but decided to stay in the hope that he could win the thing anyway. But the effort he had put into the ride was bound to cost him on the run.

When they left T2 it was shoulder to shoulder for the leaders, which meant as Smith had feared it was all going to come down to the run. Having been joined by Eggert, Marceau, Norman Stadler, Luc Van Lierde and Rob Barel, the so called non drafting triathlon was reduced to a running race in much the same way as a significant number of the drafting races on the pro circuit were beginning to develop. Smith knew the caliber of the field meant he had his work cut out if he was to take the medals and some of the runners had put in little effort on the bike, instead just drafting for the duration of that discipline.

Despite his concerted efforts, In the end for Smith it was too much to ask and when one of the better runners in the group, Mueller-Horner who had been sheltered in the peleton throughout the ride pulled away as the pack began to stretch Smith had nothing to respond with, and the German doctor eventually put sufficient space between himself and the rest of the field to ensure victory by a margin of forty one seconds from Van Lierde who had also dug deep in the last mile and crossed the line twenty three seconds ahead of Smith, which was exactly the difference in their run split. So it was that the dejected and frustrated Smith had to be satisfied with bronze.

By the time the evening ceremony took place the subdued atmosphere which still remained in the wake of the death of the young Estonian boy had become a little perkier especially when the food and drink arrived, however the drink soon ran out and the ceremonies seemed to drag on as they so often do at a presentations and formal gatherings. Whilst Smith may have only got the bronze it was hard to reconcile the fact that he hadn't won with the plethora of autograph hunters, which took him over an hour to get through, Despite not winning, Smith was clearly still the peoples choice.

After Stockholm the enquiry into the event the ETU acknowledged that in their own words that the male elite race had been, "a drafting paradise" because the bike marshals had taken the decision to focus on course safety rather than drafting infringements following the previous days events. But it was still too little too late for Smith to appeal or for much to be done to rectify the problems of that years' Europeans, and after all, a much greater cost had been paid by others within the sport.

On returning to the States following the Europeans Smith finished off his season with two more wins in August, the first in Cleveland on the 13th and the second two weeks later at Mrs. T's in Chicago where the $40,00 dollar prize purse ensured that Smith went home a little richer with a cheque for five thousand dollars, but before hanging up his wheels for a well earned rest, Smith had one more race to undertake, which would return him back to the UK, with the added benefit of meeting up with some friends and some family.

21st September 1995 Bath Triathlon, UK

The 1995 BUPA Bath Triathlon promised to be one of the biggest and best races on the British calendar and tempted by the prize money on offer a number of the big hitters had made their way to the picturesque setting of Bath, home to the mythological Blaudid, the ninth King of the Britons in 863 B.C. who according to legend made feathered wings and learnt to fly, but on this occasion it would be Smith and Lessing who would be flying on the bike whilst Bill Smith would be flying off the handle.

German Champion, Ralph Eggert, American bike specialist Jim Riccitello, and Aussie Junior World Champion Ben Bright were all there looking out for a good pay day, and then there were all the British triathletes including Julian Jenkinson, Robin Brew, Richard Hobson, and Glenn Cook who would turn up on the starting blocks with pound signs in their eyes. For the spectators though all eyes were fixed on Smith whose form had been devastating and Lessing, who was also in top form, having just won the Iron Tour.

The highly publicized race, which was televised by the BBC started under the picturesque Poultney Bridge where the crowd thronged the banks expectantly. Smith took little time to give away his game plan as on the 'B' of the bang he surged immediately to the front of the swim pack whilst Lessing reacted in his usually calculated and tactical way, holding his line as closely to Smith's feet as was humanly possible. As they exited the water together more than a minute and a half ahead of the field, the pattern for the race was set Lessing and Smith off the front and the others racing it out for third spot. The bike course at Bath was technical with three main climbs and once again Smith's tactics were obvious with a manifestly aggressive all out attempt to break away from Lessing on the bike as he pushed and punished the course, his black QR bike hurtling through the circuit with his Specialized tri spoke wheels buzzing as they cut through the wind. As Smith powered on, Lessing's tactics were arguably less than acceptable with him pulling out all the stops to stay with the young Londoner drafting perilously close to Smith's back wheel. Remembering that this was a non drafting event, whilst some may have felt the call borderline, others felt the drafting was blatant in terms of the permitted distance and eventually even the draft busters acted, despite penalizing Lessing being something that few would really want to do given the publicity surrounding the two athletes.

With the TV cameras following the action closely, the drafting was too evident to ignore and eventually going up the second hill Lessing got two footed for drafting. This was the first time he had ever received a penalty in eleven years of racing. Bill Smith was pleased with the decision having spotted the drafting out on the course, but was still angry at Lessing who then sprinted back up the hill to catch up with Smith and continued his tactic of sticking as close as he felt he could get away with. With the drafting box being a legitimate ten metres Bill Smith was clearly not satisfied with Lessing's distance behind his son and once again became visibly agitated. Bill was not one to hide his feelings and protested vociferously to those around him, and a little later in the race got the opportunity to make his feelings heard by Lessing as Spencer's only viable challenger in the race came closer than he may have wished to the six foot plus Smith senior.

With a kilometer to go on the bike Lessing sprinted past Smith as Smith furiously picked up his pace to try to keep on terms with him. The pace on the bike had been so frenetic that the rest of the field was completely destroyed with even their closest rivals losing minutes before they got to T2. Smith clung on for all he was worth, eventually making it into transition a matter of seconds behind Lessing. Being quicker in transition Smith managed to make up the deficit and they started the run together shoulder to shoulder. In making a comparison of their running styles, Lessing's long, elegant smooth running style contrasted starkly with Smith's powerhouse hard driven fashion, and in the first kilometer it was the smoothness that pushed to the forefront as

Lessing immediately picked up the pace in an attempt to pull away from Smith. Smith was wasted and in desperate need of some recovery time and Lessing knew it.

Out on the run at one kilometre Bill Smith was just a little more than visibly angry and continued to barrack Lessing, and with the BBC cameras rolling as Lessing went through Bill Smith screamed at Lessing calling him among other things, "a cheating South African bastard." Keeping his distance from Bill Smith, Lessing ran up to the camera visibly shocked and said. "I hope you got all that." He needn't of worried they had, much to the concern of the editor who was clearly worried about editing some of the more colourful language. Despite the confrontation Lessing maintained the distance between himself and Spencer continued running to the finish where he won comfortably by over a minute from Smith with the rest of the field a further three minutes adrift with Eggert taking third spot.

Lessing claimed that Smith's intimidation tactics had been happening all day, if there was dissention in the British camp it was clear which two athletes had the major rivalry and it was the best two that Britain had to offer. Whether this was because the others were so far behind that they did not figure in the rivalry is hard to determine but there was little doubt that Smith and Lessing were head and shoulders above the rest of the Brits at this time. If that point needed to be established, it had clearly been evidenced by the results of this race alone. Richard Allen who came home in fifth place which made him the third Brit to cross the line had over five and a half minutes put into him by the time he crossed the line, whilst Richard Hobson who was arguably one of the best bike riders on the British circuit had dropped to sixth place having lost over four minutes on the bike alone.

The reason for the conflicts continued to be debated, and now according to some went deeper than the mere competitive rivalry and even deeper than the two athletes themselves. They had little in common, in fact they were the antithesis of each other in many respects. Simon was based in Europe and had the same sponsors every year, a mild mannered long lean athlete, Spencer was the San Diego boy, headstrong and open, swapping sponsors continually, strong and powerfully built. But it seemed for many that on this occasion the rivalry, at least on Bill's part had perhaps gone too far.

According to Iain Hamilton it was Spencer who put an end to the feud over the drafting incident. "Spencer was sponsored by Speedo and so was I, we were sat in the VIP section with all of the sponsors. Bill Smith was trying to organise a protest because obviously Simon had won and Spencer hadn't and the protest was about the drafting. Simon got two footed but he never got a two minute penalty or anything like that. Bill wanted to do it, but basically Spencer wasn't interested. To him he'd lost the race. In a heated exchange Spencer said something like 'No dad you're not fucking doing it. Spencer did his racing on the course. I think it was always difficult for Bill not to actually get on that course and race for him. They both had bloody high passions, I mean they used to fight like cat and dog but they both wanted what was best for Spencer, there was no doubt about that. I think maybe that day was a day when there was a lot of pressure."

Bill Black who often mediated between the two Smiths when the family opinion was divided, and who had the ability to step back objectively view the situation also played a major part in the decision and confirmed later that it was, "a straight vote, two to one, myself and Spencer against Bill." That meant that no appeal was to be made. Smith senior may not have liked it, but he had no choice.

"Basically Spencer was King in Britain and Simon didn't used to come across to the UK much. Simon was still French really or at least South African. He'd raced for us but he wasn't seen around the UK like he is now," recalled Hamilton. "Spence was a British bulldog, that was the thing. Everyone wanted him to win, his dad just wanted it more." That sentiment was unquestionable, Bill was completely outrageous in supporting Spencer... but he knew it. And no one would have expected anything different from Bill. After the dust had settled and Bill had the opportunity to calm down at least a little, Bill was reported to have said. "I know, I was wrong and I hold my hands up..... but he's my son!" Bill just couldn't help himself.

By the time the season was drawing to an end, Smith had confirmed that he would not contest the World Championships in order to defend his title, but would boycott the ITU Championships by way of a demonstration against their decision to permit drafting, so with their energies spent and only one more race scheduled on the calendar, the Smiths took a break from the trials and pressures of racing for over a month, but with a prize purse on offer in Australia that could not be ignored, a short return to racing was on the agenda in November with a break in the warmer climbs thrown in to boot.

5th November 1995 Noosa International Triathlon, Australia

So it was that a week before the World Championships in Mexico, Smith would find himself racing at an event that given the timing he may not have been able to race had he been planning to compete at the Worlds.

Notching up his eleventh win of the season, whilst not anywhere near the prestige of the Worlds, Spencer and Bill could be seen grinning ear to ear when Spencer took the finish line, and the winners prize of $20,000 dollars worth of car which was not a bad days winnings, even if Spencer was unlikely to swap it for his Mercedes which he had recently purchased. After the race Ben Bright described Spencer as "hitting the run harder than a double shot of tequila." Having taken a minute out of Miles Stewart by the time the racing was done. Smith wanted to prove that had he selected to go to the Worlds, he had the form to win it and he had clearly demonstrated that to the Australian public and the top field of triathletes that had assembled in hope of taking home some of the significant prize fund.

A few hours later Bright in his usual Aussie candor, claimed that at the celebrations a few people were hospitalized at the local nightclub when Spencer hit the floor like a mass swim start. With no World Championships to concern himself with, Spencer was clearly out to enjoy a rest from the pressures of racing, but it was a rest that perhaps in secret, he would have preferred to do without.

12th November 1995 World Championships Cancun, Mexico

So it was that both Smith and Michellie Jones who had also won the Worlds in 1993, stuck by their words and boycotted the 1995 World Championships in Cancun in opposition to the ITU's acceptance of drafting in the event. They had both stuck a knife into the ITU and with its President Les McDonald having the reputation of not being one to forgive and forget there were according to some quarters some serious potential repercussions for snubbing the ITU. Nevertheless, they both thought they had made the right decision and whilst vast number of the other athletes supported their view and their cause many of those who were in agreement with Smith elected to race the Worlds anyway. After all Smith had won it twice before and had less to prove and for many of the others this would be one of their few chances of being World

Champion.

Whilst most if not all the athletes respected Smith for standing by his beliefs and not racing the Worlds, it was not so easy for them to make the same decision. Smith understood their reasons for continuing to race and expressed no criticism of those who went. "There's only a small percentage who are making a good living from the sport," Smith said later. "and the other ones haven't got much of a say." Smith knew he was in the lucky position to be able to afford to boycott the Worlds, and it was simply not as easy for those who didn't have the financial resources to walk away from a potential world title or even just a good pay day.

In congress the ITU had officially sanctioned drafting in every ITU sponsored race for the elite, so it appeared selecting drafting races was not even an option for the elites, but now a mandatory part of racing at that level, which meant that whilst the change in the nature of the sport was clearly a long term issue, a further short term concern at least for some of the athletes, was a safety one given that a number of the athletes had little real experience in racing at top speed in a pack.

During the women's race that had been set off earlier than the men's, the bike became a procession with athletes pulses barely reaching 130 and a good deal of chatting took place before the triathlon descended into a running race which saw Karen Smyers who had just won Hawaii five weeks previous kick hard in the soaring 100 degree heat, to pull away from the rest of the field and take the tape. Despite being vociferously against the drafting rule Karen Smyers had selected to race Cancun but as the elected spokesperson for the USA professional triathletes who were opposing the immediate legislation of drafting, she had already crossed swords with the ITU President, and when it became apparent that she was going to win the race, McDonald walked away from the finish line refusing to acknowledge or applaud her success. This was a win that really stuck in the ITU's throat.

The men's race as expected, followed a similar format with just a little bit more excitement as two packs of fifty riders and mayhem erupted when the first lead pack approached the transition which was considerably smaller than was needed by such a large group. With bikes and bodies everywhere congestion was so intense that it led Lothar Leder to leave his bike outside the transition area completely in the hands of a spectator who looked on incredulously as the German pushed his way past the array of athletes and marshals and into transition.

Out on the run it wasn't long before the start of the second and final loop that Lessing took the lead, maintaining a reasonable gap until the final kilometer when he turned on his class to complete the run in 31:11, almost a minute ahead of Brad Bevan who outsprinted Ralf Eggert for second place. It looked clear from the outcome that the ITU had won its battle to establish drafting as the norm for elite athletes. It had undoubtedly changed the nature of the sport, and many including Smith would say to the detriment of the sport. But it appeared that drafting had won the day.

Whilst on the face of it Smith had still been winning almost every race he had entered, according to some onlookers his achievements had seemed to stagnate in 1995 on the basis that he was not racing the races that some felt mattered most. Having boycotted the Worlds because of the drafting in the elite races, and disillusioned with the politics but never the sport, some pundits felt was losing his grip on the top end where it mattered most. He was still undoubtedly impressive, and he was still winning but he wasn't winning titles, the Worlds, the Europeans, which to some people was what was expected of him. Titles were what many people remembered most and in 1995 he had failed to deliver on that level for one reason or another.

Smith was aware of this but had felt it was the change in the sport in terms of drafting that was going wrong, not him. An event that had once been a race of truth and individuality was now compromised by tactics and teamwork as a result of drafting, and he felt there was little he could do to stop it, apart from refuse to race, but there was one option open to him but it was a big step away from what he had been racing. He had always felt his future lay in the Ironman distance and had already been thinking about going long, but was now feeling increased pressure to bring forward his plans. At least in Ironman, a triathlete who could bike could become a champion, and drafting was still considered a sin.

As Smith deliberated over his future, the political fires continued to burn on issues regarding the rights to the title of World Championships and now the ITU were at loggerheads with the World Triathlon Corporation (WTC) who staged and promoted the long distance Ironman events throughout the world. In the ITU congress the ITU executive board made it clear that elite athletes who competed in what they referred to as "self declared" world events in 1996 would not be permitted to compete in any ITU Championships or Olympic qualifying events. It was clear that after their success in getting their way with the Triathlon World Cup in Australia they were now after the same response from the Ironman. Ironman however would prove a more formidable opponent.

If Smith had intended to go long then the races at the start of the 1996 season couldn't have been in more stark a contrast to his intentions. Having raced and won a considerable number of Olympic distance races throughout 1995 Smith had earnt himself enough from racing and sponsorship deals in 1995 to get himself a good car. A Mercedes 320 convertible to be exact, so a little bit better than a good car. In addition he had won another one in November at the Noosa event but in January 96 Smith was still without a driving license so the bike always came first all be it by necessity rather than choice. Apart from learning to drive which to not do in the US was tantamount to being unpatriotic, surfing the net was another pastime that Smith had picked up in his stay in the US which was another craze that was sweeping across the States.

Despite surfing the web, which was still in its infancy, and despite living in San Diego which had at least to some degree a partiality to beach bum culture, surfing the waves wasn't on the agenda and Smith still preferred riding the bike to all his other activities. If the bike remained the focus of his intentions however, it was a love affair that saw him changing partners at a rate that even the hardiest polygamist would struggle to keep up with.

Yes, the bike had changed again and even if the proportions were the same the logo on the side said different. Still on his 650 wheels, Smith had undoubtedly become the Specialized man with a Specialized carbon fibre tri spoke both back and front, and a bright red custom made Specialized M2 steep angle frame that was the envy of many. But apart from the new bike, Smith had remained linked to many of his previous sponsors with Speedo remaining a major player and MET-Rx and Saucony who had all supported him previously also continuing to support him.

With the Olympics a further four years away, Sydney was too far off to really contemplate but on the other hand, one of Smith's other long term objective of racing the Ironman didn't seem that far off should he choose to race it as Hawaii was only nine months away in October. Given the acceptance of drafting by the ITU, Smith's interests seemed to be waning towards the longer distance, which was ironic given the fact that his season started with the short sharp formula one series on the coastline of Australia.

The series of five rounds with three races of micro sprint proportions but with lactic acid intensity saw Smith perform at less than his best with a 4-3-1 in Perth and a 12th in Melbourne before picking up his first win of the season in Canberra. His first win however was followed shortly by a poor performance in both Sydney and at the Gold Coast which saw him place 6th and 7th, and Smith was the first to admit that he clearly had a lot to learn in terms of racing over this format. A format that the Aussies had been brought up on and were accustomed to. Not one to be outdone Smith was keen to prove he could hold his own over the shorter distances and in actual fact had learnt a lot in the F1 series apart from what it was like to lose. Transitions had been sharpened up but there was still room for improvement and Smith had already stated his intention to go back to the F1 the following year.

If his critics thought that the poor start of his season was to be reflected in the rest of his season they were to be sorely disappointed the moment that Smith returned to the sort of distances that he was used to. Upon departing Australia and getting back the US, Smith immediately picked up wins in the two early duathlons he raced in May, one of the races being held in Ontario and the other in Irvine and the confidence renewed Smith planned his return to triathlon in his adopted home town of San Diego for the international tri where he was keen to prove he was back on track. If speed had been the issue in Australia it didn't seem to be a major concern when it came to San Diego as Smith took his second win of the season over the unusual distance of 1km swim, 30km bike and 10km run in a time of 1:26:22 nearly five minutes faster than Chris Legh and Christian Bustos and nearly seven minutes faster than Scott Tinley who took fourth. Clearly running on a high that had seen him post three wins on the trot Smith continued his season with yet another win a week later at the Hanover International Triathlon and then another win again a week later on June 23rd at the World Student Games Triathlon in Czechoslovakia. Medals and money in pocket Smith then returned to America in preparation for Mrs. T's which would take place nearly a month later selecting for the prestigious and well funded American event in favour of the European Championships which clashed in terms of date.

14th July 1996 Mrs. T's Triathlon, Chicago, USA

There was a $500 dollar prime for the first athlete out of the water, and whilst Smith would not have turned it down, it was not the main focus of Smith's race, which offered a significantly more substantial prize purse for crossing the finish line first. As it was, it was Victor Parine who was first out of the water with Spencer a fraction behind him but unfortunately for Smith, this was where, despite the commonly accepted philosophy that you can't win a race with a fast swim, that in fact the race would eventually be lost, even though there was a lot more racing ahead of them.

In order to get to the transition area, the athletes had to run through a chicane, which was fenced with plastic mesh on both sides. The chicane first cut to the left and then to the right. Smith had selected the right hand side of the run in the knowledge that this was the shortest route all be it by a couple of feet. Black had trained him well in checking out the course before an event, something that had been drilled into him from the very outset of his training. As Smith came alongside Parine who was struggling to unzip his wetsuit, Parine seemed oblivious to the switch to the right that was immediately in front of them and as a result cut directly in front of Smith. At this point Smith pushed Parine out of the way in an attempt to not just get past but also to prevent himself from being pushed into the fencing himself. An understandable and normal reaction at the time, and one which neither of the athletes payed little attention to.

Officials however are not always so keen to let such incidents go and so it was that an arguably over zealous official wrote down the incident and reported it to the referee. Both athletes unaware of the reporting of the incident continued to race head to head for the rest of the bike and the run sections, with Smith eventually crossing the line to take first prize, or at least so he thought.

With the incident having been reported, the race referee selected to act upon the official's version of events and duly gave Smith a one minute penalty. Ironically by the time Parine crossed the line he could not even recall the incident taking place, but nonetheless was awarded first place since his finish time was inside the one minute by which Smith would have had to beat him to retain his position. Smith was clearly angered by the decision and many felt he had been cheated out of his win.

Meanwhile whilst Smith was arguing over the penalty in Chicago, back in Europe, the European Championships scheduled for Szombathley on the same day eventually saw neither Lessing or Smith committing to the race, much to the disappointment of many, hence leaving the race open to the eventual winner the Belgian strong man Luc Van Lierde, who picked up his first European title in a year that would three months later see him at the age of twenty seven be the first rookie and the first European athlete to win the Ironman in Hawaii, whilst breaking the course record by more than three minutes with a time of 8:04:08

21st July ITGP Triathlon Koblenz, Germany

The field that lined up in Koblenz really was the who's who of the triathlon world, apart from Lessing and Smith both triple World Champions, a big prize purse had also bought Brad Bevan, the four time World Cup winner, Mark Allen, Mike Pigg and Greg Welch. Whether the $100,000 prize purse had anything to do with it, is an open question but there was little doubt that many of the athletes who would rarely been seen racing against each other in other events, could now be seen going head to head in Germany.

The Triple Super Sprint race consisted of three races of short sprint formats with the format changing for all three events resulting in a swim bike run, run bike swim and bike swim run triple race with a fifteen minute break between each race with the rest period clock set to start on the first athlete to cross the line so it was woe betide the athlete who fell significantly behind as their rest period would be severely diminished. The total distances for each discipline remained constant however with a 300 metre swim, a seven kilometer short criterium circuit bike, and a four lap two kilometer run

Given Smith's poor performance in the F1 series in Australia few expected the young Brit to perform well under such similar circumstances but Smith had been working hard on his transitions and speed work and now had a better understanding of what was required in such races.

In the first race first blood went to Lessing with Smith crossing the line three seconds back in 23:38, but this race whilst requiring full throttle speed also required a degree of tactics, and the necessity to hold something in the tank for the next race down the line and whether

Lessing would be able to hold that form with only a fifteen minute breather, was open to question. As if to prove the point in the second race Both Lessing and Smith paid for their efforts with Lessing dropping to tenth place, putting him well down in the points, whilst Smith held on to fourth behind Andrew Johns, Chippy Slater and Ben Bright.

In the third and final race Smith knew he just needed to stay out of trouble, stay near the front and stay close to Lessing and that was exactly what he intended to do. Whilst Ben Bright tried to take the win on the final run section both Smith and Lessing were too strong for him with Lessing shaking off Smith in the final section to win once again by a three second margin. But whilst Lessing had beaten Smith in two of the three races the final placings, Smith's consistency placed him first over all with a win that saw Lessing trailing him on points. The second race had cost Lessing dear and Smith had played a tactically astute game, which whilst uncommon for Smith who was most commonly regarded as an athlete who went from the gun, it nevertheless showed the ability of the young Londoner to think as well as race, and if the financial implications of the Chicago incident had upset Smith, he had more than made up for it with yet another win and a good pay packet in Germany.

Having proved a point in the short distance races Smith selected not to race in August but instead decided to concentrate on his preparation for the Long Distance World Championships, which was coming up in September. Apart from the change in training programs required as a result of undertaking the long distances involved, Smith also welcomed a break from racing and travelling which had seen him constantly crossing back and fourth across the Atlantic since May. Still at loggerheads with the ITU's acceptance of drafting however had resulted in him selecting not to race in the Olympic distance World Championships for the second year in succession, and meant that Smith left the door open for Lessing to pick up yet another World Championship gold which took place in Cleveland Ohio The third World Championship win of Lessing's career and the second one on the trot with the South African native storming home in a time of 1:39:50, twenty two seconds ahead of the ever present and in form Luc Van Lierde.

Whilst not racing, Smith was obviously not earning prize money, but he was still able to keep a finger on the pulse and a watchful eye on his pocket through the sponsorship opportunities that his father Bill had secured. He was after all a professional who made his living from the sport and with the launch of the first Speedo Aquablade fabric Smith was not only the first to get his new kit but also the first choice by Speedo to promote it on behalf of his sponsors as the, "Born in the water," Speedo campaign continued. In addition the MET-Rx protein supplement campaign also increased the Smith coffers with adverts in the triathlon press showing Smith jogging across a beach, in shorts vest and shades with the caption "Keep the fire burning." Something that Smith was keen to do when he got to Indiana.

8th September 1996 World Championships. Muncie, Indiana

Smith was already starting to pay more attention to the longer distance races that offered him an opportunity to race in what he considered to be a pure and untainted race and the middle distance World Championships in Muncie offered him just the opportunity he was looking for. At the beginning of the year when he had spoken to Scott Tinley. Tinley had asked him about Hawaii, to which Smith replied. "ninety seven. No bullshit," and then added, ".....hopefully." With that in mind, Smith had decided to try his luck at the middle distance. A distance of 1.2 mile swim, 56 mile bike run and a 13.1mile run.

The rookie Smith in undertaking the half Ironman distance demonstrated a sure sign of the direction he was heading in. Still one of the dominating figures in the swim discipline, Smith exited Prarie Creek Lake in 24:19 with a small group of leaders including Luc Van Lierde, Jamie Hunt, Greg Welch and Dennis Looze at the front, and headed up the carpeted hill to the transition area. With biking established as one of Smith's major strengths he continued through to the bike section riding solidly and pumping the big gears completing the bike section in 2:06:10 with Van Lierde and Welch entering the transition area over a minute and twenty seconds down. At this point it all looked good for the rookie, but perhaps naivety with regard to the importance of transitions even over the longer distance races Smith let his lead slip almost immediately.

Welch went like a rocket through transition two and pulled back a massive twenty one seconds on Smith just changing from bike to run. Welch obviously knew that even over the longer distance transition times can mean the difference between gold, silver and bronze and in truth Smith should have known better and there were no excuses when it came down to the fact that this had been an area that Smith had specifically worked on in preparation for the F1 series and Koblenz.

With tired legs both Smith and Van Lierde had started the run ahead of Welch, but a strong runner, it didn't take long for Welch to run down Smith, shortly to be followed by Van Lierde, and a look at the final splits for the run told part of the story with Welch posting1:12:30, Van Lierde holding 1:14:26 and Smith dropping to third with a 1:15:54 half marathon.

As a relative novice to the distance, a bronze medal was a fair achievement for young Smith. Smith was nevertheless disappointed and spoke frankly about his disappointment giving further insight into the run splits. "There was a lot of cheating going on in that race. Luc (Van Lierde) and me rode right off the front, but there was a big pack behind us. Greg Welch was the only one to come from the pack on the run, but he ran straight past us."

Welch admitted apologetically that he had been caught up in a pack that chased down both Smith and Van Lierde but shrugged saying. "There was nothing I could do." With a lack of motorbike drafting marshals on the circuit at the request of the police, the bike section had been a drafting festival with a handful of draftbusters beleaguered by the riders and Welch appeared genuine in his apology, if obviously reluctant to over elaborate or over stress the problem. Nevertheless Spencer's finishing time 3:49:21 compared favourably to the eventual winner Greg Welch with 3:47:05 and Luc Van Lierde's 3:47:54, especially given the fact that only six weeks later Van Lierde won Hawaii.

12th October 1996 Laguna Phuket Triathlon, Thailand

Come the end of the season the Laguna Phuket Tri promised sunshine which in itself was a major draw but in addition it also promised the strongest field ever assembled for the event, with Lessing, Smith, Brad Bevan, Wes Hobson, Andrew Johns and even Mark Allen and Mike Pigg in the line up. This was to be Allen's last professional triathlon and he was sure to want to win it but the competition was fierce and whilst Pigg was coming to the twilight of his career and was probably there more for the fun, the sun and the money, the likes of

Lessing and Smith were at the height of their careers.

Run over the Olympic distance, which was slightly shorter than the event was used to, the athletes were nonetheless going to face a hard task just to battle against the heat and humidity of the October Thai climate. Pigg had referred to the event as, "one last chance to kick Mark Allen's butt," which was undoubtedly said in jest but nevertheless, losing was not on the intended agenda for any who had made the journey, but the conditions were capable of kicking all their butts if they did not heed the warnings.

Whilst the race started at eight in the morning in an attempt to miss as much of the tropical heat as possible the whole field were aware that the heat was likely to take its toll, especially Allen who had the Hawaii experience behind him, and this concern at the need to conserve some energy, meant that whilst the majority of the fourteen strong field took it easy in the swim. The exception to the rule being the Sanson brothers, Ben and Jerome, who stuck to their usual strategy of leading out the swim, whilst the rest of the field started steady with none of the rest of the starters willing to commit from the outset.

The bike course, which was flat and narrow saw little real aggression from the chasing group with perhaps the exception being Allen who had appeared the keenest to catch up with the Sansons but the rest of the riders seemed happy instead to save their energies for the run. Given Smith's prowess on the bike this appeared an unusual tactic for him to follow but uncharacteristically he remained in the bunch apparently happy to sit in and bide his time.

Whether the slow pace on the bike had been a contributing factor to Smith's decision to hammer it out of T2 or whether it had always been his intention from prior to the race start was unclear but it was on the run where it all went to extremes for Smith as he set off like a man possessed.Smith had however vastly underestimated the impact of the Thai climate and blew up completely a short way into the run, literally gasping for air with eyes bulging and lungs heaving for oxygen that just wouldn't come. Whilst Smith appeared to struggle to even get a first wind let alone a second, the more controlled running of Lessing and Allen saw them pass the breathless Smith, and brought them to the front with Johns and Bevan also passing him some time later as he continued to struggle to recover from his early exertions

With a short distance to go on the ten kilometer run Lessing eventually managed to edge away from Allen pushing the pace a little beyond Allen's capability, to the tune of a mere ten seconds at the line, whilst Johns and Bevan held onto their positions to take third and fourth place more than one and a half minutes down on the leaders. Smith who paid the price throughout the rest of the run, recovered sufficiently to hold off Ben Sanson for fifth place, undoubtedly with the tune of 'mad dogs and Englishmen,' ringing in his ears.

Whilst Allen did his best to mask the disappointment he undoubtedly felt having to accept defeat in his final race, the sight of the World Champion, Lessing throwing up shortly after crossing the line must surely have been a consolation in that he knew he had taken some of the best triathletes in the world to the very limit of their capabilities and only one had managed to beat him. For Smith there was another lesson learnt, a lesson that would be well heeded should Hawaii still be on his mind. Irrespective of the competition you face, by far the most dangerous threat can often be the weather.

With a season that had once again stretched to nearly nine months Spencer hung up the bike for a few weeks, to take a break from racing and get some rest in. For Smith Senior however, it was time to focus on securing some new sponsors in the guise of sunglasses by Rudy Project, the same sponsor as Miguel Indurain, whilst sureing up the deals with his existing sponsors, Saucony, Speedo and of course MET-Rx, whose last campaign had included an advert showing a picture of the back of Spencer with the strapline. Most triathletes see just one side of Spencer Smith………..(and not usually this close). A slogan not far from the truth.

The 1997 season started exactly as Smith had said it would in 1996 with Smith returning to the Australian Formula One series but even the slightly leaner in build Smith who had dropped six pounds over the winter and now weighed in at 174 pounds was not going to find the loss in weight any benefit when it came to the short sharp stuff.

With a poor showing in the first round in Sydney and a DNF in the second round enduro at the beginning of February in Adelaide and a further poor showing in Melbourne's eliminator which saw an 18th placing followed by a DNF and the obligatory DNS, the St George F1 series looked like it was going to be a repeat of the previous year with Smith getting a good hammering from many athletes he would normally beat over the standard distances. But Smith had suffered bad starts to the season before, especially in the short F1 type events and things had always worked out ok in the long run so when he headed over to Brazil briefly prior to returning to Australia finish the series he was probably not so concerned about his form and quite looking forward to be what promised to be one of the potentially best pay days on the calendar.

23rd February 1997 Santos International Triathlon, Brazil

This race promised a good payday for those who were on form. It was such a good pay day in fact that Smith had endured a twenty seven hour flight from Australia. With a total prize purse of $60,000 and a $10,000 first prize up for grabs a not unimpressive international field came to race this early season race, but despite the field, which included Olivier Marceau, Lothar Leder, Wes Hobson and Jimmy Riccitello, Smith had to be favourite for the win.

With the confidence of a good winters training behind him, Smith made his usual start leading out the swim with Frenchman Oliver Marceau on his shoulder matching him stroke for stroke. Exiting the first transition together at about two hundred metres into the bike, Smith was in the process of putting on his shoes as he rode past Marceau, when a motorcycle official rode alongside and gave Smith a yellow card signifying a one minute standing penalty which had been issued unbeknown to Smith for illegally passing the Frenchman on the right rather than on the left.

Unable to establish the justification for the penalty or converse with the Portuguese speaking official Smith jumped from his bike and lifted the bike above his head carrying out the normal European penalty of stop and lift and went to head back off in pursuit of Marceau. Confused by Smith's actions, the official continued to try and remonstrate with Smith but Smith became impatient as the official fumbled with his stopwatch, and with the adrenalin pumping Smith decided to continue his race. Unfortunately for Smith the rules governing penalties are different in different countries and the rules in Santos required an athlete receiving a yellow card to stop for one minute. After only thirty seconds had passed Smith was back on his bike and had bolted after Marceau who in the eyes of Smith was now beginning to take a significant lead. The response from the official was immediate and swift. A red card. An immediate disqualification from the race. Smith would go home empty handed. Twenty seven hours for nothing.

What had promised to be a good pay day had in fact cost Smith a lot of hassle and a lot of money. Gutted but unable to do anything about the decision, the only thing that was left to do was head back to the airport and return home in search of some better form and some better luck. Whilst Oliver Marceau went home $10,000 dollars better off.

27th April 1997 St Anthony's Triathlon, USA

In the first ever draft legal pro at St Anthony's Smith took his first win of the season, much to his own and his fathers relief. Victory was sweet especially given the draft legal ruling but Smith remained very negative and vociferous about the draft legal racing. "To tell the truth the race was kinda boring." Smith admitted after the race, a view that was echoed by the women's elite winner Michellie Jones who also reiterated her stance on drafting stating. "Drafting sucks." Whilst both were quick to complement the promoter on a well organized event Smith made his viewpoint clear. That the St Anthony's should return to its original non drafting format a format that was for real triathletes.

Later speaking to the press Smith continued to speak out against the draft legal format. Clearly disappointed at the way things had developed within the sport over the last two years, Smith openly stated that he was no longer motivated by World Championship titles under the drafting format. A point demonstrated by his refusal to race at the previous two championships. "I came into triathlon to be the best at swim, bike and run. On my own!" said Smith, "You can't say that the winners of the ITU races in their present format are the best triathletes in the world." Which whilst not a direct attack on Lessing, could undoubtedly have been construed to be by those that were looking for a story.

Smith was careful to outline that his lack of motivation for the ITU World Championships format did not mean that he would never return to racing them as to do so would be foolish especially given the number of high profile events that were now beginning to accept drafting in their elite category races. But instead Smith went on to suggest positive proactive policies that event promoters could implement such as other race formats like time trial races that could be offered as an addition to the present races, but with the culture within the sport moving steadily towards drafting it looked more like even for Smith at that time such comments were related more to hopes rather than any real expectation.

Whilst clearly an important issue within the triathlon fraternity, drafting and triathlon however remained minor concerns to the sports media in the UK, and if the concerns over drafting were first and foremost in the triathlon media's eye then they were running a very distant second to the general sports media's interest in a young twenty one year old black golfer by the name of Tiger Woods who had just become both the youngest and the first black golfer to win the US masters. A point that continued to demonstrate that despite the successes of first Smith and then Lessing at world level, the British media had remained ambivalent and ignorant as to the importance and even existence of triathlon in the sporting calendar. To make matters worse, the general media seemed to feel it more important to focus on the day-to-day activities of the Spice Girls and a sheep called Dolly that was apparently causing a major moral controversy, rather than the successes of their British sports stars.

Cloning and genetic matching apart, the British triathlon press themselves had managed to create some controversy of their own all be it limited to a few thousand committed triathletes, when in April 1997 Triathlete Magazine was to print an article claiming that London Triathlon had attempted to persuade Spencer to race the event but claimed that Bill Smith had said he didn't want a head to head between Lessing and his son. This was the first time the rumours that had abounded the relationship between Smith and Lessing had ever been put to print and a claim that the Smith clan vehemently denied. Smith had after all raced Lessing on numerable occasions over the last few seasons and a rapid response from Bill Smith saw the claim quickly retracted by the magazine in the following edition with an apology to the Smiths for having made such accusations, but once again the gossip mill persisted.

Whilst Smith would continue to race the standard distance races throughout 1997, he still had his eyes firmly fixed on doing Hawaii at the end of the season, but if he went there he made it clear that he wanted to put in a good performance. "I don't want to go there and make a mug of myself." He had told the press. Smith was acutely aware that there was a lot he did not know about racing over that kind of distance and when asked what he saw as the big obstacles he jokingly made reference to twenty Germans, the length of the race and just about everything by way of acknowledging the demands of the race and the caliber of the competition.

Smith already trained long and the training didn't worry him but racing over the Ironman distance was something else. He had lived in San Diego for some time now amongst many of the greats in the Ironman world, and had gained some insight into their training and what it is to race at Hawaii but in the end all athletes are different and Smith knew that the only person who could tell him what it was like would be himself, when he actually got out there and raced it. Smith however wasn't generally interested in Ironman as a race or a distance. In truth he was only interested in Hawaii. There was something special about Hawaii. "I would give all my World Olympic distance titles for an Ironman title, for sure," said Smith.

4th May 1997 St Croix Triathlon, USA

Despite the plans for the end of the season, the standard so called Olympic distance remained the major focus of his early calendar with St Croix, held in the picturesque US Virgin Islands his next race. The St Croix International event often referred to as the 'Beauty and the Beast' had always been popular with professional athletes. Covering the slightly over distance 2km swim, 55km bike and 12.5km run, the race offered a good prize purse which stood at around $50,000, included a $500 swim prime, a $250 bike prime on a severe six hundred foot climb over three quarters of a mile long (the Beast) and a $5000 bonus for beating the course record of 2:30:03 set by Greg Welch in 1995. Smith saw it as a good pay day and a good race to win and looked to go home a lot wealthier than when he arrived.

Giving the swim prime up to the Russian Rukosuev who he had beaten previously in St Anthony's, Smith had his eyes on the bigger purse and went in pursuit of the victory and the course record. With Mike Pigg and Jimmy Riccitello potentially offering the greatest threat and Richard Allen the only other British athlete in the field, Smith was sure to be up there in the winnings, and stamped his authority on the race from the outset against the primarily American field. An awesome performance on the bike followed by an equally impressive run where Smith never once looked back, saw Smith almost cruise to victory with nearly a two minute lead on the following Riccitello and a further two minutes on the American pro Abe Rogers. With his sights initially on Welch's course record Smith had hammered the bike section, but had realized by half way through the run that his chances of picking up a further $5,000 was not possible and in the end the course record remained intact with Smith's finish time some three minutes and thirty nine seconds slower than Welch's course record. Smith however was pleased with the win that had made it two on the trot.

Smith's season continued with a second place in Memphis and a win in Oceanside after which he was to jet across the Atlantic once again and head home to the UK. Britain had changed some what since Smith had left in 1994 to live in the States, not least of which had manifested itself on May 1st that year when Tony Blair led the Labour Party into government in the largest recorded anti-government swing in British history, replacing the Conservative Party which had been the longest serving British government of the 20th century, almost being in power since Smith had been born. Other major stories at the time included the fact that Britain was about to return Hong Kong to Chinese Sovereignty and the Union Jack would be lowered over Hong Kong for the last time. Meanwhile back in Windsor, the home of British Sovereignty, the British flag waving spectators were doing the opposite and if anyone felt that Smith was willing to give up his sovereignty as the King of British triathlon, they had clearly mistaken the young Londoner who remained determinedly proud of his heritage.

15th June 1997 Royal Windsor Triathlon, UK

Now in its seventh year Windsor which had been the largest UK triathlon in 1996 with seven hundred and fifty entrants had managed to secure sponsorship in the form of Pepsi Max and with ideal weather conditions Royal Windsor was bathed in sunshine with a slight wind and the spectators and age group athletes could now sit back and sip freely from ice cold cans.

Unusually for Smith it was not he who led from the start but it was in fact GB international Richard Stannard who put in the fastest swim split of the day at 18:37 a good forty seconds ahead of Smith and an up and coming young athlete Stuart Hayes who was racing for Smith's old club, Thames Turbo.

Whilst the sunshine was great for the spectators, the glare it caused on the water led the unfortunate crowd pleaser, Richard "Captain Quads" Hobson to go slightly off course towing the lanky Welsh former steeple chaser Richard Jones in his wake. With a lack of foreign internationals present, it was expected that Smith would lead from the front and stay there till the line but on this occasion the predictions were going slightly wrong. With just under an hour gone the leading group of riders came into view of the crowd, but much to the dismay of his supporters, Smith was not among them. Instead, leading off the bike was Craig Ball, Tim Stewart, Peter Tiernan and Steve Burton, all accomplished athletes but few would argue them to be in the league of Smith. Whilst rumours of crashes and punctures filtered through the crowd, no one was really sure what had happened. And then a roar went up through the very pro-Smith crowd. Forty seconds down on the leaders Smith came into view, and still looking confident he flew through transition and headed out on the three lap run in pursuit of the frontrunners.

By far the most superior runner Smith ripped away at the leaders eventually taking the lead in the final lap, whilst Richard Allen followed in his wake, Allen who a few weeks previous in St Croix had come ninth more than seven minutes down on Smith was having an excellent race and continued to move up through the field, but Smith was far too strong for them all and crossed the line with a comfortable lead in a time of 1:52:52 leaving Allen to take second, forty seconds later with Stewart and Ball holding of the rest of the field to take third and fourth. For Smith the race was another win in his home territory and another pay day. For the crowd it was just nice for them to have their prodigal son continuing to return all be it infrequently. Spencer was undoubtedly still the nations favourite son.

5th July 1997 European Championships, Vuokatti, Finland

With the UK having suffered a miserable run of weather throughout July most of the British squad arrived in the small Finnish town which being only 400km from the Arctic Circle had been expected to be cold and windswept but instead found their arrival greeted by an unexpectedly warm and sunny spell. With the recent wins at St Croix and Windsor, it was apparent that Smith was on form but there was still a concern for him over the format. This was to be the first ever ETU drafting triathlon Championships, and apart from the obvious disadvantages that caused for the better bikers in the field, there was bound to be a lot of discussion concerning the continued move towards drafting first by the ITU and now by the ETU in races of such importance on the calendar. The drafting format meant that two sprint distance qualifiers had to be used to prior to the final race day in order to reduce the 100 strong elite field down to what was considered a manageable fifty for the race two days later. This in itself meant that the overall format and qualification criteria had changed significantly for the elites, with the need for them to be able to recover well between races and a danger of holding back too much in the qualifier and failing to qualify as a result. Smith who had experience of the F1 series behind him, placed little emphasis on the qualifying heat and raced a smart tactical race ensuring that he saved something for the real event comfortably qualifying ninth in his heat. Others undoubtedly with less experience spent more energy on the qualifier than they would have wished at a time when they should have been tapering and relaxing.

Come the real race day however, and Smith would be anything but comfortable. A frenetic washing tub start to the swim with all athletes trying to vie for the front positions appeared to take its toll on Smith and to the surprise of onlookers Smith did not lead the swim from the gun in his usual manner but lagged slightly behind the leading swimmer Thomas Kocar and exited the water in a surprising eleventh place with a pack of swimmers including Ralf Eggert and Willen Joackhim, Eric Van der Linden and Markus Keller to name but a few. On exiting the water the reason for the unusually lackluster time for Smith became obvious. During the chaotic start of the race where swimmers jostled for positions as the pack of tightly woven swimmers tried to navigate the first swim buoy, Smith's wetsuit had been torn undone and Smith had swum the entire rest of the swim leg with a wetsuit full of water.

Never one to give up, Smith had continued to swim on relentlessly dragging both flapping neoprene and suit full of water with each and every stroke determined not to lose too much time on the leading swimmers. After the race Smith referring to the wetsuit incident commented in his usual understated way that. "It didn't seem to affect me that much," but the opportunity to try and break away on the bike was sure to have been vetoed by the increase in energy expenditure resulting from the swim discipline.

Given that the race was draft legal and that no swimmers had managed to make a significant break away, it looked possible that it was going to be a bunch ride. The course was a four lap circuit of a pan flat course with the exception of one hill. The hill however was something that had to be seen to be believed. With an average of a one in ten gradient the fifteen hundred metre climb was a killer. To ride it well involved grinding the gears up to the top without blowing up, at which point the riders had to have the guts to descend it at speeds nearing eighty kilometres an hour. Whilst the very challenging bike course scared some, it offered the opportunity for a lone breakaway for the better riders who had the confidence on the day and when Eric Van der Linden attacked on two occasions it was Smith who had to bring him back, riding what looked to be ridiculously big gears for the terrain. Van der Linden was however the only athlete to make any real attempt to break away from the peleton.

Fortunately for Smith the lack of sustained attacks on the bike gave him the opportunity to rest a little in the bunch and get his second wind, but having said that, the Vuokatti bike section was not a course for a weak cyclist and there were limited sections where the drafting was of significant benefit. As the race progressed Smith appeared to have recovered, but having done so, instead of sitting back in the bunch, Smith continued with his usual strategy and started to hurt the rest of the field by picking up the pace. Feeling stronger as the race continued, Smith knew that if he was to win what would eventually come down to a foot race, then he would need to make a number of good runners in the field, who were taking it easy in the bunch, suffer on the bike before the start of the run.

The question in the minds of those who had identified the wetsuit problem earlier in the race was whether Spencer had suffered too much in the swim and whether he could recover sufficiently throughout the bike section to run away from the pack. In answer to that question Smith's willingness to chase down and pull back Van der Linden could have been construed as evidence enough and in addition, instead of picking up the cadence as he began to feel stronger, Smith demonstrated his confidence and recovery by maintaining his usual big gear methodology and actually started to go up a couple of gears rather than go down them. By the time the bunch was coming off the bike into T2 Smith had worked them into a sweat and was feeling pretty confident at having made some of the major challengers suffer.

Ultimately as Smith had predicted prior to the race, the result had come down to the run, all be it on this occasion perhaps to his advantage, and as a group of twenty exited the transition Smith worked hard at the front almost from the off, determined to not allow them any recovery from the bike section. His tactics almost imediately worked, with a few being dropped from the start of the run as Smith split the majority of the field apart with the exception of some of the much stronger runners, which included Stephan Vuckovic and his German teammate Ralph Eggert, Jose Barbany of Spain and Martin Matula of the Czech Republic. Smith leading from the front continued to pile on the pressure trying to burn off his European challengers and as the run pace increased it was only Vuckovic who managed to stay on the shoulder of Smith leaving the rest of the field to battle it out for third.

It was clear that Smith was working hard but it was also evident that Vuckovic was working harder and suffering more, but the German dug in and it wasn't until the final half kilometer that Smith managed to pull away from Vuckovic as the German's legs gave out, leaving Smith to take the tape just twelve seconds over two hours.

After the race Smith paid respect to Vuckovic, "He was strong and he hung on to me." Said Smith. "I made several surges and he stuck with me, but at the end of the day he didn't have the legs." With the fastest run split of 31:34 Smith had crossed the line first to add a third European title to his collection. In the end only seven seconds had separated Smith from second placed Stephan Vuckovic but it was a confident seven seconds.

Once again the race had come down to the run with the final order of the top seven being in direct correlation to their ranking in terms of time splits on the run section of the race. The fastest runner coming first, the second fastest runner coming second and so on, with only two athletes in the top ten bucking the trend. The crowds had cheered ecstatically as Smith crossed the line and ever the professional, Smith duly acknowledged their support always keen to please his fans, signing autographs and shaking hands, the Smith family were once again on top form, and Billy Smith celebrated with a few drinks, a big cigar and an even bigger smile.

This race emphasized a change that was now increasingly apparent in Smith's approach to racing. In the past Smith had always raced straight from the gun, and when unable to get away on the swim or the bike he had at times lost confidence. When he did take the lead he seemed to grow with the lead and even ran faster when he was in the lead than when he was behind. Smith had learned that he was more than just a good swimmer biker who could hold on when it came to the run. He was beginning to realize he could win lots of different ways, which opened up a tactical advantage as well as a psychological one.

After the Europeans, the Smiths made their way to Spain for a bit of training and recuperation before they planned to return to the UK to see some family and friends and then the States, but whilst in Spain Bill fell ill, all be it at first not appearing too serious. According to Barbara, at first he just complained about a headache.

Bill Smith was a tough man with a strong constitution, not one to suffer from illness or complain easily, however suffering from constant headaches his usual vibrancy and enthusiasm were missing. "He just wanted to sleep all the time," recalled Spencer. Unlike his usual self he was just exhausted all the time and showing no keen interest in the bikes or Spencer's training but what was more concerning was that he was complaining about pains in the left side of his head. "He felt so tired he couldn't even be bothered to go an see a doctor." Spencer recollected some time later.

It was on the morning that Bill, Spencer, Barbara and Spencer's nan were due to get on a plane to fly back to England, that Bill started to really suffer. The bags were packed and the tickets had been booked but Billy became worse just before they were about to set of from their hotel. Bill had said. "Barb, I can't do it," and there was clearly something wrong but no one was sure what and they thought it was just some sort of migraine that would pass shortly. Not one to make a fuss, Bill had told Spencer to just get on with the plans and take his nan back to the UK, whilst he and Barbara stayed in Spain until he felt a bit better when they would follow them a couple of days later.

"At that time it didn't appear too serious despite Bill being in considerable pain. It didn't appear life threatening," recalled Bernie. But soon after Spencer had headed off Billy just collapsed, it was almost like a stroke and in the end they rushed Bill to a the hospital in a taxi." At the time Spencer and his nan were flying out they hadn't realized how ill Bill was, and it wasn't until arriving in England, that Spencer was relayed the message that his dad was seriously ill and in a coma. On hearing the news Spencer returned to Spain immediately on the next plane.

On arriving in Spain, Spencer and Barbara were keen to get Billy back to the UK as soon as possible but the Doctors insisted it was too dangerous to move him even when he came out of the coma, and emphasized that having discovered a tumor close to Bill's brain, that the operation would have to be done in Valencia, Spain. The doctors planned to operate as soon as they felt it was possible.

In what felt like an agonizing wait and what resulted in a long complicated operation the Spanish doctors worked diligently and professionally taking out the tumor that had caused Bill's collapse, but even when the operation was concluded, the news wasn't good.

The doctors informed Spencer and Barb that the tumor was malignant and fast growing, Whilst they expected Bill to recover in the short term, the long term outlook did not look good, but Billy was a tough man and always seemed capable of doing the impossible. No matter what the odds against Billy he was one of life's survivors, he would duck and weave, he would shimmy and do a deal. Despite this being the biggest deal he would ever have to do, it was somehow believable that he could pull this one off.

If it wasn't enough with Bill being so ill things were made worse by the fact that they had sold up lock stock and barrel in England when they first went to the States and had literally nowhere to stay. Returning to San Diego was out of the question given the medication and radiotherapy that would be needed over the next few months, since the cost of such treatment would have run into hundreds of thousands if not millions of dollars.

The only solution was to return to the UK but the immediate problem was to find somewhere to stay. Barbara and Spencer were obviously concerned at the prospect of being homeless in the UK but Bill's long term friend Bernie found the solution, he would give them his house whilst Billy recovered and Bernie in the mean time would move in with some family he had in the area. A gesture that only the closest of friends would be willing to make.

After a short time recuperating from the operation in the Spanish hospital, Billy was pronounced fit enough to travel and Bill Black went over and brought him back to the UK with Barb. They flew into Heathrow where Bernie picked them up. "I couldn't believe it when they came back, no hair, big scar it didn't look like the same guy." recalled Bernie. Bernie had made it clear there was no time limit on their stay. It is only in times like this when you find out who your friends are and Bernie was more like a brother than a friend, in fact, he was closer than a brother.

On getting back to Bernie's house in Bedfont, Barb did as she always did and took control of everything around the home whilst friends and family did their best to help out. The family had a good support network of friends and family who in typical London style would pull out all the stops for their kith and kin, but the one who would have to do the most was going to be Billy himself. For a long time Bill didn't ask what was wrong with him, perhaps he didn't really want to know, too afraid of what the answer might be. Then one day Spencer just said to him. "You know what you had, don't you." To which Billy replied. "Not really." And after Spencer told him Billy just looked up and said. "Nightmare." Billy knew when to play it cool, even when it was life threatening Bill didn't want all the fuss.

Bill felt guilty about his illness, it had resulted in Spencer pulling out of the rest of the season's racing and most notably, Hawaii, but Spencer's only concern at this time was for his dad and whilst he was aware that there was nothing he could physically do to make him better he wanted to be beside him. "My dad has everything to live for." Spencer had said. "He has a lot to see." He had to see his lad win Hawaii for one thing. Spencer wanted to stay in England with his dad and his mum but Bill was more pragmatic and knew that Spencer had to get back to training and racing. He had told him that he was the breadwinner and the family needed him to do his bit which at this time was first and foremost race and win, and so it was that Bill convinced Spencer it was time for him to return to California and get into a routine. To get in some training and racing. Reluctantly Spencer agreed on the proviso he would be informed immediately on any matters relating to his dad's health.

In late September Bill had an appointment with a specialist up in London where Bill spoke at length. Never one to beat around the bush Bill wanted to know the facts, and the facts were not good. The specialist told him he had a year.

Bernie recalled that evening when he returned to the house. Billy was sitting at the dining room table eating fish and chips. "I came home and I said how did you get on today, He said. No good I said what do you mean no good? What did he say? Billy looked up from his chips and said. One year finnito. I'll never forget that. I said what do you mean? He said one year all over. I said no we ain't having that we've got to have second opinions." Ever the fighters they went in search of a second opinion and found a second specialist who whilst not able to make any promises, said he'd give Bill radiotherapy but the emphasis had been on the fact they would 'give it a go.' When you're told you've got no chance then any odds will do and they jumped at the chance. If anybody could beat it Bill could, but they all knew the chances were slim.

Bernie took him in for radiotherapy every day from Monday to Friday for weeks on end. To begin with Bill was still always in good spirits, as Bernie would chauffeur him back and forward to hospital appointments more often than not in his convertible, but his condition was slowly deteriorating.

Bernie used to come in every morning to pick up Billy, and would see changes from day to day in his demeanor and physical appearance. Cancer is an evil disease that attacks the entire system and can come in waves and on one morning in November, Bill had gotten suddenly worse. "Billy either wouldn't or couldn't speak." Bernie recalled, although at the time he wasn't sure because Bill had been losing his speech on and off for some time and being a proud man hated himself for it so sometimes wouldn't talk because he hated not being fully in control, but on this occasion it seemed much worse to Bernie.

The normal drill was to go to Ashford but Charing Cross, London was where the real specialists were and Bernie bypassed Ashford getting straight on the phone to the London specialists who told him to get Bill to them as quickly as possible. They had offered to send an ambulance but that would have taken even longer so Barbara and Bernie carried Billy to the car and headed for the hospital.

Living not far from Twickenham rugby ground, as they approached the ground they got stuck in traffic heading to the game that was scheduled, but this was an emergency and not able or willing to wait in traffic Bernie mounted the kerb and started to make his way weaving through the stationary traffic. According to Bernie there was a motorcycle cop down the road who couldn't believe what he was doing and pulled him over, but on looking inside the car Bernie explained the situation, which became obvious to the officer as Bill struggled to stay upright in his seat and started leaning into Bernie's shoulder, whilst Barbara tried to prop him up.

The policeman quick to seize the gravity of the situation offered them an escort straight to the hospital getting them there quicker than they ever could have hoped for. An hour and a half later the doctors operated on Billy again, they operated on him for ten hours and removed another tumor. In the middle of the night the doctor returned to them and said. "It's grown again and its going to do it again."

Tough as old boots Billy recovered from the operation, got his speech back and some of his movement as Bernie took him to the gym at the Metropolitan, but it was just a matter of time.

Spencer kept coming back and forth from San Diego. "He didn't know what to do the poor devil." Remembered Bernie. "He said to me what do I do? I said let's be blunt he can go on for a long time like this Spence and he needs the dough, you've got to go and earn it, he can't earn it. You've got to earn it, so you haven't got a lot of option. You've got to carry on doing what you're doing as best you can."

Only those who've lost people close to them and watched them suffer slowly day to day can comprehend the difficulty faced in such situations, the need to carry on in an attempt at trying to retain some normality in what seems such futile and unimportant activities like working is hard to deal with. When the future seems so unsure, so unreal, the idea of continuing to deal with the present and work towards it puts a lot of things into perspective but still the need to live, survive, eat and sleep is never ending and so lost between the guilt of not being able to be there every moment for the ones you love can turn people over inside. "I said it ain't gonna be easy, you won't be able to concentrate properly and do the racing." Bernie recalled. "He also was committed to the races, you have to remember that. He had sponsors to look after. The sponsors were brilliant, they stood by him, I mean he missed this race and missed that race but they just accepted it. They treated him very fairly Speedo included."

Reluctantly Spencer returned to racing on the understanding that if anything bad should happen he would be contacted immediately and would be on the next plane home. In truth Bill's illness brought an end to Spencer's season at least in so far as racing was concerned.

On Thanksgiving Day Spencer announced his engagement to his American girlfriend Melissa. She had stood by him through this traumatic period, which had undoubtedly brought them closer together, and the engagement brought a little light relief to the Smith family which was undoubtedly needed. By coincidence Smith's closest rival Simon Lessing also confirmed the rumour that he and Lisa Laiti would also be getting married. So it seemed the two athletes would even go head to head when it came to walking down the aisle.

3rd May 1998 St Croix Triathlon, USA

Away from the problems at home, In early May, Smith was back in St Croix to retain his crown, and with a world class field which included Jimmy Riccitello, Tony De Boom, Mike Pigg, Peter Sandvag and Mark Allen amongst others he was sure to have his work cut out. With the temperatures expected to soar, the promoters invested in an early 7am start that saw the sun just beginning to rise off the sea as the elite men plunge into the throng.

Given the run of luck the Smith family were having it would seem fair that Spencer would have some luck in this race but as the field roared down to the front Smith hit the floor before he hit the water slipping on the beach, which left him a considerable amount of work to do in the two kilometre swim if he was to get onto the front. Angry and bruised Smith proceeded to thread himself through the other swimmers, which sometime included swimming over them, when it provided a more direct route, and inevitably Smith eventually surged to the front, effectively splitting the field with only a small number of the top pros able to stay with him including eight time St. Croix veteran Jimmy Riccitello.

As they exited the water, Smith must have felt that his share of bad luck, at least for this race was over and looked forward to the opportunity to make the difference on the bike on the "Beast" of a hill that they would find themselves facing twenty miles into the thirty two mile course. The beast which would require even the best of the riders to go in search of a 39/25 dinner plate of a gear would unfortunately only add to the bad luck that Smith had faced in the swim when after only ten miles of the course complete Smith found himself left stranded with a puncture.

With the pace as high as it was, Smith would decide that a leisurely ride back to the hotel in time to tuck into some pizza was the best option left open to him, leaving his title behind him to be picked up by Riccitello, who just held off a rapidly closing Sandvag. St Croix was not a good day at the office for Smith.

His racing continued but his bad luck seemed to continue to plague him and despite a win at Kapello in May, a stomach upset in the following race and a false start of all things in Milan, were poor omens for the season ahead. As predicted it wasn't going to be easy for Spencer "His mind wasn't there," recalled Bernie, "he had punctures and that, he said he was finding it hard to train and concentrate and it was only expected that that was what happened to Spencer during that period." Then at the end of May, glad to be back with his family at least for a short time Spencer returned to England to race on home territory to pick up where he had left off the year before in Windsor.

Bill Smith was conspicuous by his absence and his battle cry of 'come on my son' was sorely missed but Spencer's mother Barbara had come to cheer on her boy and the sun shone brightly on Windsor on race day, much to the relief of the competitors who had sat in the race HQ the previous evening listening to the sound of torrential rain on their windows and fearing the worst in terms of racing conditions.

But with the race kicking off mid morning, and the sun shimmering on the Thames, Smith exited the water in 20:30 just six seconds behind Robin Brew, with a bunch of ten swimmers coming into transition together shortly after, which meant from the start of the bike that the draftbusters were likely to be on a losing wicket as the chance of splitting such a tightly knit group was almost impossible.

With the problem faced by the officials and the penalize one and they would have to penalize them all catch twenty two dilemma faced with the peleton that had formed at the front of the race the draftbusters may have well have given up and gone home when none of the riders proved willing to fall back. Having accepted the inevitability of drafting in what was supposed to be a non drafting event the only job they could do from then on was ensure that the riders did not endanger themselves or the public by breaking the law in their pursuit of the medals.

Despite the obvious benefits gained by the bunch, as the race reached the turnaround point so Richard Allen who hadn't had the greatest of runs in 1998 decided to try and put some distance between himself, Smith and Johns knowing that if he were to stand any chance of a win then he would have to get at least some time advantage on the bike, although attempting to do that to Smith was like offering a red rag to a bull. Surprisingly however Smith did not take up the challenge and Allen found himself taking the British trio of Stuart Hayes, Richard Hobson and Glenn Cook into the second transition with a significant lead on chasing group that included not only Smith but perhaps all of the most likely winners.

Having stuck within the highly suspect drafting second group of racers for the remainder of the bike ride, Smith didn't show his usual aggressiveness on the bike which meant he had his work cut out when he found himself starting the 10km run, some eighty seconds down on Richard Allen, which had led some to believe that the stress over the past few months would be the factor that would see an end to the reign of Smith wins at Windsor, but Smith clearly had other ideas.

On leaving T2 Smith's visibly aggressive surge saw him cut swathes out of Allen's lead with a 9:55 split for the first of three laps which covered 3.33 kilometres. Not simply satisfied with a podium spot, though none would have blamed him, Smith continued to dominate the run picking off the leaders one by one. Despite the quality of the field being good in British terms it was admittedly lacking in international athletes, but Smith knew that the newly crowned UK champion Andrew Johns who had formally raced under an antipodean flag was no push over and dug deeper in pursuit of Johns, who he would also be facing a month later at the European Championships. With a courage for which he had been renowned since the early days Smith continued to put on an awesome display of running strength that saw him cover the 10km run in a split time of exactly thirty one minutes, leaving Johns to take second with a run split some forty nine seconds slower, and in doing so was serving due notice to the British triathlon community that he was still the British number one and letting Johns know that despite previous form he was still someone to be concerned over at the Europeans.

Unbelievably, Allen found later that he had been demoted to fourth place having received a two minute time penalty for crossing the transition dismount line by half a wheel. A penalty that seemed totally out of line, given the extent of illegal drafting that had taking place in the race. Whilst more incredibly a highly disgruntled Hobson, Hayes and Cook had all been DQ'd for crossing a white line in the middle of the road. It seemed for once that the bad luck was now plaguing some of the other athletes. In truth however none of it would have affected the overall result for Smith who had demonstrated once again his pedigree in the British ranks. The hometown victory against a strong field in Windsor, seemed to put a stop to what had already been a terrible year in so many ways, but the next race would involve him testing his metal against the best in Europe.

4th July 1998 European Championships, Velden, Austria

With the race format being draft legal Smith expected it all to come down to the run again, but since his thirty one minute run split in Windsor had shown that his running form was good, there looked to be a pretty good chance the they could be raising the Union Jack at the presentation ceremony.

If it had been expected to be a close run thing, then the race which was based in the south east region of Austria certainly lived up to expectations. With a tightly compact field lined up on a pontoon that had been considered too high to safely dive from, the swimmers dropped into the water more like stones than like swimmers and made a mad dash for the first buoy on the two lap swim course against a strong swell.

With an undramatic and uneventful fifteen hundred metre swim completed, Smith exited the water in his usual manner, that is at the front, and headed up the steps towards the grassed transition area with only a matter of seconds separating him from the majority of the field which offered little advantage except for a bit more space for a fraction of a second in a frenetic and crowded transition area prior to heading out on the six lap bike course.

The bike section like the swim, saw little in the way of attempts to break away with the peleton to big to make such an attempt viable and the ride proceeded with the almost the entire field riding wheel to wheel and elbow to elbow through the 40km route with the exception where the riders had to climb a steep 500 metre hill at the beginning of each circuit. But if the bike became a procession, then the second transition and the run were to prove a more interesting spectacle.

As the group exited the second frenetic transition it once again became a foot race, where by the fastest runner would undoubtedly win. Prior to the race many of the athletes had anticipated the field staying together most notably Stephan Vuckovic who had stated. "In the running there are five, six guys who can be in front and especially Spencer. He's the main favourite for me." Ralf Eggert too identified Smith as one of his major concerns but also made the point that Andrew Johns who he slightly mockingly referred to as having, "just turned into a British Citizen," was also racing well. But there was no doubt that Smith was still considered the major threat to many of the other competitors "He's so fast, he is looking so strong this year." Eggert had said of Smith.The question of whether he was able to live up to the other athletes expectations was now to be put to the test with a tough three circuit run course which included a steep downhill section on each lap that presented itself just before the finish line. Smith sticking to his race plan went out hard from the start, and continued to look strong on the run throughout both the climb and the flat section, on each occasion that Smith descended the hill however, he seemed to falter almost breaking his stride in an attempt to control his legs. Whether it was the bulk that Smith carried or simply his running style which was more powerhouse than smooth, Smith was clearly having problems on the descent whilst the three athletes who remained in contention with him in the guise of Andrew Johns, Jean Christophe Guinchard and Vladimir Polikarpenko seemed much more comfortable on each descent.

On the final circuit and with only a matter of a few hundred metres to go whilst Smith shortened his stride and almost staccatoed down the hill, Johns who Smith had demonstrably outclassed on the run only weeks earlier simply flowed down the incline with an ease that contrasted so painfully with Smith's descent, taking the tape and the European title in a time of 1:50:09 with Jean Christophe Guinchard who had also descended significantly more smoothly than Smith in his wake. As they crossed the line only one second separated the first three, but by the time Smith crossed the line to take fourth behind Polikarpenko, his faltered and dejected frame had lost a further ten seconds over the last few meters as he struggled to keep his balance on the downhill section. Smith literally walked across the line clearly despondent at the final outcome whilst Guinchard remained prostrate on the floor having collapsed with exhaustion following his sprint against Johns.

Whilst Smith had been concentrating on the longer distances in his training in preparation for Ironman, This did not seem to be the reason for the loss of pace at the end and whilst some onlookers had speculated that he didn't have the pace when it came to the final push, the main reason for his inability to outsprint the competition was less related to form and more related to the course and his running style. Smith however had been quick to congratulate Johns and headed over to shake his hand immediately after crossing the line, but was undoubtedly naturally disappointed at the final outcome.

As Spencer continued to race, so Bill was becoming increasingly ill, a point that brings home the fact that despite any attempts to control, there will always remain many things outside of an athletes control, that still can have a profound affect upon their lives. Some of these things are close to the surface and their effect is manifest and obvious like his fathers illness, but in other circumstances however things that seem sufficiently removed and seem to bear little relation to the everyday life of an individual can also have a wider effect on the environment in which they find themselves. Spencer had always liked to be in control, and had tried to only share that control with those around him who he really trusted most notably, his father and mother, but following his fathers illness it had become painfully clear that the cocoon that his family and friends had surrounded him in for so many years could be penetrated and impact directly on him, and things over which he could have no control could manifestly affect him.

To this point, one area that at this time he may have felt bore no relation to his life was professional cycle racing but it would be something in which he would later become more closely embroiled in and at this time was an area that was soon to hit the headlines throughout the world, but for all the wrong reasons and wrong reasons that would directly affect each and every sport and cut to the very moral fibre of every athlete. The issue was drugs.

Whilst Spencer's involvement in professional cycle racing would not emerge for a further year, the controversy revolving around the 1998 Tour de France, would nevertheless be something that would impinge upon and affect the lives of many athletes as a tsunami of moral panic flooded across the entire sporting spectrum and most notably affected the actions of the federations in their pursuit of a clean image for their sports. Away from triathlon but intrinsically interlinked with the sport of cycling Spencer had through triathlon had become a keen cyclist and secretly dreamed of riding the Tour de France. As a result Smith kept a close eye on the world of cycling, like many a British triathlete and cyclist Spencer was wholeheartedly enthusiastic to see the Tour de France come to the south coast of Britain some years earlier and now the Tour was to make a further trip across the water from mainland Europe, but this time to the emerald Isle of Ireland. Whilst the emerging stories that came from the 1988 Tour could in no way be seen to directly affect Spencer, the result of the problems faced by the Tour de France in what has been described as its darkest year, had a profound affect upon cycling and sport in general at the highest level and as such affected every athlete, every federation, every journalist and every sponsor involved in professional sport and thereby indirectly would affect Spencer.

Having successfully competed against bids from Belgium and Italy, Ireland had secured the opportunity to host the start of the 1998 Tour de France. The project had been put together, by none other than Alan Rushton the Managing Director of Sport for Television, who had been responsible for staging the Triathlon World Championships in Manchester in 1993. Now five years later the Tour would be coordinated in Ireland by L'Evenement, a name change that had replaced Sport for Television but the cast remained the same where once again Rushton would be joined by Mick Bennett and Pat McQuaid. In this case liaising with the Irish government and Jean Marie Leblanc, who was the Directeur Generale du Tour de France, L'Evenement had been able to cite the successful hosting of the Tour de France in Britain only a few years earlier, which they too had coordinated and in doing so were able to convince the Societé du Tour de France to bring the event all the way across not just the Channel but also the Irish Sea.

The Tour would bring with it 200 riders, 3,500 accredited personnel, 1,000 media, 13 helicopters, 4 fixed wing aircraft, 500 radio channels and an estimated television audience of 950 million viewers world-wide. For Ireland it was a big publicity coup, in the end a much bigger one than they ever could have realized. The benefits to Ireland in hosting the Tour were sure to be substantial in terms of increased tourism expenditure, which the organizers claimed perhaps rather ambitiously to be in the region of £30 million but given that the Irish government had forked out the necessary £2m in state funding required to bring the Tour to Ireland, it was a figure that they sincerely hoped would be achieved. Irrespective of the funding, the worldwide publicity that the Tour would generate for Ireland was sure to be significant, and in the end, events that surrounded the 1998 Tour, did indeed generate more publicity world wide than even it had ever achieved in its long history. All be it not quite the publicity the Ireland really wanted.

The Tour de France would spend three days in Ireland commencing with a 7km prologue time trial in Dublin City Centre on Saturday 11th July. The day after the prologue the first official stage starting from Dublin would, cover 110 miles of the surrounding regions and then finish in the Phoenix Park back in Dublin City. Publicity wise this was the same day as the Football World Cup in Paris, so it was sure to play second fiddle, but nonetheless, the press would be out there in force.

On Monday 13th July the riders and their entourage would transfer to Enniscorthy for a stage start to commemorate the 1798 Rebellion and cover a hundred and twenty five mile route, just over the Ironman distance that would lead them through the streets of Waterford and Carrick-on-Suir, the home town to the legendary Irish cyclist Sean Kelly and down south finishing in Cork City, Ireland's second capital. Ireland was certainly up for the craic.

Alas for Ireland, the events surrounding the Tour that would generate the most publicity in 1998 would be stories surrounding doping accusations, drug scandals and team expulsions in a race that would be shaken to its very foundations. Rather than the sporting achievements of the athletes involved, or the beautiful scenic Irish countryside full of myth and folklore, the media eventually focused closely on the world famous event more out of morbid fascination for the dirt behind a race that had traditionally been characterized by a spirit, courage and sacrifice and suffering that few people could imagine with riders covering 3458.2 kilometres over twenty one days of racing. Racing in heat and cold and rain, racing up mountains day after day and descending along hairpin turns at speeds that would have the average boy racer in his car reaching for the brakes, this Tour instead of acknowledging and praising the prowess of one of the toughest sports and events in the world, was to be a catalyst for the emergence of a moral outcry by not just the cycling fraternity but the sporting fraternity as a whole and society in general, against the use of doping in sport.

Whilst Mr. Enda Kenny the Minister for Tourism and Trade was preparing for what he referred to as the, "biggest sporting event ever held in Ireland," and the multicultural and multilingual fete that was sure to surround it, the French customs officials were also preparing, but they were preparing for the bespectacled Belgian Festina Cycling team soignier, Willy Voet, who was approaching the French Belgian border in his Festina emblazoned team car and a boot full of banned EPO performance enhancing drugs.

As Voet's car was checked by French customs, little did he know that the findings of the customs of the French officials would result in such an explosion of truth within the sport of cycling that it would challenge the very nature in which his sport and indeed other sports would be viewed at an elite level. As the customs uncovered the 230 banned doses of erythropoietin, commonly referred to as, EPO substantial vials of human growth hormone, (HGH), various steroids and syringes and an abundance of masking agents it became obvious that the drug abuse that many privately knew had been prevalent in professional cycling for many years, and a problem that for as many years the sport had refused to acknowledge or do little about was being unflinchingly and uncompromisingly laid bare by the French Judiciary. What wasn't apparent at the time was the official stance that would be taken on it by the French authorities. Would it be seen as an isolated case where one Belgian team official would be sacrificed for the said, 'good of the sport,' or would it be taken further.

In the past riders who had spoken out against the drugs problem in cycling had been accused of, 'spitting in the soup,' and in a sport as tough as professional cycling where allies were needed in some cases even to get through a race let alone win, it was a brave if not somewhat foolish thing to do. Those who did, soon found themselves looking for another profession. In the case of Voet however, the quantities uncovered were sure to have a greater impact. The quantities were so large that it seemed unlikely that the drugs were meant solely for just the Festina team, which he had been a part of for many years, and so other teams were under suspicion, as a matter of course.

As the ongoing saga of accusation and denial, police raids on team hotels raged over the next twenty five days, so the media presence grew on the Tour and the headlines joined in with accusations that led to a moral panic on doping that reached far beyond the Tour and cycling in general. Sport was dirty, it was official, anyone who won was a cheat, infact anyone who was any good was a cheat, and every sport had to prove otherwise. At first it was just the Tour de France that suffered. It was however a catch twenty two situation for all sports and all sporting federations. The logic ran that if you didn't catch the cheats, then you weren't looking hard enough. If it was possible for the Tour de France to go unchecked for so many years and then all of a sudden to find what appeared to be the whole peleton taking drugs then, it must be happening in all the other sports. Or so the logic seemed to say.

The media warned that the federations needed to be tougher, they needed to catch more dopers as evidence that they were really trying to do something about it. The concerns however were that some sports federations were beginning to fall prey to the witch hunt mentality which could endanger not only the sport themselves but also the validity and the manner in which the athletes were tested. In the wake of the media attention focused on such a high profile event it was no surprise that the International Olympic Committee called a special executive board meeting for next month to deal with the doping crisis in sport. The committee said President Juan Antonio Samaranch would convene the 11-member board in Lausanne on August 20th, "with a single item on the agenda: the fight against doping in sport." The crisis had gone right to the core of sport and in the months ahead both triathlon and Spencer Smith would find themselves caught up in it.

However, as Marco Pantani crossed the finish line on the Champs-Elyses in Paris on Sunday the 2nd August 1998, resplendent in his yellow jersey, Spencer had other things more important than the Tour de France and the ensuing moral panic about drugs on his mind and greater things to worry about. His father's condition had become worse.

Smith ever the professional had grown to love the bike.

TRANSITIONS NINE & TEN
Irretrievable Losses & The Big Island

In the end Billy's condition deteriorated so badly that it was no longer possible to take care of him at home and he had been transferred to a convalescence home at the top of Kingston Hill. During the day Billy would drift in and out of sleep, sometimes oblivious to who it was that was by his bed but most often he would be at his best when Spencer and Barbara arrived. In his usual way, Bill would often create a scurry of activity around the ward when he would pull the pulse monitor from his finger setting off an alarm, a practice the nurses attributed to the fact that he found the monitor uncomfortable but that some of those who knew Bill better would have perhaps put such actions down more to his mischievous nature and his sense of fun. But his sense of fun was soon to be irretrievably lost when three weeks after being admitted Billy passed away.

Close friends and family had known all along that there was no real hope of recovery for Bill, but nevertheless, the death of a loved one is always a shock, even when it is inevitable and prolonged. Putting on a brave face the family arranged what they had to and did it in the way that Billy would have wanted.

On Tuesday 18th August 1998 at Hanworth Crematorium, Billy's family and friends assembled to pay their last respects to someone who had taken on so many roles throughout his life, over three hundred people came to pay their respects, so many in fact that some had to wait outside. A father, son, husband, compatriot, a competitor in his own right, a lovable rogue, an advisory, a shoulder to cry on, a business man, a tyrant when he wanted to be, an enthusiast, a motivator, an entertainer. Billy was going to be sorely missed, not by just a few but by many. Billy was never one to be down or dower and it seemed a strange thing for many to be in such a solemn atmosphere but when the vicar had finished his speech he stepped aside to make way for Bernie who as Billy's closest friend, had been asked to say a few words the atmosphere changed.

Bernie started his speech with words that would set the tone for the rest of the day. "Bill was a very religious man. He never swore or drank or even told a lie." The congregation of close friends and family laughed, as Billy would have, had he been there. Bernie then paused or a second and then continued. "If you will excuse me a moment, I would just like to make Bill feel a little more comfortable with the proceedings." At this point Bernie removed his dark jacket and put on the brightest red waistcoat imaginable, in a tribute to Bill's fashion sense that had always been to say the least, loud. "Right Smudge," he said, "we've got this off on the proper footing..."

Bernie started the speech by offering on behalf of the congregation his sympathies to Bill's family. "Our hearts and love go out to Bill's family, Barb, Spencer, his mum and dad, Ann and Bill, and June his sister," but he couldn't let Bill go without saying a few words about his life and his style to all the footballers, market boys, car traders, bar owners, neighbours and friends from the triathlon world, who had come to pay their last respects.

"Bill was a big man. A big man amongst men where ever he went. He was a man's man with a strong character we will never see again. He touched everyone who ever met him and the one thing everyone ended up doing was laughing their heads off when they met him. Bill always took the P... out of you and he could take it when you had a go back. This invariably ended with one of his favourite phrases that started with a 'B' and ends in 'locks'." Bernie went on to recall the first time that he had met Bill at the Loose Rein wine bar in Chelsea back in the 60s, where he had told his mate Peter to. "Lose him." Then Bernie stopped and said. "Well, thirty one years later I lost him.......and it hurts."

Bernie recalled a few of his own special memories, like the time in the 70's when the miners came out on strike for the second time, Bill and he purchased a couple of hundred boxes of candles. He recalled going to a market in the East of London where when things were going slow. Bill decided they needed to be a little more proactive so stood on two boxes and bellowed out at the top of his voice. "Who likes sex! Those who like it in the dark stand on my left, and those who like it with the light on stand on the right, because have I got the candles for you." They sold the van load. He also recalled that when they got back to the garage, they still had about two thirds left, which led Bill to take one look and say to Bernie. "Market's too slow, we're going to have to hit every shop we can and quick before the prats go back." For the next two days they hit every shop in West London, with Bill going in with the spiel of the miners strike and the fact that the candles were filled with the best whalebone fat ever made, whilst Bernie used to sit in the van waiting for his big beaming face to lean out of the door with a smile on it and say, "four boxes boltman." They sold out at ten o'clock Tuesday night. The miners went back Wednesday morning. When Bernie saw him Wednesday afternoon Bill's remark was. "F.. me.....that was a bit tight son."

Bernie had the assembled audience in fits of laughter at some of Billy's antics and his irreverent speech was in line with Bill's philosophy of say it how it is and sell it how you can. According to Bernie, three quarters of west London wouldn't be able to tell the time if it wasn't for a Billy Smith watch, and they would be on floor boards if it wasn't for his carpets. "I even brought a carpet and a watch from him myself," Bernie admitted, "…as shrewd as I am."

Bill's ability to sell and negotiate well was recounted in Bernie's tales of dodgy deals and close calls which included the time he saw Peter Meluish, Bill's greengrocer partner, personally buy three TV sets from him, "I said to Pete, surely you can only watch one at a time Pete, he's done you again. To which Pete smiled, crooked his head and said. I know Burn, but he knows I can't refuse him." Whilst another story Bernie recalled included a tale about an old silver Fiat Strada which needed a £300 repaint to which Bill had reluctantly agreed. Somehow by the time Bill came to pick it up however, the deal had been mysteriously negotiated down to a snide Rolex watch and a crystal rose fruit bowl with no £300 to be seen.

"I could go on for hours with the strokes Bill pulled," Bernie said, "but we all know why he got away with it, it was simply because we loved him for it. I personally had hundreds of deals with Bill, and when you had a problem and went to try and get your money back you were told, 'you're over twenty one son'. I remember when he had cause to come to me. 'Now' I thought ' I've got him'. I stood there and delivered the immortal line 'You're over twenty one son.' Back came the reply 'Piss off I'm only eighteen gis me money back."

Bernie continued. "The last year I not only shared with Bill, I also shared it with his wife Barb, and I can say from first hand knowledge the love, devotion and care she gave Bill in his time of need was above and beyond anything we can possibly imagine. I won't go into details, but take it from me Bill was a very, very lucky man to have Barb as his wife. Also such a devoted Mum and Dad whose love we can all see today and not forgetting June, who constantly gave Bill so much love and encouragement in her many visits to the hospital. I don't have the means to calculate Spencer's love for his father, they were just inseparable. Bill enjoyed, through Spencer his son, tremendous success in the triathlon world. Success, which bought them World Championships fame and friends throughout the world. My humble little phone at my home has borne witness to this. I have received calls from the four corners of the world to give Bill encouragement. Bill and Spencer were a team and Bill would love you all to give Spencer every support you can to keep up what he started."

Finally, Bernie concluded his speech with the way he wanted to see it from now on, a final tribute to Bill. "Bill was a winner and he loved coming first." He said. "Now if we could just look at it this way, Bill hasn't gone. Remember how when you were drinking in a bar with him and he always left you to go to another, well, that's exactly what's happened, and one day we will all walk into that bar and guess who will be sitting up on a stool with the champers, and the first thing he will say will be 'Fuck me, you took your time coming!"

Spencer also gave a short reading, highlighting what everyone knew already, that the two had a special close and tight relationship that only a father and son can have, but theirs went much deeper than even that a lot of people were going to miss Billy.

From the crematorium at Mortlake the congregation made their way to the Winning Post just outside Twickenham and a stones throw from the Metropolitan Health Club which Billy used to use as his office where they played Frank Sinatra singing 'My Way' the lyrics so fitting a man who did it in his own inimitable style. "You had the guys from the market," recalled Bernie. "You know hard working guys, you had the car dealers, you had the triathlon people, you had journalists from the Times, you had everybody there, and even the people from the Met Club, you know the top old bill, all those turned up. It did look well with them all mixing together." Bernie smiled. Only Billy Smith was capable of bringing people from so many walks of life into the same room for a few hours. "He would have loved that day." Bernie said. "He went out in style Bill, we had the old champers on."

Spencer and Barb kept it flowing all day, just the way Billy would have wanted it. The world of triathlon had over twenty representatives, and from this you can gather that over three hundred others came to pay their respects from all the other facets in his life and Champagne glasses were raised to his memory in what was truly a celebration of his life and how he would have liked to be remembered a fitting tribute to a man who had the canny ability to drink anyone under the table and still be up before them again the next morning. "There's nothing that hasn't already been said about Bill. You know, he spoke from the hip, kicked from the heart." Said Steve Freestone some time later and I think it may have just summed Billy up.

Bill would not only be missed on the UK side of the Atlantic and Scott Tinley who was based in San Diego showed the feeling was felt in the US as well. In a posting in which Tinley proposed a Irish style wake in Bill's honour Tinley wrote. "I for one, would like to hoist a few in his honor and tell a few off-color stories about this old bugger we will so miss."

Bill Black who had been so close to Spencer and Bill throughout the ups and downs of Spencer's career was asked to write a piece in. Triathlete in which he tried to sum up Billy's life within what had been one of the most successful sporting teams in the world. "Bill was a big man," he wrote, "a larger than life character, a one off, a sharp dresser, a loveable mischief maker, a shrewd business man, a devoted father, a husband and a loyal friend. Nobody outside the team can ever comprehend the amount of work Bill did behind the scenes, over the years he became an excellent bike mechanic, a tour operator, a marketing manager, a financial director and an assistant coach." Bill was going to miss him and the triathlon world was going to miss Bill's familiar shout, "Go on my son!"

With the passing of Bill, Bernie continued to help out on the business side for Spencer having started to get involved in the triathlon side of things when Bill became ill. He had been to only a few races in Spencer's early days and whilst a shrewd business man, still somehow found it hard to decipher why a lot of people would run around in wet underwear and put themselves through the torture of a swim in a dirty lake or river, a twenty five mile or more ride in the same soggy, kit and then embarrass themselves by running around in it for a further hour or so, all for the sake of a T-shirt that they could have bought on the market for a couple of quid. When you start to think of it rationally he was probably right, it didn't make sense.

For Spencer and his mum very little at the time made sense, but

Barbara was sure of one thing and that was with respect to Spencer, it was time he got back into training and she made that point clear to him. A strong woman, whilst she went about putting her life back together without Bill, she had told Spencer that he had to do the same, and after the funeral, whilst Barb stayed on in the UK with her family, Spencer returned to the States in preparation for Hawaii, a race he was determined to compete in as a tribute to his dad.

Bill Black had always been aware of the importance of Bill in Spencer's motivation to train and to win. His motivation had always been to make his dad happy and now that motivation had been ripped away, but it wasn't only Bill who was acutely aware of that fact, Barbara was also concerned for Spencer. Bill Black recalled. "Certainly when his dad died, Barbara said 'you're going to have to race for yourself now Spencer.' Billy was a big guy, a big character and was a major part of the team. There was the family team and myself and each had their own job."

How Spencer would cope with the loss was open to speculation, the loss of a loved one can never be underestimated or its effects predicted as each individual comes to terms with their grief. There was no doubt that Spencer was a tough cookie when it came to training and racing but this called upon something much greater than physical and mental strength and would call for him to dig deeper than perhaps he had ever been asked to dig when for so long he had been enveloped in the support and love of his family, most notably his dad. Spencer was now going to have to race for himself.

In preparing for Hawaii there was little doubt that his dad remained a major contributing factor to Spencer's motivation. In terms of adapting his training from the shorter Olympic distance to the Ironman distance Smith had previously believed that he wouldn't have actually needed to start specific training until after his last short distance race which had been planned for early July but it was now August which left him only a matter of weeks to get his final preparation right. And even given his original plan was somewhat unconventional given that most athletes planning to put themselves through the ordeal of an Ironman would have been upping their distances at least three months out from the event if not significantly more. On the plus side, Smith liked to train long anyway and wasn't fazed by the longer distances involved in the Ironman and simply planned to increase his longest bike ride from 2-3 hours to 4-5 hours and his longest run up to 2.5 hours. "I already run two hours" said Smith philosophically, "so it's not like it's double. Everything would be increased slightly, but with less tempo," assured Smith. It sounded simple enough but even Smith was aware that this would be one of the hardest tasks he would take on in his triathlon career.

Asked why he has now decided to move up to Ironman, Smith's reply was revealing. "I guess I'm at that age, where it seems like the right time." He stated, "I was too young before. The training takes a lot of time and it can be too much for younger athletes. As you get older you get stronger, you can push more but not so intensely." This old school philosophy that Smith seemed to accept here, which claimed that athletes mature into endurance events from a speedy background, like long distance runner's, seemed at odds with the current scientific thinking and new breed of young long course specialists who eat, sleep and breathe Ironman, and marathons, but Smith could easily be described as an old head on young shoulders, which maybe underlay this thinking, and in the end it wouldn't really matter what he thought but what he did. It was deeds not thoughts that would take the prizes, and whatever the reasons behind the move to Ironman, Smith was there, and this time not as a spectator. He had also made it clear that this one was for his dad.

In order to assess his preparation for Hawaii, Smith had planned to compete in the MetRx half Ironman in Perris on August 9th, a month away from the real thing, but things did not run smoothly for him in the build up and despite the intentions, Smith ended up pulling out with back problems so preparation clearly hadn't been perfect. Coupled with the back problem that eventually seemed to have subsided, things took another bad turn when a couple of weeks out from the race Smith became concerned at his general state of health, he wasn't feeling at his best, and feeling constantly tired and a little sick he phoned home for a little moral support and some advice. "He rang me up a couple of times and told me he wasn't well," recalled Bernie, "and he spoke to Bill Black who told him to go and check it out."

On Black's instruction, Spencer went to see the official Ironman Doctor Dr. Joseph D'Armas before the race to have a medical to see if he could identify what was wrong, and following a detailed examination, Dr. D'Armas diagnosed him as being anemic and duly prescribed and administered some painful iron jabs which he had had to endure in his rear. All this at a time when Smith would have preferred his butt to be left alone "The doctor said he was a little anemic and suggested he take some vitamin B jabs," recalled Burnell. "Even then he wasn't feeling in top form."

"He gave me a thorough medical including blood tests and prescribed B12 shots and told me to eat steak daily to improve my iron level." Smith later recalled. "I ate a large steak every day right up to the Ironman and my mother administered the B12 shots to me." Fortunately for Smith it appeared that the diagnosis was right and following the prescriptions and the steaks, Smith began to slowly feel he was recovering his strength and started to feel like he was getting back on form, and it was becoming increasingly clear he would need to be on top form for this race as the best triathletes in the world started to assemble in Hawaii.

Despite the problems in preparation 1998 was a good year in some ways to be competing in the Hawaii Ironman and a bad year to be there in others. On the plus side, the 1998 Hawaii Ironman was more wide open than any other year since Mark Allen decided to drop out of the 1994 race. On the minus side, whether by accident or design, the 20th Anniversary Ironman World Championship had attracted the strongest field in its history, with all but one of the top fifteen men from 1997 returning for more.

Perhaps or the first time ever there were ten men who, on their day, were each good enough to be crowned World Champion and Smith would have his work cut out if he was to make top ten. With about five major contenders whose pedigree had been clearly stated, and another five or six who could certainly not be discounted from making a podium place, few of those in the know believed Smith had a legitimate shot at winning the 20th anniversary race, perhaps even Smith was in all honesty not expecting to do more than at least be up there at the finish. Top ten… maybe. He knew this race would be a baptism of fire.

At the top of the list of athletes looking for the win were Thomas Hellriegel, Lothar Leder, Peter Reid, Luc Van Lierde and Jurgen Zack.

Of the Germans, Hellriegel who had won in 1997 had to be one of the major favourites, since despite having bad Ironman in Germany, where he finished sixth, he had never previously finished worse than second in his three Ironman appearances and therefore was clearly expected to be one of the front runners. In addition Lother Leder, who had been the first man to break the eight hour Ironman barrier in 1996 at Roth was clearly looking for a good result despite historically never seeming to perform at his best in Hawaii. He had however posted the fastest run split in 1997 with a 2:49:15 marathon split off the bike in exceedingly unfavourable conditions which had given him third place on the podium, and whilst many felt that Leder preferred to concentrate on the German based Ironman and preferred to win on home territory the pull to win at Hawaii always brought Leder back year after year.

Luc Van Lierde was also back on form and following his ITU long course World Championship win at Sado Island two weeks previously, he was obviously hoping for a repeat performance in Hawaii. A powerfully built athlete, now it was time for the ultimate test of that fitness and given the fact that Van Lierde had one Hawaii title already under his belt as a result of his surprising 1996 rookie win where he had broken the then record by over three minutes, he was clearly an athlete who was sure to be up there on his day failing serious accident or harm, even given the injury-riddled season that he had endured in preparation for the 1998 race. Lierde was determined to make an impact and as the current world record holder there were few that would bet against him even if some were questioning the extent to which he could have recovered from Sado.

Given the quality of the field, few spectators and even supporters of Smith probably expected him to win it at his first attempt if indeed finish on the podium, it was just not something that ever happened with the exception of Van Lierde. Newcomers were not expected to figure to heavily in the top placings and conventional wisdom had long dictated that the athletes who put their bodies and souls on the line at Hawaii had to pay their dues to the Kona Gods before success could even be considered. For those that were unsure they only had to ask Mark Allen.

But Van Lierde knew that Smith is not entirely without experience in longer distance races since he had seen him place third in the World Long Course Champs in Muncie in 1996 when they had both been pipped at the post, and he could testify to his staying power over an increased distance, and after all, Van Lierde had proved that irrespective of the odds, on the day, first time Hawaii Ironmen can still take gold, so there was little doubt that at least one Belgian would be taking Smith's challenge seriously.

Even now it had only been in the last couple of months that he had returned to training full time since his father's passing and whilst few who knew the mental and physical strength of the young Londoner believed he wouldn't finish, not many were putting money on him. Smith however had supreme confidence in his own abilities, something that his father had instilled in him throughout his career and something of a prerequisite for success in Hawaii. With enough big race victories to ensure the event would not intimidate him, Smith would be going into the event with the confidence of a former World Champion and a point to prove to not only himself but also to Van Lierde among others.

To add to the field of Germans who were on the Kona coast, 1997 Hawaii Ironman Champion, Jurgen Zack who was also the 1998 German Ironman Champion was also in attendance and despite having never run particularly well in Hawaii, he was a good bet for a place in the top three if he could control the race by leading on the bike. On the bike the, 'Zack attack,' could make all the difference and he had a thousand dollar score to settle with Smith just for good measure.

Away from the European dominance that had seemed to prevail in Ironman over the previous few seasons, the best hope seemed to come in the guise of the Canadian, Peter Reid. Reid had already had a great season with a win at the Ironman Australia and remaining in top form Reid knew he had the opportunity of winning in Hawaii. Having finished fourth for the last two years Hawaii offered few surprises for Reid who as one of the strongest runners in the pack was capable of coming off the bike a few places down and still running the likes of Zack and Van Lierde down, but like Leder, Reid would have to work hard on the bike to make sure that the gap didn't get too big. Perhaps an outsider but nonetheless a possible good odds bet was Chris Legh who had come second to Reid at Ironman Australia earlier in the year.

Having crossed the line only a mere fraction behind Reid he was clearly on good form, but his debut experiences in Hawaii the previous year had undoubtedly scarred him physically and the question in 1998 was whether they had also scarred him mentally. In the previous year's Hawaii, a late run collapse towards the end of the marathon saw his ambitions for a podium place crumble but in his determination to finish the race he eventually suffered a complete physiological breakdown, which resulted in him being hospitalized and ultimately losing a large section of his colon in a post race operation. Whilst the result in Australia outlined the physiological recovery was complete, a return to Hawaii would undoubtedly still offer the potential for a psychological barrier which he would have to overcome, and those who raced in Hawaii knew that the race was as much physiological as it was psychological.

Added to this phenomenal field, were the likes of Cameron Widoff, Cristian Bustos, Tim DeBoom, and Ken Glah and with such an outstanding pack of triathletes on the starting line up, the race offered the potential for something special, so much so that Smith must have asked himself what he had let himself in for. All of these guys, had proven themselves at Ironman before and Smith was a definite outsider, so much so that to those who felt themselves to be in the know, Smith was just a rookie who would have a lot to do just to prove himself a pretender let alone a contender.

Even away from the sharp end, where the title would be won or lost, the names were no less illustrious. The original 'Big Four' of Dave Scott, Mark Allen, Scott Molina and Scott Tinley, were all on the island who between them had won no less than fifteen titles in a period of American domination the like of which would probably never be seen again. Whilst Allen and Scott were simply there in a supportive and promotional role Tinley and Molina were both actually taking part and it seemed even if you weren't there to be race, you still had to be there.

A year earlier Smith had been discussing the main differences between Olympic distance races and Ironman and despite having never raced an Ironman before he was aware of one significant difference that he would now have to contend with. Over the Olympic distance he had said. "You're either there from the gun and you're feeling good, or you feel crap and you're crap all the way through." One small mistake and it could be all over in the shorter races but Ironman was different. Over the longer distance he recognized that it could be good, bad, good, bad all the way through, he would have to be mentally stronger, but that again was an area where Smith was not lacking. In the longer races Smith was intensely aware that you were always in the running. Away from your own performance you could never be sure of what was happening to the athletes in front of you, they could be about to blow and that meant you had to keep going because you were always in with a shout. A point that had been proved by one of Smith's boyhood heroes, Mark Allen, the eventual winner in 1995 having been over two miles down at the start of the run.

When it came to the major challengers, naturally Van Lierde's name was the first ones Smith uttered but with one of the strongest fields ever at Hawaii there were so many possible winners and without detracting from the superb field assembled in Hawaii, many independent, and some not so independent observers were clearly hoping for a head-to-head between Smith and Van Lierde. An unlikely but nonetheless interesting proposition. Even perhaps both athletes were secretly looking forward to meeting each other again, with a chance to settle old scores.

As for strategy, Smith's reputation of being aggressive from the start of the race and leading the races from the front, naturally resulted in a question as to whether he would adopt the same tactic when it came to the Ironman, attacking hard on the bike in an attempt to weaken the opposition and then attempt to hold on for the run, but despite Smith's lack of experience over the distance he was the first to counter such suggestions stating that it would be, "foolish to get off the bike not feeling fresh." A good point that many who had blown up on the run could attest to.

Smith even went so far as to state that he didn't feel it would be sensible for him to even go off the front given the heat and his inexperience over the distance but contrastingly acknowledged that it would be prudent to try to stay as close to the leading riders who may be making a break on the bike in an attempt to avoid the gap becoming too big. But having said that, Smith had played his cards close to his chest by expressing that point in the third person rather than saying that they would be his tactics. He was too aware of the things that could go wrong over that distance to make specific predictions about what he or others would do in given circumstances, but left that instead to the journalists, commenting only on the dangers of being too far behind the leaders into T2. "It's hard to increase your pace on the run to make up even a four or five minute gap." Smith admitted. "If you ain't there on the bike then you probably ain't there."

Smith's vision of the race and its unforgiving nature, seemed to be a reflection of the perspective two time winner Scott Tinley had of it when in 1985 he had stated that Hawaii offered, "no margin for error, absolutely none. If things aren't going right, they're going wrong." Tinley had said. "There's no middle of the road, you're either awesome or you're beat." Smith accepted that this was a learning experience for him but was looking for more than just finishing. "I want to enjoy the race." Smith said acknowledging that it might not be possible. Nonetheless he felt he was in good shape and could, "do well." But to be brutally honest his preparation for the race to date had hardly been ideal and what the term 'well' would come to mean by the end of the race he wouldn't say.

Even though his immediate goal was success at Ironman, beyond Hawaii, many wondered what the future would hold for Smith and what impact success or failure in Hawaii would do with respect to Smith's future choices between the shorter distance races and the Ironman events. With only two years to go to the Sydney Olympics some wondered if a successful move into Ironman would result in a permanent move or if Hawaii was just a one off transitory foray into the world of the long distance.

Some of his comments from earlier in the year seemed to identify a clear and planned progression into the longer distance races as he matured but if anyone though that he was going to forsake a place at the Sydney Olympics he was soon to put them right on that score. "I'll be going for the Olympic team so I'll need to check the situation on that," replied Smith when asked if this would be his only Ironman race. As for a quick one off try at Ironman, Smith was less committal and replied. That he would, "see how it went."

Whilst some believed the reference to 'how it went' referred to his concerns over his future performance in Hawaii, those on the inside were aware that his comments had more to do with the problems Smith had of fitting in an Ironman race between Olympic qualification races rather than any personal doubts about his own performance. A supremely confident athlete he clearly believed he could compete successfully at both distances but recognized the importance of specific training and the fact that obtaining a qualification spot for the Olympics would mean that he would have to temper his enthusiasm to go long because he knew how much he would have to suffer going long and the problems of recovery from such exhausting events.

Even if Smith and his supporters were looking forward to the race, there was one person who perhaps wouldn't have been so keen to see Spencer suffer in the Kona heat, but sadly that person would not be there, that person was his father Bill. Whilst Spencer was dedicating his race to his dad, ironically, Bill was the one person who never really wanted Spencer to do Hawaii. "He thought it was too hard," said Spencer. "He would never want me to suffer like that." Bill had said that if he ever saw his son in trouble he would pull him out the race. "Fuck the sponsors and the race." Bill had said to Spencer. A reflection of the father, rather than the manager, but now Spencer had to face up to the race on his own.

3rd October 1998 Ironman World Championships, Hawaii, USA

In 1998 Hawaii Ironman had come a very long way from its small beginnings twenty years earlier and with its present day organization involving a myriad of organizations and parties encompassing sponsorship, and television, administration and logistics, Hawaii Ironman was now big business in the world of sport. If this fact was in question then a look at the prize purse which totaled an astonishing quarter of a million dollars with $35,000 going to the winners would soon put pay to that viewpoint. Whilst in terms of golf and tennis this may have not been considered such an impressive pay day, for triathlon such a payout was considered untold riches for those who dared push themselves to the limit in terms of not just distance but also time. If the prize money was obviously important to the professionals such as Smith who made their living from the sport, for the majority of the 1,500 athletes it was not about winning or the money that was on offer but just about finishing what could be arguably called the most demanding one day race in the world.

One would imagine with such frightening distances in the race, that the preceding week on the island would see the athletes all taking it rather easy but even the taper and reduction in intensity of training for most if not all the competitors didn't seem to result in a reduction of the sporting activity around Hawi.

The early morning swims off Dig-Me beach continued, as did the steady runs around town and would be competitors could still be seen pedaling the tarmac from sunrise to sunset. If this was tapering, then many Ironman competitors appeared to be failing abysmally in their attempt to follow the rule-book and the tapering tradition which stated do less and less frequently and if you must then do it at a lower intensity. The good news for those who made it to Hawaii is that race day weather conditions around the island rarely suffered the wild fluctuations that could be inflicted on the competitors at other Ironman qualifiers throughout the world, especially in Europe where it had been hard for athletes to predict if it would be calm or windy or hot or cold. Pretty important factors when selecting race kit.

The bad news for those in Kona however is that the conditions whilst fairly constant are always difficult. It is always hot, with a blistering and unforgiving sun for most of the day, and it is always windy, ranging from exceedingly, to extremely and 1998 was to be no different.

On the morning of the race, it appeared that the weather gods had brewed up a storm for the anniversary race and the consensus among the athletes and spectators alike was that this was to be one of the hardest racing days in Hawaii ever. Today was not a day for the weak or the meek and the 'Mumuku,' the wind that comes from all directions was sure to take its toll on one and all. The water would be choppy, the bike would be tortuous, and the run would simply blow some away.

A few minutes before 7am with the sun shimmering on the waters, a field of fifteen hundred 'would be' Ironmen started their journey. As the starting canon blasted its warning that now was the time to be resolute, the shoal of swim capped athletes stuttered and then began to froth and bubble as one, slowly heading away from the Beach. Given the months of intense training endured by all that were assembled, it seemed almost ironic that so many of those who had counted down the months, the weeks, the days, the hours, the minutes until the start of the race, seemed so unprepared for the start, as the shock of the boom that echoed across nervously silent waters first halted and then triggered the realization that the defining moment had arrived and they were on their way.

Smith and the rest of the professionals enjoyed the benefit of a ten metre head start on the rest of the field. A policy implemented to help avoid them getting caught up in the throbbing washing machine start of flashing and tumbling arms and legs of slower but no less determined athletes, and as the field of fifteen hundred thrashed through the water, the ranks of the professionals made a clean start and started to vie for positions pulling neatly away from the rest of the field as its members tussled and tumbled in their attempts to put order into the chaos which is one of the enduring spectacles of the sport of triathlon. To describe it as chaos is not to criticize its structure, but to cherish its nature, as out of its chaos comes order. The strong would lead and the weaker would follow.

Whilst there is considerable status associated with leading the field in the swim there is little glory, which is saved and guarded for the finish line, but despite this, over the race's short but notorious history there have been a series of outstanding swimmers who have had the benefit of being able to enjoy the distinction of having led the field in the world's most prestigious triathlon, all be it in some cases for only a few minutes, as in many a case it wouldn't take long before the lead swimmer would be swallowed up by the big hitters who would dig deep on the bike and relegate the swim leader to the relative obscurity of a placement outside the top ten.

Among athletes who had gained this reputation for leading the swim were Rob Mackle, and Lars Jorgenson from the USA who had achieved such a distinction but not quite adhering to that principle of now you see me now you don't, German triathlete, Wolfgang Dittrich, was one of those awesome swimmers who could also do it on the bike and for a few years in the 90's, he arguably spent more time in the lead on the bike section than any other athlete, having led out the elite field in the swim on five occasions, firstly in 1989 with a 48:13 as compared to Mark Allen's 51:17. This in the year when Allen won his first Hawaii with an awesome 2:40:04 marathon split head to head with Dave Scott. On this occasion the German managed to take 10th place overall.

Unwilling to be dissuaded from bucking the trend, Dittrich kept up the habit in 1991 when once again he exited the water at the front of the elite field in a time of 48:02 leaving Allen and the rest of the field nearly two minutes down, on this occasion his reputation among his compatriots for leading out the swimming and keeping on going stood him in good stead with him even managing to maintain his lead on the race until the early stages of the marathon improving his overall standing from the previous year with a 5th place just off the podium.

Not satisfied with twice but choosing to make it three in a row Dittrich led the field out again in 1993 with a 48:30 but Allen was at the peak of his career and took the Ironman title once again despite being two minutes and ten seconds slower in the swim, 1993 however was the best year for the tenacious German which saw him get his just deserts for all the work he had put in over the past years with a podium spot and a bronze medal for his endeavours. But despite his continued efforts in Hawaii and despite leading the swim again in 1996 and 1997 Dittrich never again managed to get back in the top ten.

Notwithstanding Dittrich's capabilities, his non appearance in 1998 meant the responsibility of leading out the swim had fallen squarely on the shoulders the swim specialist, Lars Jorgensen, who had just out sprinted Dittrich in 1995 to win the swim prime and had set the swim record for the event, but despite Jorgenson's strength in the water, he was a significantly more prone to dropping back after the swim section than Dittrich, and had yet to match his swimming capabilities with respect to the other two disciplines. As would have been expected Jorgensen who was based in San Diego quickly assumed his rightful position at the front, leading the rest of the field away towards the turnaround boat and by the time he had reached the half way mark he had established a clear lead on the field with the exception of Aussie Paul O'Brien who was sticking closely to his feet.

It was Jorgenson who held the course record 46:44 set in 1995 and with a strong powerful stroke and no let up in pace, it looked like he could be on target to beating his own record, confident in his capabilities Jorgenson picked up the pace, while the elite field struggled to stay in touch watching him determinedly stretch his lead over the major contenders to two minutes. To the elite field however Jorgenson was not a threat, they had bigger fish to fry and the swim was the shortest of the disciplines and he was left to take the prime having slithered a mere three seconds inside his own course record with O'Brien in his wake.

Two minutes adrift, the chasing pack included some serious contenders for the podium places. Van Lierde was out of the water sixth, in a time of 48:48 with the antipodean swim specialist Bryan Rhodes on his shoulder, whilst closely following on from the Aussie was Smith in 49:02 and the DeBoom twins only ten seconds behind him. Smith was looking strong and having had a good swim found that he had put nearly a minute into Lothar Leder and three minutes into Peter Reid, Thomas Hellriegel, Swiss rookie Christoph Mauch and American Ironman veteran Cameron Widoff who all exited the water within seconds of each other, but if it was going well for Smith, it certainly wasn't going well for Christophe Legh, whose body had suffered so badly in 1997.

Suffering from severe cramps in the swim section Legh finally exited the water in 55:12 more than six minutes down on the main contenders at the front of the pack. It later appeared that severe cramps had forced him to pull out of the lead pack and drift back through the field of flailing arms and legs. Determined not to give up Legh had eventually realized that he would have to rely on breaststroke just to keep him going, but of course it cost him valuable time, and severely affected any possibility of him making a real impact on the race. He knew now that if he was to medal he would have to pull out all the stops and that in truth their was little hope of him achieving what he had dreamed of on his return to Hawaii, but not one to give up easily Legh kept on going. If the Kona gods thought that cramp would be enough to stop him they had obviously forgotten his determination the previous year or had underestimated his tenacity. Whilst he would not be taking home a winners medal, one thing that Legh would be able to take home with him was the well acknowledged belief that it is always possible to lose Hawaii in the water even if it is not possible to win it there. It seemed that for the second year in a row the Kona Gods had not looked kindly on the young Aussie.

One of the things often not acknowledged by triathletes, even some of those who are experienced, is the extent of the depletion of fluids that can result from swimming. A normal swimmer can lose in excess of two pints of sweat in an hour session, a considerable amount, which can have a considerable effect on performance, so there is a danger of dehydration before the second leg is even started, coupled with this the waters around Kailua Bay are extremely salty which whilst helping add to the buoyancy for the swimmers can lead to athletes feeling nauseated by the time there out of the water, so it was not unusual to see a significant number of the field, including the top contenders, take time to guzzle some fluids, the minute the got into transition, Smith included.

For the elite athletes the first part of the race was over with Van Lierde leading the major contenders out of the water in a time of 48:48 followed closely by Bryan Rhodes in 48:49. James Bonney 48:59, and Smith at 49:02, fourteen seconds down on the Van Lierde, but in a race of this distance fourteen seconds was nothing and they still had another seven and a half hours of racing in front of them.

There are two major fears attributed by athletes to the Hawaii Ironman bike section, firstly the length, which remains constant to all Ironman events but secondly and perhaps most concerningly the conditions, and Hawaii had both of them this day. A hundred and twelve miles of riding ahead with an estimated four and a half to five hours in the saddle for even the strongest riders there is little opportunity for relief from either the gale force winds or the scorching sun and 1998 had both. As if to warn the athletes of the oncoming terrain, as the course headed out of Kona and the first thing the riders faced was a sharp incline before the course turned left onto the Queen K Highway at which point they would find themselves on their way to Hawi and it would seem even to the most committed triathletes with plenty of miles under their belts a hell of a long way, even to the turnaround point.

Officially the road that the majority of the bike section is raced along is called the Queen Kaahumanu Highway but over the years it had been affectionately shortened to the Queen K, though why anyone would have affection for the forty mile two lane highway which is constantly scoured and bombarded with vicious and shifting winds and punctuated with long gradual hills that sap your strength before you know you're on them, god only knows. And on this gusting but heavy and hot October morning the likelihood of any triathletes looking upon it affectionately, at least whilst racing on it was unlikely.

For those that race, as the day progresses so the black tarmac starts to shimmer and sizzle under the scorching sun, with the heat maintaining an almost uncanny ability to both radiate down and then rise again. According to even the best triathletes who have won in Hawaii· there is a common acceptance that the Queen K is never conquered, never beaten, and Smith having been to Hawaii before was aware of that. It would be back there the following year and the year after that and the year after that, in much the same way that Smith hoped he would, but for that moment in time, all Smith could hope to do was survive it and hope it didn't take too much out of him before the run.

Far removed from the holiday brochure images of Hawaii with sun drenched beaches and lush vegetation, the Queen K is a sight of desolate volcanic rubble and rocks where nothing grows save for the handfuls of sparten yellow brown grass that sprout up between the volcanic wreckage. The Highway from Kailua-Kona to Kawaihae is a sea of black that pushes through the brown burnt and scorched rocks that rise up to the horizon with its distant backdrop of Mauna Loa and the nearer slopes of Mount Hualalai. The highway at its worst is a blast furnace, an oven, which can burn the energy out of the strongest legs and scorch the mind into submission. Even when the wind blows, it blows only hot air, which suffocates rather than relieves and adds the burden of intensifying the effort needed just to turn the gears over. And Smith was now beginning to face up to those obstacles.

Even in the morning before the swim start the winds had threatened to bring added impediments to the race and it kept its promise. The ferocity of the wind was so acute that riders had to work hard just to keep their line and avoid crashing in on each other as gust after successive gust bombarded the field on a clear course. So strong was the wind at times that it was possible to see riders actually leaning their bikes into the wind in an attempt to stay upright, whilst standing up on the pedals, even on the flats just to turn the gears over. Any plans that had been made in the way of pre-selection of gears for specific parts of the course could be safely thrown away. Today was not going to be a typical, if there is such a thing, for the Hawaii Ironman and was certainly not going to be a day for those whose weakness was the bike. The day would be about strength and this would suit Smith well.

Early in the ride it was Belgium's tough man, Luc Van Lierde who pushed to the front with Jorgenson quickly dropping down the ranks. Paul O'Brian, had however been resolute in his determination not to be swallowed up so quickly and having managed an eighth overall in the Australian Ironman earlier in the year must have been feeling confident about his performance. Obviously enjoying the opportunity to ride at the front with Van Lierde they took it in turns passing each other as and when each was feeling a little stronger. In truth O'Brien may have been a little out of his league when compared to the biking prowess of Van Lierde and whilst they maintained their lead for the first forty or so kilometres, it was almost inevitable that O'Brien would eventually drop off the pace.

If Van Lierde's strength on the bike was undoubted then Jurgen Zack's was legendary, and pretty soon after the 40km marker the rhythmic whir of wheels emanating from of the German Zack attack could be heard at the back of the leading duo. The Zack attack had commenced the moment he put his foot to the pedal, and with the race just less than two hours old, Zack took the lead from Van Lierde, whilst Smith with James Bonney and Tim DeBoom moved up the ranks closely behind him and filtered their way along the Queen K highway to make up the leading pack.

Some time after the race Smith recounted how when Zack went past him early on in the race that he had been astounded at how fast Zack had been going. Working closely to a predetermined heart rate Smith said. "He went past me…I had a heart rate monitor on and there was no way I could keep his pace." Leading from the front Zack proceeded to assert his authority on the race, and the chasing group, which included Smith seemed to remain happy not to chase down his lead and so Zack moved clear with little challenge. Whether tactics, fear or common sense were the underlying reasons for this it was difficult to establish at the time but Smith later confirmed his reasoning. Smith had decided to put his faith in his heart rate monitor and was sticking to his game plan. For Reid however, and the defending champion Thomas Hellriegel, letting Zack gain too much too soon was not something that they could allow him to do and they began to dig deeper in search of that extra something.

Whilst Smith continued to ease into his Hawaii debut, Hellriegel and Reid who were riding together clearly decided that they needed to respond. A minute or so behind Zack, Hellriegel's face was scarlet from the effort of chasing him down, there is a fine line between riding at the limit and overcooking it and Hellriegel certainly looked on the wrong side of the equation as he gasped for air whilst the wind gusted and blew around him. Fighting against the 40mph wind, which was now directly in his face Hellriegel looked distinctly uncomfortable as he pushed around the gears which also looked uncomfortably big. Whilst Hellriegel seemed to fidget and change his position on the bike, in contrast, Reid who was a mere fifteen meters behind him, still looked in control, turning over the gears rhythmically whilst his upper body remained solid and unflinching. There was no doubt that Reid was having a better day of it on the bike, at least for the time being and as the bike progressed so Reid slowly began to move ahead of Hellriegel. At this point some may have been willing to scratch Hellriegel from their top three list but as Hellriegel recovered his composure a few kilometres down the road it was clear that the Canadian's advantage over the German was to be short lived. It had undoubtedly been a rough time for Hellriegel, but in an Ironman you expect a few of those along the way.

At this point a chasing group of contenders which included Smith had formed about three minutes back remaining slightly adrift from Luc Van Lierde, who still maintained a small advantage. Alongside Smith, the group contained three Americans, Tim DeBoom, Glah, and Bonney, and another rookie to keep Smith company in the guise of the Swiss triathlete Christoph Mauch. But nobody in the group seemed willing to commit themselves at this point in the pursuit of the leaders, after all there was a long way to go and two of them were very unsure of what lay ahead. Up ahead, Zack continued to pile on the pressure determined to make the best of a tough bike section that he was most suited to. As he approached Kawaihae, which was protected by surrounding higher ground the wind seemed to drop and one may have been forgiven for asking if the gods were choosing to smile on Zack, in much the same way as they had seen fit to make Legh suffer, but an experienced Hawaiian triathlete as he was, Zack knew that as he made his way up the long climb to Hawi the wind would pick up and if anything would become stronger as he climbed. In addition, Zack knew that Kawaihae was a favorite stomping ground for Hellriegel, and it was common knowledge that this was a point where he liked to attack, just when many riders were struggling to hold on to the pace.

It was a tough part of the course and historically had been a place where many would crack and so Hellriegel would take the opportunity to help them on their way to breaking point by upping the tempo. Given this fact and in the knowledge that Hellriegel was not too far behind, Zack must have been acutely aware that the pace of the chasers may well pick up on the hill up to Hawi in an attempt by the rest of the field to stay with Hellriegel but Zack maintained his tempo selecting to ride his own race, rather than be dictated to by the tactics further down the field.

Strangely, the surrounding environment becomes more attractive and green up at the top of the hill where the winds blow hardest, but neither Hellriegel nor Reid were in the mood for sightseeing and now that Hellriegel had recovered from his previous exploits, Reid was increasingly aware of the likelihood of an attack. At this point it was about becoming mentally prepared for it and Reid had been preparing himself. They broached the climb together pushing it harder than perhaps either of them had intended and then according to Reid, at the top Hellriegel turned to him and smiled and said. "We are now clear." Whilst Hellriegel may have felt that he had broken the following pack, Reid was acutely aware that the biggest threats at present still lay in front of them. Firstly the man mountain that was Jurgen Zack and secondly, the rest of the race!

Whilst things may have been going well at the front for the leaders it was not however going to be such a good day as it had first appeared for Lars Jorgenson who had led the swim from the start and beaten his 1995 record. Suffering on the bike Jorgenson had been forced to pull out during the bike section and so his new record of 46:41 would not be allowed to stand. Jorgenson was obviously devastated but such are the ways of an Ironman. At least some may say that his physical and mental suffering had ended for the day, but for Jorgenson, it was months of training and nothing to show for it.

Given the ferocity of the wind and the pace at which the group were riding, Smith remained looking comfortable perched on his yellow Specialized bike with matching helmet and continued to ride smoothly with his tri spoke wheel whirring steadily over the smooth tarmac surface. Holding a much more upright position than was traditional for the shorter distances that he excelled in Smith almost looked more like a bikie rather than a triathlete, all save for the telltale signs of the tri bars.

Whilst the obvious sufferings of Hellriegel had manifestly subsided, Reid continued to appear relatively more comfortable than Hellriegel, after the climb despite the fact that it had been the German who had dictated the pace. Reid had the utmost respect for Hellriegel who he had affectionately referred to as 'Cyborg' in his description of the mechanical and powerful way he would bike through the toughest conditions, but now Hellriegel was beginning to suffer at the hands of the Canadian who two years previously he had comfortably dropped him in the Canadian Ironman. But two years had been a long time in Reid's race resume, including two wins at Ironman Australia and one in Lanzarote and Reid's current winning form was beginning to show through.

Behind them, Van Lierde was doing most of the work in the chasing pack whilst Hawaii 'veteran' Ken Glah and rookie Smith were content to sit back which was perhaps the smart move in the tough conditions. Meanwhile back in the field it seemed that Christophe Legh, was still challenging the Kona gods and despite struggling with the first part of the bike he was making good progress on the Queen K and actually starting to put a dent into the time advantage that Smith and his compatriots had over him. The wind continued to play its part in the race for all of the competitors, and descending the hill from Hawi, the tail and side winds made life difficult for all but the most experienced cyclists causing innumerable crashes with some athletes ending their race right there with the wind literally blowing some riders from their bikes. Whilst the more cautious accepted the time losses as they braked their way off the descent, others took the inevitable risk associated with riding in the potentially dangerous conditions, and some paid the price.

By the time Zack reached the lava fields again, much to his relief, the winds offered up a more consistent tail wind as is the norm for the return leg but his relief soon turned to frustration when a puncture threatened to cost him the entire race. As Zack waited for a replacement wheel to arrive so his frustration and agitation began to show, it was clear that the wait was not only losing him time but also affecting his concentration and costing him more in terms of wasted nervous energy and anxiety, all of which were tantamount to committing racing suicide. As the seconds dragged on to minutes so the energy and power that had taken him into the lead and maintained him there seemed to drain from his muscular frame.

Some two minutes later, climbing on his bike for the second time, having received the spare, Zack looked coarsely at the photographers who surrounded him knowing they had a good picture and commented that they must all now be happy. Whilst they had been frantically clicking away, Zack's impatience had become more and more manifest in his expression which had grown increasingly strained in the knowledge that the possibility of winning in Hawaii in 1998 was slowly ticking away from him. With respect to Zack, this was strike one to the Kona gods, and if the puncture on the bike was not enough he was soon to face further misfortune just a few miles into the run.

Despite his puncture, Zack remained just over a minute ahead of Hellriegel and Reid at the 90-mile marker and maintained his lead as he approached Kailua whose tree lined boulevard promised some respite from the burning sun in the last eight or so miles of the ride.

As the first of the athletes to come into the town he was the first to receive the screams, and cheers of encouragement from the waiting crowds who had gathered within earshot of the PA announcer who had whipped the spectators up into a frenzy of expectation which undoubtedly spurred him on as he began to once again refocus on the task in hand. Just as the cheering started to subside as Zack departed, so it started again as barely a minute passed before the two chasers also made their way into the town of Kailua emerging from the black, hot, and desolate lava fields into the throng of the waiting crowds once again.

Whilst the throng spurred on the riders, Zack who had raced Hawaii before, knew that beyond the crowd there remained a final short, sharp and steep climb up to the Keauhou shopping centre before the final downhill to the Kona Surf resort where he would end the bike section and make his way into the second transition, but more than that, he knew that he would then have to face the marathon, when he had spent so much energy on and off the bike already. Once past the last hill and the decent that he would have to endure on the ride, Zack arrived in T2 with his lead still intact, but at only 1 minute and 15 seconds, it was far less than he would have wanted it to be. His transition was methodical practiced and quick and he was already out on the road starting his run, by the time the roars of the waiting crowd signalled to him the arrival of the powerful frame of Hellriegel who was followed like a shadow by the noticeably less muscled and leaner Peter Reid.

Further back into the race Smith had continued to lose time to the leaders which given his biking prowess may have surprised many but the distance and the conditions were taking their toll on the rookie, so much so that going into T2 Smith was down to ninth place, nearly nine minutes behind Hellriegel and Reid, who were in second and third. It was not all bad news however for the Londoner as whilst the three leaders were ripping the field apart with devastating times, Smith was only giving away less than two and a half minutes to the rest of the field that currently stood, Sandvag in fourth at 7:27, Van Lierde at 8:27, Legh at 8:30, DeBoom, 8:44, Mauch, 8:55 and Glah: 9:30. For Smith, being nine minutes and fifty five seconds behind the leader, had clearly put him in the reckoning if he could put in a good run, and even though he had never previously seriously considered the possibility of a podium finish as a novice to the Hawaii Ironman, he now was beginning to believe it may be within his grasp.

Smith had never expected himself to finish on the podium, but instead had acknowledged this race to be the beginning of his apprenticeship, and with that in mind Smith looked like the possibility of achieving his own objectives were still in the offering and perhaps even better. Prior to the race he had sat down with his girlfriend Melissa and contemplated what he expected from the race deciding. "Top twenty is good, top ten is very good, top five is what I'd like to go for." Now coming off the bike in ninth place with the knowledge that he was one of the better runners, he knew that in terms of top five he was certainly in with a chance and if the front runners were to falter then anything could happen.

Lothar Leder on the other hand was having a very bad day. As a veteran to the race who would normally have been up there in contention for a podium spot, a twelve and a half minutes deficit to Zack after the bike signalled that something was very wrong and it was evident that he was suffering badly. As the bike splits began to be relayed, the splits themselves told the tale, Hellriegel 4:44:39, Peter Reid 4:44:45, Christophe Legh 4:48:50, Peter Sandvag 4:50:55, Christoph Mauch 4:52:26, Ken Glah 4:54:15, Tony DeBoom 4:55:02,

Luc Van Lierde 4:55:11 Rainer Mueller-Horner 4:56:02 Troy Jacobson 4:56:05 and Spencer Smith 4:56:25. Even with the 11th fastest bike split, Smith had lost 11 minutes and forty six seconds to Hellriegel.

As the leaders were contemplating the run, so it was that much of the field of age group competitors were still struggling on the bike but if the news of the tail wind had filtered back to the bulk of the competitors, any celebration on their part was undoubtedly premature as the 'Mumuku' remained true to its reputation and swung around full tilt resulting in a full on head wind offering no respite or help to those who were hoping for an easy return to T2. Once again the Kona Gods were playing their part. Whilst the wind was relentless, and seemed to get stronger as the day progressed, there was at least some relief from the scorching sun as cloud cover moved in to cover some parts of the course in the early afternoon making the run, a little easier than 1997 at least for some.

As if to warn of the impending suffering, the start of the run is in itself sufficient to make many an athlete consider whether or not to take on the third discipline. As the athletes leave transition two, so they are faced with a steep hill as the course heads out onto the Queen K again, this time with a twenty six point two mile run ahead of them. Some athletes walk up the hill trying to stretch their legs out in the hope that they will be able to pick up their pace as they get further into the run but now where time is so precious very few of the professionals can be afforded such a luxury.

Even if the majority did not expect Zack to manage to hold on to his slender lead, Zack was not one to give up so easily and started the run solidly with a look of stoic determination, but even at this point Zack knew he was in big, big trouble. Out on the bike he had been suffering difficulties with his hydration, and now his trepidation was shifting from whether or not he would get caught, to whether his body would hold up sufficiently to allow him to finish the race. The dangers of a water mineral imbalance are acute amongst athletes and can lead to the complete breakdown of the body which is not only a severe problem in terms of racing but also of significant risk to both life an limb as the body fails to absorb the water needed for it to function even its basic needs. And whilst Zack was aware of the risks he continued to try and focus on the race hoping that his body would start to respond as he attempted to hold off both Reid and Hellriegel who were gaining fast.

In the early part of the run there appeared little to separate the two chasers with perhaps surprisingly Hellriegel looking the stronger of the two despite not taking advantage of that fact. Unbeknown to Hellriegel, however, Reid and his coach had agreed on a run strategy prior to the race that involved Reid consciously running slower on the hills and faster on the flat in an attempt to save energy. To this end, the indication that the Canadian was suffering more on the hills was in fact a misrepresentation of the physiological suffering that Reid was going through. As the race progressed so the picture began to change with Reid eventually beginning to show his strength as he strode past Hellriegel on the way into the 'Pit' and then convincingly set his sights on the struggling figure of Zack less than a mile later at a pace that highlighted Zack's suffering.

Whilst Reid was clearly feeling confident at this point and a challenge from Smith was highly unlikely, despite the fact that he could put in a thirty minute 10km, things had been known to go horribly wrong for even the most experienced runners at Hawaii and there remained two Ironman world record holders in the guise of Van Lierde and Leder, neither of which had given up on the possibility of tracking down Reid and both of whom were more than capable of running a two hour forty five marathon off the bike. But Reid looked smooth and in control as he headed into his sixth mile on Alii Drive, whilst Zack continued to maintain his resolve digging deep to remain just under two minutes down, with his German counterpart, Hellriegel coming up close behind.

Van Lierde was a good seven minutes down on Reid but was undoubtedly one of the biggest threats to him and looked strong on the run despite what he had felt to be a disappointing ride, whilst Smith remained in sixth place only thirty seconds behind the Belgian with Tony de Boom and more surprisingly Christophe Legh holding their positions on the road only a matter of seconds behind him. If Smith was surprised at his current placing in the event then so was Lothar Leder, though for somewhat different reasons, having started the event as one of the race favourites Leder now found himself a further two minutes behind Smith and after a less than characteristically good bike, was in need of a somewhat special run if he was to even get on the podium let alone the possibility of challenging Reid.

Whilst Leder's bike had been poor, despite the problems Legh had suffered in the swim, he had produced an incredible bike split of 4:48:50 which had not only been bettered by Reid, Hellriegel and Zack and had seen the Australian hammer his way back into medal contention and brought him back on terms with the leaders, though whether his exertions would cost him in the run was open to conjecture.

In comparing the athletes who now headed the field, the stature of the majority of the leaders contrasted significantly from the solid musculature that Smith had brought with him to Hawaii with perhaps the exception being Zack. Despite having tried to lose weight for the race Smith's powerful physique and unyielding commando type stride remained unmistakable, almost misplaced among the more graceful stick like figures that the Hawaii elite was accustomed to seeing at the front of the race, but he continued to appear in control and measured in his attempt to maintain his position, unlike Zack who looked increasingly uncomfortable with his muscular frame accentuated by a distended stomach which continued to refuse to absorb the fluids he was desperate to take in. As he struggled to maintain his place in the field, his short stride length gave indication to the rest of the field that for Zack, the battle for a medal was almost over as the gods of Kona saw fit to reducing this Ironman giant to what looked little more than as shuffle. For Zack it was the second strike to the gods.

If Zack was to take in any solace in his predicament, he was not alone in his suffering as Hellriegel stopped several times, to hold his back, a sure indication that the efforts put in on the bike were beginning to take their toll as his run began to slow and then to visibly collapse.

With the placings now set, and little that could stay the pursuit of his first Hawaii win, Reid continued strong to the end continuing to break the field behind into splinters with a run that comfortably distanced himself from any danger of being overtaken. With arms aloft Reid crossed the finish line in a time of 8:24:20 some seven minutes and thirty seven seconds ahead of a determined looking Van Lierde who just managed to hold off Lothar Leder by exactly a minute.

Picking up the placings outside the top three, Mauch had just put enough extra in on the run to distance himself from Smith to take fourth and Smith in turn had outrun Legh in the final stages to take fifth in a time of 8:39:07, a mere minute and one second down on Mauch's fourth place and only six minutes and eleven seconds away from a time that would have seen him on the podium. Having crossed the line the exhausted but jubilant Smith was immediately ushered into one of the medical tents where he had to be administered two intravenous bags to aid his recovery from the dehydration he had suffered. The heat, wind and duration of the event had undoubtedly taken its toll on Smith as it would do on all the athletes who had raced, but at least for Smith the race was now over, whilst for the unfortunate Zack the battle was far from completed.

Hellriegel, had been suffering more and more as the run continued but remained persistent in his struggle to the finish eventually dropping back to a creditable but disappointing eighth place, but of the Germans it was undoubtedly Zack that suffered worst, his inability to get his body to rehydrate, destroying any chances of a top ten place and eventually reducing him to a shuffle that saw him finally covering the marathon in four hours and forty four minutes, and correspondingly plummeting from first place to 246th over the course of the run.

The Kona gods had thrown all they could at him, but they couldn't manage the third strike and his determination had seen him most definitely remain 'in.' In a similar vein Matt Belfield who had been one of the other British podium hopes prior to the race had also suffered on the run and despite starting the run in the top thirty, a 4:28:53 marathon which was way outside what he was capable of, also saw him relegated to an uncharacteristic 286th place overall.

For an athlete who had been through so much in the preceding months on a personal level and had for much of the season primarily concentrated on Olympic distance racing with only the odd venture into the longer distances, Smith had achieved more than many had believed him capable of. Reflecting on that after the race Smith commented. "I sensed that not all the critics were with me," but was honest enough to recognise that with no previous record of competing at that kind of distance the lack of faith in him was at least justified if not perhaps misplaced. Smith was clearly pleased with his performance and with regard to returning the following year Smith made it quite clear that Hawaii 1999 was definitely on the programme, but he was the first to admit that the pressure on him would be somewhat greater now that he had raced it once. "When I come back it's going to be harder." Smith stated, citing that at his first attempt expectations of him had been considerably lower. "Next year that's over, I've got to win it now, but that pressure is very good. It's what motivates me." Few athletes would have dared to have stated such an objective so emphatically, but Smith had been World Champion before, all be it at the shorter distance and his own expectations and confidence were at a high. He was an official Ironman but he now wanted to be the Ironman World Champion.

Smith still maintained his winning ways at Windsor 1998.

Bill and Spencer embrace at the Worlds in New Zealand 1994.

TRANSITIONS ELEVEN & TWELVE
Accusations and Battles & Return to Racing

Three days after his successful debut at the Ironman distance and whilst still in Kona, Smith married his long term girlfriend Melissa Simon in Hawaii with his mum at his side. The ceremonies and formalities over, they then planned to head off to the French Rivera on their honeymoon for a break. It had been a tough last two years for Smith, but now a new start beaconed with a beautiful wife, and Smith save for one major person missing was almost back on top of the world. With the season officially over, this was at last a chance for Smith to relax and enjoy himself, but he was still feeling a little unwell following his diagnosed anemia prior to the race and so he called Bill Black for some advice. Taking on board Smith's ailments, Black arranged an appointment for Smith with he British Olympic Medical Doctor, Dr Rod Jacques for when he returned to the UK after his honeymoon, in the mean time Black told him to go and relax and enjoy his honeymoon. But the honeymoon period, as brief as it was, was soon about to end.

At Hawaii shortly after the race Smith had been required along with a number of other athletes to provide a urine sample as part of the drug testing procedure for the race. This was not an uncommon procedure for major events and Smith had thought nothing of it at the time, but early into November, whilst still on their honeymoon, the British Triathlon Association notified him that his alleged sample from the race had contained 8 ng/ml of the steroid nandrolone. He had tested positive. Smith recounted this as what he termed the, "second lowest moment of his life," after the death of his father. Having only just told the press after Hawaii. "I'm gonna be back next year for sure and then I will concentrate on short course racing up to Sydney 2000." It now looked like he would be doing neither unless he could get to the bottom of the accusation. The positive test meant an immediate ban. "When I heard it I was shaking and shivering." Smith recalled. "Melissa had to control me." Smith couldn't believe it, there had to be something wrong. "I was devastated and cannot put into words how I felt when I read that letter," he recounted. Smith immediately called home again, to talk to his mother and seek advice from Burnell who had been there for them throughout all their recent troubles. "He came on the phone in tears to me," recalled Burnell, who then told him to get home as soon as he could so that they could get to the bottom of the problem.

Whilst Smith was sure of his innocence he was immediately given an interim suspension after the positive test. Nandrolone was and still is a banned anabolic, androgenic steroid on the current IOC list of banned substances, a list adopted by both the ITU and the BTA so the ban was immediate pending an enquiry. Whilst the ban was effective immediately, under the guidelines of the IOC there was an embargo on any public announcement of the alleged positive test which was to remain in place until the second sample was tested, but nonetheless, Smith would not be able to compete again until after there had been an enquiry into the case and then and only then would he be able to race again if he could prove his innocence. If the test was proved to be genuine and valid, then there was little doubt that the ban would be significant for Smith. Nandrolone is a drug that belongs to the steroid family which are a type of drug that are usually synthesized from the male reproduction hormone testosterone and have a number of performance enhancing benefits, hence the reason for them being on the banned list of all the major sporting federations and organizing bodies.

The major benefits obtained by users of such drugs are the reduction of the onset of fatigue associated with training, and the reduction in time required to recover after physical exertion. In addition to this fatigue reducing element, as a result of the stimulation of protein production in the body, nandrolone also promotes the development of muscle with an associated increase in strength and power. But as in the case of most drugs, the benefits of use of usage go hand in hand with a number of negative side effects and in the case of nandrolone, some part of the increase in muscle bulk is derived as a result of the laying down of water and minerals as opposed to muscle, hence the increase in strength is often not as pronounced as the muscle growth indicates.

Whilst this in itself could cause problems, additional physiological drawbacks suffered as a result of such anabolic steroids is the promotion of growth and activity in other tissues in the body resulting from the release of the hormone testosterone which disturbs the body's natural equilibrium and can result in damage to many of the body's major organs. With the liver, being one organ which is particularly susceptible to risk and the heart a significant other, the dangers can be acute, and since the heart is made of muscle tissue its expansion through the use of steroids can ultimately lead to heart attack. Apart from all this, there is also an apparent increased risk of cancer in the cases of prolonged abuse or usage.

Alongside the internal changes in the body, some obvious indicators of use of steroids can potentially be identified by even the non-expert. Since steroids also promote the growth of bones, particularly facial bones such as the jaw and forehead, severe changes to facial shape with widening of the jaw line can result in gaps developing between the teeth, which don't grow, giving what is often referred to as the 'dopey giant' appearance which some users get, reflecting the image sometimes portrayed in children's books. Other visual side effects can include the development of inappropriate sexual characteristics such as breasts in men, and facial hair in women, deepening of the voice, baldness and male impotence which comes about as a result of the body not producing its own testosterone due to its own finely tuned system picking up signals that there is already sufficient testosterone in the body.

Despite these horrific side effects, some athletes have undoubtedly continued to use these drugs in an attempt to improve their performance, but Smith was determined and resolute in his claim that he was not one of them. Whilst many athletes undergo the drug testing procedures, few are aware of the complexities of such procedures or the processes that the sample needs to go through, but for Smith this was now something that he would have to learn about if he was to find the cause of the alleged positive test and clear his name.

When athletes are tested for the steroid, scientists actually search for nandrolone's waste product, 19 norandrosterone. If this is detected in urine it is regarded as proof that nandrolone has been present in the athlete's body and results in a positive test for the athlete subject to the quantity present in the system, which in some cases may be naturally produced. At this time, for men, the IOC (International Olympic Committee) limit was stated to be two nanograms of the waste-product per millilitre of urine, whilst for scientific reasons the women's limit was a slightly higher 5ng/ml.

At first glance it would appear that the testing procedure itself holds no particular mystery although the conditions in which the sample is collected and stored are of paramount importance to ensure the sample is neither damaged or open to tampering, and a process to ensure this is the case is well documented with procedures should be well known to the staff initiating the test. As long as the procedures and protocol are adhered to there should be no problem in identifying the waste products where present, and thereby identifying a positive test, the problem, however for the federations and governing bodies responsible for implementing it, is that once detected, no-one can be sure how the substance arrived in the body.

The problems for the federations at this juncture appeared that there were three possible reasons for the identification of nandrolone in a sample. Firstly, it could have been injected, with the intention to dope on the part of the athlete, although it would have to be said that this is unlikely where testing procedures are known to be put in place, since athletes know it is easily detectable. Whilst the federation had to consider this a possibility, Smith was resolute in his denial of this and at least for him this was not an avenue of investigation he had to pursue.

Secondly, it could arguably have occurred from the somewhat bizarre possibility of eating a large quantity of wild boar offal or alternatively contaminated meat, although a diet of wild boar offal was out of the question and in respect of other contaminated meats, scientific research at this time seemed to suggest that this was again extremely unlikely. But unlikely outcome or not, Smith had to consider the possibility of contaminated meat, especially given the extent to which he had been consuming steak following his diagnosed anemia. Thirdly, and perhaps more likely was the possibility that it may have occurred after pills, supplements or even food containing steroid derivatives, were digested knowingly or otherwise. Clearly a much more likely possibility than the first two options, and again an option that Smith would have to pursue, on the basis that he had unwittingly taken a supplement that was contaminated.

Around this time scientific evidence seemed to show that minute amounts of nandrolone occur naturally in the body, though testing had established that this rarely exceeds 0.6 ng/ml, which threw serious doubt over the Smith case in which he was alleged to have 8.0ng, significantly more than the 'generous' limits permitted by the IOC. But on a closer view of the nandrolone issue it becomes increasingly obvious that its detection and the determination of its source is not as simple as first thought.

Whilst not related to the Smith case a leading expert at the time, Dr Mike Wheeler, who was based at St Thomas' Hospital, London, when speaking to the BBC outlined some serious problems relating to food supplements that contain allowable steroids, which the body readily converts into the banned nandrolone. "I went out and bought some in a sports shop this morning," said Dr Wheeler in interview, emphasizing the ease with which unsuspecting athletes could buy over the counter supplements that would see them banned. "Athletes may in all innocence be taking supplements which contain steroids they don't know about but which will result in a positive test." Add further to the problem of identifying the source, the suggestion by some scientists that nandrolone can be found in meat injected with steroids, which is an increasingly common practice in farming and the scientists and the athletes would find themselves not so far away from the apparently ridiculous wild boar scenario which may have appeared at first to have no credibility and the concerns become greater.

To further complicate the matter, whilst not a concern for Smith but undoubtedly a serious worry for female athletes, is the fact that in women, the increased presence of nandrolone in the body may be due in part to pregnancy or the use of some contraceptive pills, this in short showed the sort of problems that could arise in cases of athletes being tested positive and highlighted that a potential positive test is a much more complex issue, even if we look at the simple case of whether the drug was present in the athletes system or not. Clearly, the major problem for the authorities should have been whether athletes knowingly took pills or other products containing the steroid or whether their 'natural level' is higher as a result of either lifestyle or diet.

At this time Smith was in a position, which left him needing to question a number of possible reasons for the alleged positive sample. Firstly he needed to establish whether the sample was in fact his. Secondly if it was, how did the nandrolone get into his system? And thirdly whether UCLA's lab testing, could accurately measure a specific amount of nandrolone metabolite found in a urine sample.

On returning to the UK Smith would find he had his work cut out. Burnell picked him up from the airport, and the first word Smith would utter to his manager and confidant were. "I don't know where the fuck this has come from." Those were his exact words recalled Burnell. Whilst Burnell admitted that he didn't believe Spencer had knowingly taken any drugs, he admitted that he had to ask him face to face if he had, "I trusted him, but I had to ask him," recalled Burnell, to which Spencer had made it clear with a definite and heartfelt no! And a no from Bill Smith's son was good enough for Burnell who promised Spencer they would get to the bottom of it.

Over the next week Bernie sat down with Spencer and produced a log of every thing Spencer did and ate in the week leading up to Hawaii. Every piece of food, every vitamin, every restaurant he ate in and every item was gone over with a fine toothcomb. Smith at this point was still clinging to the hope that there had been a mix up on the sample tested by UCLA, and that an administrative error would show that the sample that allegedly belonged to him was in fact someone else's. Alternatively he concerned himself with the possibility that it had not been kept in conditions that been necessary to ensure an accurate and untainted readings and this would put a finish to the problem when it came to light. In short, had there been a mix up or had there been a cock up, either way he wanted a quick end to the problem. For Smith at this time who had little knowledge of the scientific background to nandrolone, these seemed by far the most likely reasons behind the whole issue but as he would soon learn there were far greater complications to his case.

Having returned to England Smith also went to see his former coach Bill Black to ask for his advice. Despite Black not playing such a major role in his coaching any longer given the distance between them, Smith had continued to keep in touch with him right up to the Hawaii event, and had spoken to him a week after the race, when he was still complaining about feeling unwell. At that time Bill Black, had agreed to make him an appointment with Dr. Rod Jaques, the British elite squad doctor when he returned to England, and now that he had returned and given the new circumstances that surrounded his return, the need to keep that appointment seemed all the more important.

Bearing in mind that Smith wouldn't have known anything about the positive test result, when he had originally spoken to Black, it would seem almost inconceivable for an athlete who had been knowingly taking drugs to arrange an appointment in which he would undergo blood tests, and this would be a point that would be strongly made at the subsequent inquiries into Smith's case.

To add additional credence to Smith's case it seemed strange not only in the case of planning to see Dr. Jaques but also having been to see the doctor at the Ironman immediately prior to the race that Smith who had been now accused of having taken drugs had no apparent fear of doctors or the tests that they may undertake on him. Clearly not the actions of an athlete who was knowingly talking drugs. Later Burnell would comment on this saying. "One part of our defense that was very strong was the fact that if you were on drugs, why the fuck would you go and see a doctor a few days before a race, not knowing what tests you were going to be subject to, and he was subjected to tests, blood tests and the like. Now Spencer didn't know what these guys were going to find, he was going with a genuine problem so if he was taking drugs, the last place in the world you would want to go is to see one of those guys."

The appointment in place, on November 9th 1998 Smith underwent a series of blood tests in the presence of Bill Black and under the supervision of Dr. Rod Jaques, the result of which would be negative, and in addition according to Burnell, Jaques told Smith that he had been diagnosed wrongly by the Ironman Doctor, and confirmed that whilst he was anemic he also had a parasite in his gut, which Jaques duly treated. It seemed that the plot was thickening.

From Smith's point of view the case was simple. He didn't take it and he was innocent. If the drug was present in the sample then clearly the sample wasn't his. So adamant that he was innocent of all charges that if it hadn't been such a serious charge, the thought of him taking nandrolone would have almost been laughable. As a heavily built athlete racing in an ultra-endurance event like the Ironman, the effects of using nandrolone seemed more likely to be detrimental than beneficial to his performance.

Whilst Smith was silent at the time having been advised that it would be more appropriate to stay so, he would later put his case clearly and concisely having had time to study the consequences of nandrolone ingestion, when, if not a little controversially when he stated. "There is no way I am going to take nandrolone," he argued. "I weigh 180 pounds, and I do not want to run that marathon weighing 185. I've done well in the sport, and I can certainly afford my drug of choice if I was a cheater, and it wouldn't be nandrolone, or some other stone-aged drug you can test for. It'd be EPO, and no, I didn't take that either." It seemed a good point.

Smith knew he would have to prove his innocence in front of his governing body, the BTA and whilst he believed that it must have been a mix up in samples was advised to check for all possibilities of how the drug may have inadvertently got into his system. If the sample was his and nandrolone was present, Smith would have to account for it.

Two weeks after he was notified of the positive dope test Smith had written to the BTA Technical Committee reiterating his innocence and outlining his present course of actions in trying to prove his innocence. In the letter Smith stated. "I have never knowingly used nandrolone or any other anabolic steroid. I am in the process of re-checking medical treatment which I received to determine whether that may have been a source of contamination."

So it was that the highly organized and thorough Burnell, and Smith ran through all the products that Spencer had used prior to the race in minute detail. Everything had to be checked and double checked, even to the point of having the vitamin B injections prescribed by the Ironman doctor, translated from German to English and having the beef steak from a restaurant in which he had eaten sent to a laboratory for testing. The checking and rechecking was time consuming and labourious, but Burnell was determined not to let anything slip through, but whilst they were doing their best to discover any potential sources of contamination, so it was that they were to be dealt a further blow but this time from the other side of the Atlantic.

Whilst in America, prior to returning to the UK Spencer had been advised to get a legal representative, and had duly done so. Because he was in America, he got one in America, but suddenly out of the blue, the lawyer who had initially agreed to take the case, and had been given all the information relating to it was to phone Smith in the UK and inform him he was no longer in a position to represent him. The lawyer in question outlined the fact that he had identified a potential conflict of interest in the case because his company also represented the laboratory where the tests were done. Stating it would be inappropriate for him to continue with the case he advised Smith that he should get himself another lawyer. "He said, I'm not charging you a penny," recalled Burnell, who immediately thought the whole situation 'stank.' "We were then left with no representation, with a hearing looming up, with the BTA and we had to get someone else."

As it turned out, the loss of the American lawyer may have been a blessing, because in the end on advice from a number of sources, Smith took on one of the best and most publicized London Attorneys around. And so it was that Smith was to be represented by the notorious

Anthony Morton-Hooper who had represented Dianne Modahl, in a case that contributed to the eventual folding of the British Athletics Federation.

In Modahl's case, after successfully fighting a four-year ban for 'failing' a drugs test and being sent home from the 1994 Commonwealth Games, Modahl, who had to sell her home to fund the long-running legal battle, had sued the BAF who had been placed in administration in October 1997 with debts of around £2million. She contested that by acting on the findings of the laboratory in Lisbon, which detected testosterone in her urine sample, the BAF had acted inappropriately. Modahl claimed that the lab was not accredited by international athletic bodies and the BAF should not have acted on its findings. Four years later on, her remaining argument with the BAF was that there was bias on the part of two members of the original disciplinary committee, which imposed the four year ban. Whilst the fact that Modahl had won her case, may have been a good thing for Smith, the fact that it had taken years of expensive court battles and had cost Modahl her career must have been playing on his mind.

Upon contracting Morton-Hooper to represent him the first thing Morton-Hooper was concerned with was the 'chain of custody' of the sample which is the term given to the process that starts even before the athlete urinates in the bottle. From the time the athlete crosses the finish to the time a lab tester has the athlete's sample, there is a clear, strict and uniform protocol that in theory should protect the athletes sample from being tampered with and ensures that the chain of custody for the sample is not broken. The crux of Smith's alleged doping case at this point seemed to centre on the chain of custody of doping samples from the Ironman site in Hawaii to the UCLA lab in Los Angeles. Smith was becoming increasingly conscious of the seriousness of the case and was desperate to prove his innocence, and although Smith lived and trained in California, given that the British Triathlon Association was his national governing body, it was they who were responsible for the doping hearing and they who he would have to face at the initial enquiry to prove his innocence.

Despite the drugs allegations against Smith not formally being made public, rumours were starting to circulate in the triathlon fraternity, but loyal to Smith, his sponsors continued to support him and even expanded on his involvement in their promotional strategies. He had kept silent about the whole affair hoping it would be sorted out quickly and without media attention that could harm his image, which he was maintaining in the UK through the sponsors despite not racing regularly in Britain and to this end, for the first time Smith was to star in a cinema advert for Speedo. In an advert which depicted Smith being tracked by a thermo camera running through the city streets, whirring through an urban area of railway tracks and desolate buildings, rushing through a forest and diving into a lake, a frenetic drum and base soundtrack cut to silence until Smith was seen in close up emerging from the water with a caption that read. ONLY EVER CAUGHT ON CAMERA— Speedo –No Barriers. Now It would appear, at least according to the American scientists, that Smith was caught at Hawaii.

As if Spencer didn't have enough to think about since his father's death he had found himself feeling increasingly isolated from the close knit extended family of support that had been evident when Bill, Barbara and Bill Black had been the support crew. Living in San Diego without the constant support of his dad had put significant physical distance between himself and Bill Black who had remained in the UK with his family. Whilst Melissa and Barbara were there to support him and the usual array of family members who could always be called upon in times of need, there remained a huge gap in Spencer's life that had always been filled by his father. Black had previously said that Bill, Barbara and himself had done everything to take the pressure of Spencer with the exception of racing, but things had now changed irreparably.

Black had continued to set the programme for much of Smith's training, but Spencer had begun to feel he needed support from people closer to him in the US and in December had told Black that he wanted to work with another coach. Whilst Black was clearly disappointed, he understood Spencer's reasons. This could have been seen as an unusual move for an athlete who had achieved so much under Black's guidance especially from an athlete who admitted that he didn't like a lot of change. Since even when it came to training schedules Smith had always been a creature of habit, who liked a set routine in his training that some athletes would consider too monotonous to be motivating. "It's not fun," Smith had once said of his training programme, "it's too hard to be fun. But I get good satisfaction from it."

Clearly the relationship between Spencer and Bill had been initially formed partly due to the original friendship between Black and his father Bill, and now with Bill gone, so had some of the bond that had linked them over the past eight years. "We were very close but when one door opens another one closes," said Black.

At their annual end of year discussion where past events were scrutinised and plans were made for the forthcoming season, Smith told Black that he felt it was time for him to "move on." Smith felt he needed someone closer to him who could travel round to the events with him like his father had done in the past and Black knew that he could not offer that kind of support.

"I have no problem with Bill Black. He's been fantastic," said Smith later, "but now because dad's no longer around, I need someone to travel around with me like my dad did." Smith was aware what Black had done for him, he had been there from the beginning but now he needed someone close by. There were no hard feelings between Black and Smith and they continue to this day to keep in touch with each other either by phone, or when Spencer returns to the UK.

Having been phenomenally successful under the watchful eye of Black, there were concerns as to how Smith would fair with a new coach, who had new views and new philosophies. Whilst many coaches now seem to focus heavily on one particular event with all preparation leading to peeking for one major race, Black's philosophy had been somewhat different. "We never really technically built up for anything not even a World Championship," recalled Black. "We just programmed to see how things are going in that year, we didn't train specifically to win a World Championship. It was just what was good for Spencer at this particular time at this particular race." Whether Smith's new coach would follow that philosophy or would focus on individual events, only time would tell.

In looking for a more manifest kind of support, Smith had found a new coach in the guise of Mick Gillingham, an Australian coach who had worked closely with Australian international, Chris McCormack. Gillingham was in many ways a very similar make up to Spencer's father. Loud, confident and vocal, above all, passionate and as Spencer put it. "A bit crazy." In much the same mould as Bill, he was an excellent motivator. They had first met up a number of years previously when Spencer was racing at Noosa. Smith Senior and Gillingham hit it off like a house on fire and travelled with them during the St George series, now some years later they had linked up in San Diego and whilst Black had continued to set the programmes for Spencer's preparation for Hawaii, Gillingham had also been involved in the training schedule and so the relationship and confidence in Gillingham's capabilities had grown. But now that input would be much greater. Once again as Spencer put it, "it's all under one roof again."

By a twist of fate Black found himself being offered the position of British elite men's coach literally a couple of days later, which meant he found himself working more closely with Andrew Johns, Tim Don and Spencer's previous advisory Simon Lessing. Black was undoubtedly one of the most accomplished triathlon coaches in the world and having spent most of his time focussing on the needs of Spencer, now with more time on his hands, Black had little trouble finding new athletes in the UK who wanted to work with him and apart from national duties soon found himself increasingly busy with GB junior Stuart Hayes and GB female senior Annie Emmerson on a private basis.

19th April 1999 BTA Hearing, London

The first hearing took place in the Pall Mall at the Institute of Directors on April 19th 1999. In the case put before the BTA, Smith's attorney demonstrated that the chain of custody was not without serious potential flaws and made serious criticism of the testing procedure and protocol and this whilst not directly challenging the validity of the findings of the laboratory tests on the sample would be sufficient if proven to question the fact that the sample belonged to Smith. One example at the lack of rigor in terms of security in the testing area was highlighted at the hearing and backed up by evidence from the Hawaii events doping director Dr. Elmore Alexander, in his post event evaluation, who commented in the report that a reporter had breached the security and entered the doping control area immediately after the first finishers had crossed the line, posing as an athlete representative. Whilst eventually the journalist in question was identified and ejected from the doping control area when he attempted to interview Peter Reid, the breach of security was highlighted which in itself was sufficient to establish that the doping control was not secure.

Apart from the criticisms of the procedures, there were also other concerns relating to the drinks stations. "My coach had reservations about open drinking vessels on the course, a fact my solicitor was very concerned about." Smith stated later, arguing that the organizers had not undertaken procedures to remove the possibility of tampering or contamination. Morton-Hooper criticized the organizers for engaging an inexperienced testing crew and argued that the sample was not proven to be Smith's since the chain of custody was open to question.

Apart from his criticisms relating to the organization of the race and the testing procedures Morton-Hooper, also complained that despite having corresponded with the ITU and USAT and asked them for documentation relating to the chain of custody, neither party had seen fit to forward the documentation. "It transpired by the time we got to the hearing no chain of custody documentation had been produced," recalled Burnell. "No one would answer Anthony Morton-Hooper's requests." After about half a dozen calls to track down the elusive documentation and no response from either party, the BTA themselves had requested it since it was required not just in the case of the defense on Smith's part but also by them in order to prosecute, but even at the BTA's request the ITU were not forthcoming and so the hearing had to go ahead without the documentation. It seemed obvious even to the layman that without such evidence there was nothing to show either whose samples were present or tested or any proof that there had been no contamination or tampering.

From a prosecution point it would appear that a serious error had been made by the ITU and USAT in not submitting the relevant documentation. Whether as a result of mis-administration, incompetence or just arrogance Smith would have no case to answer.

The simple logic was stressed by Burnell. "You have to use something to prosecute, you can't just go into a hearing and say we have no evidence." To prove Smith was guilty they had to at least provide something but they failed to.

In addition to the criticism of procedures in Hawaii, the BTA using their own records to research into Smith's drug test history noted that of all the previous doping tests undertaken by Smith, four in total, all four had been negative, including two in-competition and two out-of-competition. Most notable however was the date of the latest negative test, which had been undertaken by Dr Rod Jaques on November 9th, 1998 only five weeks after his alleged positive test in Hawaii. The BTA on considering the evidence put before them made the only decision that was open to them. There was no case to answer. Smith, Burnell and Morton-Hooper were delighted with the decision, all be it a decision which they had expected all along. The United States Triathlon Association and the ITU were undoubtedly not going to be so impressed.

To make things a little worse for the prosecution, on the 14th May there seemed to be some additional problems for the ITU along the same lines as the case Smith had been facing, when Swiss duathlete Oliver Bernhard was cleared of a doping offence for nandrolone by the Court of Arbitration for Sport (CAS) on the basis that the nandrolone metabolites identified in the test could have occurred naturally within the body. Bernhard had claimed that his body had produced the performance enhancing drug naturally and his evidence included scientific testimony that strenuous exercise could naturally raise the body's levels of nandrolone metabolites, which was in direct contrast to previous evidence surrounding the subject. In response to the findings, the ITU released the following press release.

ITU Press Release:
CAS overrules IOC doping limits

The Court of Arbitration for Sport today lifted sanctions against Swiss duathlete Olivier Bernhard after he tested positive for levels of nandrolone metabolites in excess of the IOC doping limits. Bernhard finished first at the 1998 ITU Powerman Long Distance Duathlon World Championships, where he tested positive. The three member panel of arbitrators announced that Bernhard had succeeded in demonstrating that the presence of nandrolone metabolites in his body could have a natural origin, thereby giving rise to serious doubts as whether this was in fact a doping case and an infraction. ITU strictly adheres to the IOC Doping Control policy and pursued the case based on the IOC established maximum of nandrolone metabolites. ITU has immediately reinstated the 1998 World Championship title to Bernhard and ordered payment of any withheld prize money.

ITU Anti-Doping Commission Chair Mark Sissons issued the following statement: "The International Triathlon Union (ITU) cares first and foremost that its athletes compete on a level playing field. Every athlete must have an assurance not only that those caught doping will be punished, but also that no innocent athlete will unjustly be found guilty of a doping offense. The system only works if all athletes take full responsibility for what they put in their bodies. Normally, unless there is a glaring defect in the collection process, the presence of a banned substance in the body of an athlete is sufficient evidence of a doping violation. This system depends heavily on guidance from the IOC Medical Code, particularly with respect to the amounts of the banned substances found in the urine necessary to constitute a positive test. In the Bernhard case, the International Triathlon Union followed its own ITU Anti-Doping Rules as well as the instructions of the IOC Medical Code. Clearly, the Court of Arbitration for Sport does not agree that the specific amounts of nandrolone metabolites as stated by the IOC Medical Code (greater than 2ng/ml) constitute unequivocal evidence of a doping offense.

The ITU will recommend to the IOC that, if the IOC wishes to retain any semblance of control over doping in sport, the Medical Code immediately be amended to reflect amounts of nandrolone metabolites that will withstand future CAS appeals. The same recommendation holds true for other substances and/or ratios. In the absence of such immediate amendments, reputations stand to be irreparably harmed and tens of thousands of dollars wasted every time a positive test is appealed."

Clearly from the tone of the statement the ITU and most notably Sissons felt they had been let down by the CAS decision, but the CAS decision had been based on what had been considered right and fair in a court of law and was not politically prejudiced towards the protection of the image of the sport but was based on the legal premise of innocent until proven guilty, and there were clearly questions on the extent of nandrolone that the body can naturally produce.

Whilst some may have felt that in the wake of the 1998 Tour de France ensuing dope panic the ITU had been just to try and show the media that triathlon was a clean sport, the CAS panel had to work within the law and could privilege no such media agend. And given the queries relating to the new scientific evidence relating to the natural metabolism of nandrolone in the body they had no option but to find Bernhard not guilty. Whilst all of this may have made interesting reading at the time, none of it was immediately relevant to Smith's case, which had hinged at his hearing on the chain of custody rather than the levels or presence of nandrolone it was a clear acceptance by the CAS panel that issues relating to nandrolone remained a problem.

Whilst Smith was already aware of the findings of the BTA panel, on the 21st May 1999 the British Federation, formalized their decision in a twenty nine page report that acquitted Smith accepting the criticism made against the doping control rigor and the chain of custody of doping samples between the event and the UCLA Olympic Analytical Laboratory, outlining their ruling that there was 'no case to answer.' Although immediately some individuals would be sure to argue that Smith had got off on a technicality, it was a technicality which threw serious doubt onto the case and the credibility of the testing procedures. The BTA clearly felt the criticism of the security and protocol undertaken at Hawaii was justified and this had been reinforced by the lack of any documentation to demonstrate the chain of custody had remained intact by the ITU. "No chain of custody meant there was no case to answer," recalled Burnell. "They threw it out on the fact that they couldn't even consider anything else when the chain of custody wasn't intact or even produced. It was proved to the board that strenuous efforts were made. Numerous times. So we won it on that."

With his interim suspension lifted, Smith could now get on with his training and his racing. He had spent seven months on the sidelines and despite continuing to some extent with his training Smith had found it difficult to motivate himself. Smith's hearing before the BTA tribunal, had taken over ten hours, almost two hours more than it had taken him to finish the race, and resulted in a twenty nine page document, which exonerated him fully. Whilst those that believed Smith innocent and were pleased that Smith had been cleared, there remained rumblings and whispers claiming that the first hearing, won by Smith, was a whitewash on the part of the BTA strictly for either political or financial reasons.

In the past, the British Athletics Federation (BAF) had gone to battle with Morton-Hooper on behalf of two of his clients, and one federation bankruptcy later, it could have been argued that no British governing body would want to tangle with Morton-Hooper again. Other conspiracy theorists, especially some of the more cynical within the sport argued that the motivation of the BTA would surely be to support the innocence of one of their top athletes rather than find them guilty of doping. Whilst other accusers believed that the BTA, whose funds were clearly lacking in comparison to some of the other world federations, would prefer to dismiss the Smith case and let it be fought by one of the richer federations with the kind of financial base that could fund a long and drawn out court battle. After all if the USA didn't like the findings of the British hearing then they could appeal against it.

In the BTA's defense, its hearing had lasted ten hours, much longer than one would expect if it was all just a sham. In fact the duration of the hearing would eventually be in direct contrast to the subsequent appeal hearings which despite any possibility of partisan objectives working in favour of Smith, would not last anywhere near the same amount of time and whilst the whispers would continue, as they always do, neither the ITU or USAT was ready to formally accuse the BTA of not taking the case seriously or question the legitimacy of its findings. At least not straight away, but soon the war of words was to start.

If when Smith, was acquitted in May with 'no case to answer' he believed the nightmare was over he was in for a shock. No sooner had the celebrations started than his nightmares were to return. It was barely a couple of weeks later in mid April 1999 that he was informed that his case was to be reopened. The American Federation (USAT) had appealed the BTA's decision to the ITU. Both Smith and the BTA were furious, but USAT were determined to continue their fight. In its twenty page appeals brief, USAT claimed the British Triathlon Association continued with its hearing despite knowing it lacked all the necessary evidence to try the case properly, a clear reference to the chain of custody documentation that the BTA and Smith had tried to obtain to no avail.

It became apparent that USAT were taking no responsibility for their lack of evidence at the hearing but instead chose to berate the BTA hearing, arguing that the BTA had clouded the issue of the chain of custody of Smith's urine samples between the Ironman site at Hawaii and the UCLA drug-testing lab in Los Angeles. The criticisms of the BTA's hearing and subsequent acquittal of Smith's case bit to the very core of the BTA executive. In a four-page "private and confidential" letter to ITU Anti-Doping Commission Chairman Mark Sissons, the Acting Chief Executive of the BTA, Graham Schuil-Brewer complained about the filing of the USAT's appeals notice, which challenged the BTA's May 21st acquittal ruling. In the letter Schuil-Brewer who was obviously concerned not only for his athlete but also about the image of triathlon in the UK especially since this could affect funding of triathlon in Britain stated. "It would cause great damage to our standing generally and our relationships with the English and UK Sports Councils (our principle funding agencies) for the allegations against us to be made public without our position on those matters being considered." On a more hard hitting note Schuil-Brewer continued. "The BTA resents the nature of the accusations made against it, and refutes the truth of such accusations. Many of the

USAT's accusations in the brief are false." Schuil-Brewer was angry that the BTA's hearing process and its motives were, "repeatedly disparaged," by the American Federation, with accusations of the British Federation being partisan and disinterested in banning Smith.

Because of Smith's standing in the sport the BTA were both angered, appalled and shocked at what they described as USAT's, "unfounded accusations." The bitterness felt within the British Federation towards USAT could be felt within the context of the letter in which Schuil-Brewer went on to admonish the criticisms made of them. "Equally the BTA strenuously resents and refutes the implication that it did not and does not treat the issues of drugs in international sport with the requisite degree of seriousness. Such musing is outrageous." He contested. The BTA were sticking to their guns. Spencer Smith had no case answer to in relation to the positive sample provided at the 1998 Hawaii Ironman.

Apart from the BTA being appalled by the accusations made by the American Federation, Smith was so incensed by USAT's decision to reopen the case. In an attempt to prevent the case going any further, he challenged their legal right to reopen it on the basis that the ITU Doping Hearing and Appeals Board had no jurisdiction to hear a USA Triathlon appeal of the BTA's nandrolone-doping acquittal. If he won, the case would be closed for good and he could get back to racing, if he lost he would have to go to a second tribunal, but this time the prosecution would be USAT.

Whilst the battle in the courts raged on Smith continued to the best of his ability to keep training and racing. As a professional it was how he made his living, as an individual it was how he focused, relaxed and lived. Triathlon had always been his life and at least he could return to training, all be it pending on the findings of the next hearing, if it got that far.

Interestingly, at the time it was not only Smith who was standing accused of drugs violation but other triathletes, duathletes and sports stars were also facing the same problem, with many of them being accused of using the same drugs, most notably nandrolone so CAS were finding themselves increasingly busy and federations were finding themselves under increasing scrutiny. Tied to this, whether the throwing out of Berhard's case had served as any comfort to Smith is questionable and whilst not argued on the basis of the chain of custody, it had clearly reflected on the procedures, practices rulings and methodology put in place by the ITU.

The Bernhard case had clearly hurt the ITU's credence with regard to drug testing and the fact that the arbitrators conceded to the possibility that an athlete could demonstrate the natural presence of a low concentration of nandrolone metabolites in their body seemed to point to the conclusion that this ruling also gave serious doubts as to whether Smith's was in fact a doping case at all.

At first this ruling may have appeared to bode well for Smith as well as a number of other high profile athletes who were fighting to prove their innocence including British sprinter Dougie Walker and the Czech born former Australian Open tennis champion Petr Korda, who was due to appear at the CAS shortly to defend himself after testing positive for nandrolone at Wimbledon in 1997. But in hindsight Smith may have looked back on it as one of the catalysts that would lead to the ITU's and USAT's even more prolonged and determined battle against him in an attempt to restore their credibility. With no opportunity to challenge Bernhard further, Smith's case would be the next high profile case which they would have to win to prove their credence.

Whilst the legal issues remained in the forefront of Smith's mind, as a professional athlete with a family to support and the potential for an expensive legal battle ahead Smith now had to return to racing, if for no other reason then to make up for the seven months of lost earnings that the original ban had placed on him. How he would perform however given the amount of time he had spent working alongside Burnell on his defense was something only the races would show.

23rd May 1999 Bally Total Fitness Triathlon, Los Angeles, USA

If the pressure of the court case was building it certainly wasn't showing when Smith's first race back commenced with a win at the Bally Total Fitness USTS-Los Angeles, where Smith would once again meet up with Tim DeBoom who had last raced Smith in Hawaii. Like Hawaii, Smith had that little bit extra when it came to the run when and pulled away comfortably to out sprint DeBoom in the last mile after running shoulder-to-shoulder for much of the previous 10km. Whilst the win was a nice start, it was clear that Smith was just pleased generally that he could race again on the basis of his acquittal by the BTA and despite knowing that the second case was potentially imminent, he was confident in his innocence being proven and determined to continue to race for the rest of the season and get some form back. In addition he was especially keen to return to Hawaii in October despite the fact that this had been where all the problems initially arose. In the mean time however, after the California race Smith would return home to the UK but this time to face the athletes and his British supporters rather than an appeals panel.

20th June 1999 Royal Windsor Triathlon, UK

Smith continued with his racing programme and headed once again to the Royal Windsor Triathlon. A winner since 1991 Smith loved to race on home turf. Windsor was a prestigious race on the triathlon calendar not least because of its heritage as a race but also because of its location and connections with the Royal family. A Royal connection with Windsor has existed for more than 1000 years, which was a little longer than the races history, but the first fortifications, following the Norman Conquest of 1066 that subsequently became Windsor Castle made a perfect and alluring backdrop for this picturesque and heavily contested race on the British calendar.

Before William the Conqueror established a fortification on a chalk mound on a bend in the river in 1070 the area where Windsor Castle now sits would have been just another hill, a hill that many an athlete would curse as they would be forced to run up and down it three times in the course of the race, Clewer Hill as the original site of the Castle was known, was sure to sap the strength from the weaker runners in the field but Smith seemed to relish the opportunity to take it on, especially since in more recent history Smith had clearly established his own fortifications around the Royal Windsor Triathlon title, a title that he clearly felt was his to own and one that he would not give away easily. Smith knew the course well and was even said to enjoy the hill, which was an unusual thought for an athlete of his stature and size, but he was determined to return to home turf and do well at an event he described as his favourite in the UK.

The proximity to the River Thames was no doubt the prime reason for choosing the area for the Castle back in the eleventh century and made it a perfect location for the race in terms of both, the swim and the number of participants who could easily attend the event. The waterway and now the motorway being the main highway to London, the event was always assured of a good size field, but had never seemed able to attract a significant foreign contingency. Not that that had ever been its aim. The race was quintessentially British. Windsor was a well known location in triathlon circles and whilst many knew the venue and the Royal association few knew the origins of its name, which strangely enough could have a significant bearing on the race.

In the naming of the location Windsor it has been argued by many historians that the name derived from the 'winding' meaning 'meandering' shores which the river certainly had in this part of the Thames, and a point which would be well considered by all swimming in this section of the course. This winding stretch of river coupled with its current, results in the need for those who wish to excel, to keep close to the shore on the outward stretch and stick to the middle of the river on the return leg to gain the benefits of the river flow. And whilst the location had rarely seen any action in the way of war, with the exception of a siege in 1193 when, Richard Coeur de Lion's brother, John, had attempted to seize the crown. It now appeared, that young Tim Don was attempting to do the same to Smith, but like his predecessor, Smith was not so keen to give up his crown either. Smith had always been the king of Windsor to the British public but Don was now running a close second in terms of the affections of the home grown triathlon fraternity, especially since winning the Junior World Championships in Lausanne in August 1998 at the same time as Lessing had won the senior race.

With Smith and Don the clear favourites for the win, the elite field made their way to the river following closely on the heels of the 1,500 age-groupers who had already been set of in waves earlier in the morning, and Windsor Castle prepared itself for just a little more action. As the hooter went, the field surged forward and in a close fought battle with a group of three clearly leading out the swim, the new young talent from his old club were with him all the way in the guise of Don and Stuart Hayes and the battle to hold on to his title commenced with the first blood going to Smith as he exited the Thames to the screams of a red, white and blue army of support. A rush through transition saw Smith lead the field out into the surrounding countryside but he was followed closely by the new army of talent on the British circuit and it didn't take long before the top elite had come together and were surging in a pack towards Great Windsor Park.

With the race having now established itself as a draft legal event, whilst the pace was high there remained little opportunity for any of the leaders to make a significant break away and by contrast to previous races at Windsor, by the time they got off the bike some 40km later, the three leaders had swelled to seven.

Out on the run however it was a different matter with the field quickly splintering as Smith pounded the course from the front, a tactic which left Tim Don the only other athlete stay with the prodigal son. Smith continued his purge putting a number of yards between himself and Don, but Don was an accomplished runner with a good turn of speed, and managed to chase back, eventually coming shoulder to shoulder as they headed up and down the hill for the last time, and it looked for one moment that Smith may lose his crown, but as Don came level so he seemed to falter.

Don was no doubt in the shadow of Smith despite being an awesome talent, and It is possible to conceive that for a young athlete like Don who had always looked up to Smith as a role model, actually being there with Smith had led the young Junior World Champion to stop and ask himself 'what the hell am I doing here?' Right up to the point of contact Don had been catching him, catching him and catching him, but as he came alongside, Don's stride visibly shortened. Whether it was the confidence that held him back or the sheer exhaustion of trying to chase Smith down it was hard to tell, perhaps he simply didn't have the legs, but the games and tricks the mind can play on an athlete during a race should not be underestimated, and a moment of doubt can cost speed, distance and medals and undoubtedly Smith had the upper hand in that department, at least in this race. "We always kid him that he bottled it when he caught Spencer on that hill in Windsor," joked Steve Freestone later, who had been looking after Sigma juniors that day.

The one place that would appear theoretically at least, the most appropriate place to attack an athlete as well built as Smith would be on the hills and at Windsor Smith had looked a little uncomfortable going down the hill as well as up it despite being in the lead, but Don had not attacked. Comparing the physiques and running styles of Smith and Don at Windsor as they ran shoulder to shoulder could not have more clearly highlighted the difference in their running approach. Smith was powerful, and had a frame that meant he looked like could have carried himself as well in a power sport. If you looked at the physique of Bill his dad, he could have gone into front row in rugby, rowing or even middle weight boxing. Don on the other hand was slight, even wisp like, with raised shoulders and a running style that almost skipped where Spencer's thundered. But the style was not just genetic, at least in respect of Don. Instead it was a highly perfected and coached style specific to a particular scientific approach to biomechanics.

Graham Fletcher had been coaching Don in his running since 1994 and was a keen advocate of the 'pose' method of running. Don had been developing his running in line with its principles since the previous winter, and since Fletcher had been involved with Thames Turbo and for some time the young south Londoner had been improving steadily under his watchful gaze. The pose method of running which had been originated by Dr. Nick Romanov was still a relatively new theory on running but when Fletcher had met up with Romanov out in Colorado University he had been convinced of its potential. The method involves in a very simplified explanation running on the balls of the feet as opposed to the heel toe rolling gate often acknowledged by most distance runners. It is claimed to be very efficient as it doesn't actively use the quads, which are used extensively throughout the bike in triathlon, but only uses them to stabalise the body position and instead uses the hamstrings in a pull up motion.

The prime argument in favour of the system it is that is based around forward motion and places significant importance on positioning the body to facilitate forward motion around a center of gravity forward of the body line, which as a result reduces the braking motion that the foot would normally initiate when it makes contact with the running surface. From a scientific approach, it was a technique that had started to receive much acclaim from a number of high profile athletes and federations. Don in developing the technique for himself had gone to train in Colorado the summer before and had basically just learnt to run again, he had spent twelve weeks running, worn out four pairs of running shoes, and couldn't walk out of bed because of the tightness in his calves, but on completion of the three months training, there was little doubt that his speed had significantly improved.

So it was at Windsor that the sheer power and brute strength of Smith was pitched head to head with the pose technique and fluidity of Don but in the end Smith was just too strong, and despite a concerted effort by Don towards the end, the pace was just too much, and Smith pulled away with a ten yard lead as he headed into the finishing straight much to the celebration of the crowd, although in fairness many were happy to see either of them win. This time however the score was Spencer one, pose method nil.

Smith claimed after the race that he had not felt at full capacity, which he put down to the early season and the fact that he had started his training programme later this year than normal, for obvious reasons. Don on the other hand could have either put his loss down to nerves or lack of confidence when having to face up to an athlete which he had once idolised. "Spencer is triathlon. I remember Tim saying that to me," said Freestone. "I think Spencer inspired so may people to get involved in triathlon." Freestone continued, a point that was backed up by Don once again who was clearly pleased with his performance, commenting through his breathlessness that. "To get that close to Spencer Smith was a real buzz." Respect indeed from one of the best new generation of athletes that the UK was to produce over the next few years.

Perhaps leaving it with only five hundred metres to the finish may have been naive of Don when it came to racing Smith, because he was never likely to out sprint Smith who as a power athlete was always odds on to take the tape first, but Smith and Don had both put in a good performance and for at least a short time Smith was able to concentrate on what he loved best. Racing and winning. In consolation for those who were left in Smith's wake, the race in Windsor also proved a field day for British athletes, who picked up all the points in their quest to improve their standings in the intensifying and all consuming race for ITU points which could lead to Olympic selection. With not a single continental triathlete making the trip over the Channel, the Brits were left alone to pick up all the points available.

At the all British awards ceremony in the Town Hall, Spencer presented a number of the prizes to the winners and then finally presented the perpetual Bill Smith trophy in tribute to his dad who loved the race and had been one of the characters who had been most vociferous on the course when his boy was out there racing. Having spoken very eloquently and very movingly about him, so the triathletes made there way home with medals, trophies, sore legs, stories and no doubt memories of races in Windsor past where Bill had been shouting "go on my son!"

Notably for Don, Windsor was his first high profile race against Smith despite the fact that both athletes had originated from the same area. Strangely the whole Twickenham, Richmond, Hounslow area just seemed to be a hub of triathlon excellence in the late nineties, with Don also from Hounslow, and the up and coming Stuart Hayes based a mere five miles further down the road.

The reasons behind this geodemographic cluster seemed hard to fathom but in part it may have been due to the fact that whilst facilities in the UK as a whole were well behind our European, Australian and American counterparts, in that area, south west of London, there were some good roads to ride on, a number of tracks and some reasonable pools to swim in. In addition there were also some good clubs and some dedicated and committed coaches who could bring that talent on. To cap it all there was also in the guise of Smith, a local role model who could not only instill belief in the youngsters, but would return home regularly to do it in person. There was little doubt that Spencer has been the biggest influence on the youngsters who had come into the sport especially those who were initiated into the sport in his native Thames Turbo Club, but as Freestone pointed out this is a double edged sword.

"We've kidded Spencer before that he is the best thing and the worst thing that ever happened to Great Britain triathlon, because so many people have tried to follow in his footsteps and just burnt themselves out. He was the only junior who came out the other end of it." A look at the style of Smith's racing which focused on riding the big gears and training like a monster were undoubtedly characteristics specific to Smith that had worked for him, whilst many other athletes attempting to emulate him had suffered burn out prior to achieving their potential, but now there was a different breed of athletes on the scene in west London, some of who would soon be challenging Smith on the European and world stage.

With Windsor over and the Olympic selections not too far away Smith was acutely aware that apart from winning another battle against the drug allegations, he also needed to continue picking up points in the ITU races if he was to get one of the coveted Olympic spots. With an in-form Smith on the starting line up the battle for selection seemed not to cause too much concern and a trip to Spain in mid July saw him pick up a win and some valuable points in the Graus International Triathlon, moving himself up into the ITU top 100, but the second battle in the courts was proving somewhat more difficult.

Whilst Smith had been fighting it out on the streets of Spain, his London based lawyer, Anthony Morton-Hooper, had filed a petition against the International Triathlon Union and USA Triathlon in the Supreme Court of British Columbia aimed to preventing the USAT's referral of his case arguing they had no right to a re-trial. The Canadian

Judge who presided over the case however did not agree with the argument laid out in Morton-Hooper's petition, and over a month later on August 27th, Smith was informed it had failed his to prevent an International Triathlon Union review of his nandrolone doping charge. So with an appeal date set for September, it seemed the problem would not go away.

One question that many asked at this case was why the United States Triathlon Association appeared so incensed with the decision by the BTA to dismiss the Smith case that they would not only openly disparage the actions of the BTA enquiry but also take it so far as to appeal to the ITU's three-person arbitration panel knowing that such and appeal was sure to result in a costly and drawn out court case for their federation. From a positive and altruistic approach to the case some argued that money should not be the issue and that USAT's actions were for the benefit of the sport as a whole, and indeed in his federation's brief to the ITU, USAT's attorney Howard Jacobs had stated. "As the sport's image suffers, so does its future," and whilst the need to rid its sport of drug cheats was undeniable, not everybody was so sure that this was why they were willing to spend so much time and money on the case, especially Smith and Burnell.

For Burnell, the need for USAT to save face was also believed to be a major influence on their decision to appeal. Since USAT conducted the tests, if they were to accept the findings of the BTA enquiry they would be accepting the criticisms of their own organization which clearly undermined their perceived professionalism. Hence in order to maintain the integrity of both themselves and UCLA's lab testing capabilities they had to appeal. Part of the political problem they faced was that if their testing procedures, security and accuracy could be thrown into question, then the viability and reliability of their decisions would crumble under the immense pressure both from the athletes and one may assume their funding agencies. Outside of the political and funding issues, the fact that that USAT was seeking up to a maximum two year suspension against Smith, which would knock him entirely out of contention for the Olympics, the case was so high profile in terms of media, that they could not afford to back down.

Whilst the benefits to USAT in finding Smith guilty were manifest, It would have appeared from the very early stages of the reopening of the second enquiry that the International Triathlon Union were also backing the American Federation's case, which also seemed a strange position for them to place themselves in since their job, one would have assumed was to act as an objective observer, but they too had concerns over the credibility of the sport and had to be seen to be coming down hard on suspected drug cheats, but their understanding of the scientific issues relating to nandrolone seemed a little hazy. A point demonstrated when Mark Sissons, ITU secretary and one of the major players in the development of the ITU's anti-drug programme stated. "There's no doubt in my mind, Spencer Smith's urine contained nandrolone metabolites when he crossed the finish of last year's Hawaiian Ironman. The only question is. How did it get there? If you agree with the IOC medical code, it could only be there through the use of a banned substance." This once again seemed a strange argument given the fact that Sissons was acutely aware of the findings in the CAS case against Bernhard, which seemed to be in direct contradiction to what Sissons was saying.

Given that the amount of norandrosterone present in Smith's urine, reportedly calculated by UCLA's drug lab at an estimated 8 nanograms per milliliter, was above, according to most involved in the drug testing milieu, any amount which might naturally occur in one's system, perhaps Sissons was merely following protocol. But the fact that Sissons continued to refer to the International Olympic Committee anti-doping code, which all international federations (such as the International Triathlon Union, or ITU) are required to adhere to, he seemed to still be arguing the case that the presence of any level of nandrolone was a doping violation.

According to the IOC medical commission at that time, there was previous evidence that humans did not synthesize significant levels of nandrolone or its metabolites despite establishing the low levels deemed permissible in their testing protocol, however this ruling was not based on fact but was simply a viewpoint and it appeared in the light of new evidence, a number of scientists and doctors clearly disagreed with this view and had evidence of their own, to the contrary. In Bernhard's case, the acceptance by the panel that the human body could either generate or naturally ingest nandrolone, was a significant finding in the Court of Arbitration for Sport's (CAS) decision to deem Bernhard's 2.5 ng/ml result a potential 'false positive,' with the evidence put before the court suggesting that up to 5ng/ml of nandrolone metabolite could be naturally produced.

Despite the Bernhard case, Sissons was clearly unconvinced by the possibility of the human body naturally generating higher levels of nandrolone metabolites, and instead took the side of those who believed this was not possible. Whilst to the onlooker who had little knowledge of recent cases regarding the testing for nandrolone, this may seem an acceptable viewpoint, but it would appear a strange stance to follow this in a legal arena given the previous case of Olivier Bernhard, a case with which Sissons was undoubtedly aware. Considering also that Sissons was neither a lawyer nor a qualified sport scientist one would have to look upon Sissons' opinion as little more than that, an opinion.

Given that the facts of this case were already known to Sissons and the ITU, with the precedent accepted by CAS that the generation of higher levels of nandrolone could be synthesized in the body, It seemed surprising that either USAT or the ITU would continue with their present stance and continue to accuse Smith of a doping violation, but some protagonists argued that the alleged amount in Spencer's case was still higher than the amount previously accepted as naturally occurring by CAS and hence they were right to pursue the case.

Whilst on the face of it this would appear to be a fair and justified course of action, from a more objective and holistic perspective, it may have been more prudent to review the issues relating to the testing procedure and undergo a thorough and detailed evaluation of the evidence surrounding the determination of what actually constituted a positive test relating to nandrolone charges, rather than continuing to accuse athletes who on the grounds of new evidence would appear to have done nothing wrong. One had only to remember that previously, some athletes had undoubtedly been declared guilty of cheating because original thought was that it was not naturally possible to have even the smallest trace of nandrolone in the urine without being a druggie.

Following that acceptance the levels seemed to be adjusting on a yearly basis. Last year zero ng/ml, this year 2.5ng/ml, what next year and the year after, twenty ng/ml, thirty ng/ml?

Given the adjustments in the acceptable levels, Bernhard's case had opened up the possibility of the ITU and other governing bodies being sued by athletes previously banned on nandrolone offences, A precedent that could signal the demise of yet more federations, and clearly something that the federations and most notably Sissons felt he had to fight. Whilst in hindsight there was little doubt that more research needed to be undertaken on nandrolone, at the time Smith was under no illusions that he would be afforded such a luxury and would have to face another court battle to clear his name.

8th August 1999 World Cup Triathlon, Tiszaujvaros, Hungary

Whilst Smith's battle to clear his name continued to rage, he tried to cling onto some of his earlier form and some sanity by continuing to race, but despite a good start to the season the pressure of the case was beginning to ware on him, which was demonstrated in a poor performance in Tiszaujvaros with an uncharacteristic fifth place in the World Cup series, in a time that saw him considerably behind an in form Hamish Carter who took the tape. The race was at least a release in part from the pressures Smith had been facing but his mind was obviously otherwise occupied. Smith admitted to Burnell that he had been struggling to concentrate on his training and this was evident in his performance, it was however notable that he was still the best that Britain had to offer in this race with the now Olympic certainty Lessing over two minutes adrift and Olympic hopefuls Richard Stannard, Andrew Johns and Richard Allen taking 22nd, 25th and 29th place respectively.

29th August 1999 Mrs. T's Triathlon, Chicago, USA

Whilst concerns over his future continued, Smith, as a full time professional athlete had no choice but to return the States, in an attempt to sure up the coffers which a second hearing would ensure he had need of. With his sights on Mrs. T's Chicago Triathlon, and the significant prize purse that the world's largest triathlon offered, Smith headed to Illinois for a race that also served as the U.S. Pro National Championship.

Mrs. T's had always been a major race on the calendar and always managed to ensure a top quality field, and once again this year the money on offer had attracted the very best and had resulted in a starting line up that resembled more of a World Championship than a National Championship, with all but two of the past men's World Champions in attendance.

When it came to toeing the line, only Simon Lessing and Mark Allen were not in attendance and given that Allen who won the World

Champs in 1989 was now retired he could be forgiven. With former winners in the guise of Greg Welch (1990), Chris McCormack (1997), Miles Stewart (1999) and Spencer Smith (1993, 1994) as well as the formidable presence of Cameron Widoff, Alec Rukosuev, Miles Stewart and Ken Glah the promoters must have been more than happy with the caliber of field that had made it to the line on a warm but windy day with sufficient chop in Lake Michigan for it to be decided by the organisers to reduce the distance covered in the age-group swim. For the elite field however it remained the standard Olympic distance 1.5km swim, 40km bike, 10km rand with the wind the course was undoubtedly going to favour the better swimmers and the strong.

Those that had kept a close eye on Smith's performances were aware that his form had started to wane but on this occasion as the race got under way it was clear that he was looking more his old self and more to the point was racing more like his old self, constantly in the action and racing from the front. But despite his endeavors he still didn't have what it needed to make it to the finish first. After just ten minutes short of two hours of frenetic all out racing in the end it was the irrepressible and lean looking Aussie Greg Welch who took the tape, with his trademark leap across the finish line, whilst Hunter Kemper retained his U.S. men's pro title by placing second behind him in 1:51:20.

Whilst he may not have taken the top spot, Smith's efforts were still paid in part with a podium place and he had not been out of the running until the last part of the race.

Whilst disappointed at not winning the race outright Smith admitted that he had been generally pleased with his overall performance having taken the third slot in a time of 1:51:51, just thirty one seconds down on Kemper. He had at least picked up some winnings and it was clear that his form was improving even if he wasn't in the kind of shape he wanted to be in.

Having been very quiet about the allegations of doping it was undoubtedly the case that he was finding it hard to keep focus on his training and despite the fact that only a small number of athletes and members of the triathlon fraternity were fully acquainted with the case, he knew that rumours would eventually surface and ultimately accusations would lead to some people believing the worst of him, despite this he had been warned at the time by his attorney not to discuss the case.

It had become clear by now however that the rumours had already started to leak out and so it was that Smith shortly after the race, found himself talking openly for the first time and posting his first statement to the triathlon world. It read in part as follows:

8th September 1999. Statement of Spencer Smith:

"There is no easy way to start this statement but I feel I owe this not to the people that know and believe in me, but to the people who simply just do not know the facts. Firstly I apologise to those people, as I have had to remain silent due to the fact that I was told to keep all of this confidential, although as this has now been leaked from other quarters I have decided to speak out. My sponsors support me, which I thank them for. I have been cleared by my federation, the BTA, and have their full backing in this matter. I thank them also. I have never ever taken drugs."

Smith went on to explain the events leading up to the present day including the conflict of interest that had forced him to change lawyers and again reiterated his innocence. "I have had many tests before. If you are a high profile athlete and finish first it comes with the territory, so if you were taking drugs it would be stupid to finish high up the list. I have won dozens and dozens of races including World Championships and European Championships, and as I said I have had many tests, all negative. I entered the Ironman race in memory of my late father who had died two months earlier and I defy anybody to believe that I would have brought shame on his memory."

Smith also referred back to his visit to the British Olympic Medical doctor Dr. Rod Jaques, immediately after Hawaii and prior to being informed of the findings of the drug test stating. "Does submitting myself for medical tests each side of the Ironman sound like a good idea for someone allegedly taking drugs? I have never taken any drugs to enhance my performance. Anyone who knows me in the world of triathlon knows this fact." Explaining the attempts he had made to prove his innocence Smith continued, "I engaged at great expense a top analyst Dr David Black, who tested all my health supplements and I even had steak flown from Hawaii to his lab for tests, although it was now three months after the event. All his tests were negative."

Smith then went on to give an account of the hearing before the independent tribunal set up by the BTA and chaired by a QC confirming that. "After listening to both sides they found that I had no case to answer. A unanimous decision. They also instructed all parties to keep its findings confidential. The BTA and I kept to this, but others did not and leaked it to the press."

Smith then went on to criticize USAT and Mark Sissons, the Chairman of the Anti Doping Commission of the ITU for their inability to provide the relevant evidence for the hearing in March and their accusations of bias towards the BTA hearing. "It still has not been shown that the sample was mine or that there was no contamination or tampering. It seems to me that someone is being very vengeful after being inefficient." On the question of vengeful Smith also confirmed that he had been refused a wild card entry for the World Championships in Montreal in September, which through up some serious questions as to the allegedly unbiased approach to the case that many felt the ITU should have been taking.

Making reference to the fact that the BTA was not even notified that USAT intended making an appeal to the ITU and the accusations that USAT had made with reference to alleged bias on the part of the BTA, Smith made it clear that he felt he was now, "caught in the middle of that row between two federations." In closing his statement Smith went on to outline a number of theories that could go some way to explaining the possible existence of nandrolone in the body including, chain of custody, the possibility of producing it naturally under duress and dehydration. The eating of contaminated food, citing the fact that American beef had been banned in England because of its link to steroids, and the use of energy supplements.

Again, before he concluded he put it to the public to act as adjudicator. "I ask you to judge me, if it was my sample (and that has now not been proven) then I cannot say how the adverse findings occurred but I do know there are a number of explanations all of which are consistent with my innocence. Personally I am now asking all the athletic bodies to investigate this drug. With all these positive results happening there would seem to be something drastically wrong because I have never ever knowingly taken any banned substance. From the bottom of my heart, I want to thank all of those who have supported me in this long and arduous battle for my innocence. If you feel strongly about this issue, please let the governing bodies of the triathlon world know."

Smith's posting was heart felt and open meanwhile, away from the politics that was souring the sport, and the leaking of the drugs allegation story which was clearly an embarrassment, Smith was determined to put that behind him at least until the next hearing, but whilst his racing needed to continue for him to earn a living, with the ITU preventing from racing at the Worlds it seemed clear to some that in order to prevent any possible embarrassment to the federation their agenda included preventing Smith from racing, at least at their high profile events, which in turn affected his earning potential.

With reference to the World's snub, Smith stated. "I am not suspended or banned and should be allowed to race anywhere in the World." A point of view echoed by both the BTA and most fair minded triathletes. The drugs issue had now been hanging over Smith's head since November 1998 and even though he had enough on his plate to contemplate with yet another court case, he had hoped that at least he could use his preparation for the Montreal World Championships to help overcome the stresses and strains that the drug allegations were having on both him and his family, but it was not to be and both he and those close to him believed this to be little more than a political move by the ITU and muted that the refusal to allow him to race was rooted in the ITU's and USAT's drug charge against him.

Why Smith, two-time former Senior World Champion and arguably one of the most celebrated characters on the triathlon circuit, who was only six places out of an automatic bid based on points, was not permitted to compete at the Worlds, yet far less talented and even lower ranked athletes were, didn't appear to need much explanation as far as the British triathlon supporters and officials were concerned. Whilst the ITU refused to identify Smith's impending hearing with its Doping and Appeals Board as the reason for excluding him from World Championships, few believed them. The ITU claimed its decision to exclude Smith was based on their policy of awarding wildcard places to athletes from poorly represented countries, but by turning down the BTA's request to include Smith in the Montreal field it appeared to many that the ITU had shown its hand.

The ITU's poorly represented countries argument simply stuck in the throat of many, who were present in Canada, especially the British camp and especially since historically, the wild card system had always been used ensure representation of the best athletes in the world, not simply athletes from as many countries as possible. In evidence, against the claims put forward by the ITU, historically their entire system of qualification had been based on a points system, which was specifically weighted against inclusion of lesser athletes irrespective of country, with the World Championships field kept intentionally small to keep out the also rans.

Whilst the true reason for his exclusion will never be proven, one thing that the ITU undoubtedly failed to do here was take the opportunity to prove that they bared no personal malice towards Smith. Whatever the real reason, it was clearly a political one rather than a judgment on Smith's ability as an individual athlete and one that potentially didn't bode well for his future appeal in front of the ITU.

Apart from the rumours of drugs allegations starting to surface it was clear that being informed of his exclusion from the World Championships, had really been the main catalyst for Smith deciding to speak out publicly for the first time since Hawaii. He was now clearly angry as well as frustrated at this treatment by the ITU. "I am devastated to be excluded from the World's," said Smith. " I have kept quiet all this while, when everyone has been talking about me for months. Now it's time for me to speak out." Until now Smith had been hoping to clear his name quickly and quietly, but since his acquittal by the BTA things had only got worse and not usually at a loss for words Smith made his case clear and loud.

Smith's protests apart from being clear and based on evidence were also heartfelt. "I have nothing to hide or be ashamed of," he reiterated. "I swear, in my father's memory, that I have never taken drugs. I know that I have done nothing wrong, and I am determined to clear my name."

Whilst to those who did not know the real Spencer Smith or were not familiar with the extremely close bond between him and his father Bill, these may have sounded like the typical claims of a sportsman who tested positive simply arguing their innocence despite their guilt, but in Smith's case the final statement said a lot more than the simple words could ever explain. For Spencer to swear on Bill's memory would mean more to Spencer than his own life. Spencer's relationship with his father had gone far beyond the normal bounds of a father son relationship, and those who knew Spencer knew he would rather suffer the admittance and shame of cheating rather than sour the memory of his dad who meant so much to him. For many who already believed in his innocence this statement just went to reinforce their belief in him. Obviously for those who didn't know him or his dad, the statement meant little. Added to the personal views he had on his own case, Smith continued to raise the question that many involved in sport had been asking, a very valid question, which was. Why does everyone seem to be testing positive on the same drug at the same time?

Whilst Smith's case got little mention in the national press, the media at the time was rife with nandrolone charges of other more high profile sports celebrities. If it had been a new drug, or a new testing procedure had been developed, it may have not been such a surprise but nandrolone had been around for years and was not even considered by many scientists to be a particularly effective drug, leading one doctor to describe it as a dinosaur.

Unlike Smith, the high profile British sprinters Dougie Walker and Linford Christie cases both hit the front pages. Both like Smith were cleared on nandrolone charges by hearing panels of their national sports federations, only to face further hearings on the international level. This epidemic of positive nandrolone tests led some athletes to fear the testers more than their competition.

If the World Championships was a loss then it was one that Smith felt he could live with, after all he had refused to race it previously under protest of the implementation of draft legal formats, but Hawaii was a different matter. Since the beginning of the season, at the top of Smith's racing agenda was the word Hawaii, underscored no doubt to emphasise its importance and despite it being the race where the whole drugs nightmare had started, Smith was intent on returning, to prove his innocence and his pedigree.

Since Smith was entitled to race the event given his initial acquittal by the BTA, a few days after returning from Chicago Smith contacted Lew Friedland who was the President of the World Triathlon Corporation in order to confirm some details about his entry assuming it would be a formality. But Smith's entry into Hawaii was not to be such a simple affair. Friedland had told Smith that whilst he would personally really like to see him race at Hawaii, and would have been happy to extend him an invitation, unfortunately the WTC felt they could not offer him an entry into the race, despite his qualification for a place, until after the ITU hearing and then obviously only if no penalty was imposed. He told Smith that he would have to wait until the ITU appeal was held, which in the circumstances whilst not strictly in line with ITU protocol which stated that Smith, following his clearing by the BTA panel was entitled to race anywhere in the world did not seem unduly unfair as he would still face the second hearing before Hawaii anyway.

In addition, given that the WTC Hawaii Ironman was an invitation race and not held under ITU rules and regulations, they thereby reserved the right to refuse to allow any athlete in their events so they could of course refuse to let Smith to race in the same way as the ITU had done. But the WTC decision appeared to be more of a delay than a refusal to allow Smith to race based around a public relations exercise to protect the Ironman image of a clean sport, and since Friedland had confirmed that the WTC would abide by the ruling of the panel this in Smith's book this meant that if he was acquitted, which he was confident he would be, he would be able to race Hawaii.

Smith was without a doubt disappointed by this decision by the WTC but given the fact that he had a further appeal pending it seemed an inevitability anyway that a conviction at the second hearing would mean Smith would not be able to race irrespective of the invitation. Apart from Smith, Friedland, also personally assured Smith's attorney Morton-Hooper in a separate phone conversation that Smith would be allowed to race Ironman if he got through the ITU appeals panel without a ban imposed, and as Smith was confident he would, initially he made no big fuss about the delay but the concerns about legitimacy and possible ulterior motives behind the delay still weighed heavy on him.

Whilst Smith may have been confident that he would win the second appeal, Robert Burnell still had grave concerns as to the political influences over the panel and the pressure put on them for a conviction. Whilst it was the right of the USAT to appeal, Burnell felt that it was really the ITU in the guise of Sissons who was behind the appeal and as such the influencers had an agenda, political clout and a need to find Smith guilty. Burnell admitted at the time that he felt Spencer was walking into a 'kangaroo court.' "For the USAT it was convenient for Spencer to be banned because it was another Brit out of the way for the Olympics," claimed Burnell, who also strongly believed that Sissons too wanted him banned. Spencer had after all been a thorn in the side of the ITU, having boycotted three World Championships and been vociferous in his criticism of a number of their policies, they too wouldn't mind him missing out on the Olympics. In short he believed they didn't want him coming along and winning the thing because that would stamp all over the ITU's Olympic parade.

Burnell had done his best to continue to protect Smith from the pressures of the case as much as possible in an attempt to help him concentrate on his training and racing. But now even his racing seemed to be something which they were preventing him from doing before it even got to the second appeal. Smith was clearly none the less upset by the news and posted the following statement on the refusal to let him race at firstly the ITU Worlds and now Hawaii.

16th September 1999 Second Statement from Spencer Smith:

Firstly I would like to thank everyone from all over the world for sending your support. I have read the vast amount of e-mails and letters personally and would like to invite you to make yourselves known to me whenever I race near you. It has been a tremendous comfort to both myself, my wife Melissa, and my mother Barbara. Secondly, I have just been given a new blow to add to my disappointment of not being able to compete in the ITU World Championships.

The Hawaiian Ironman organisers have just told me that they cannot take a chance and invite me to the race in case I either finish high on the list or even win and then I might be banned. However, if the appeal hearing on 21st September finds in my favour they will change their minds and let me enter. This is a very hard decision for me to accept especially as I am not banned and allowed to race anywhere in the world.

As stated before, I won my case in March, but reluctantly I can see it from their point of view. Because it is a race that my late father and I adore and because I have the utmost respect for it, I will accept their condition. So where does that leave me? All the weeks of training, six hours a day, in preparing for the race could all be for nothing. Do I continue? With the above condition applying it could still be for nothing if this particular hearing can't decide. Nevertheless, the fight to clear my name would still go on I can assure you. With the strongest belief in my innocence I have decided to continue training for this race, because as I have said I love this Ironman race and desperately wish to take part in it.

I believe in myself and have nothing to be ashamed of and I have to trust in the fair-mindedness of the people involved in the appeals hearing. But most of all, that which will make me stronger and stronger, is the belief all of you out there have shown in me, also my family, friends and my uncle Robert Burnell.

I have been asked to explain the 'conflict of interests' I referred to from my earlier statement. The American lawyer told me he had found out something from Hawaii and because he represented the Collection Agency he felt he could not continue to represent me, but would not elaborate on this. This later was discovered to be the chain of custody documentation, which failed to arrive for my BTA Hearing in March.

I have now been informed by several sources that at an ITU pre race briefing in Lausanne on 29th August 1999, comments were made to the athletes, coaches and managers etc that were present. The President of the ITU, Les McDonald, referred to my case and then proceeded to totally lose it (words described to me) continuing through the whole briefing to blacken my name. This is very disturbing to me because the ITU are supposed to be unbiased in order to give a fair judgment. I am going before an ITU Appeals Board on 21st September and quite frankly, with the conduct of the President of the ITU at that race, I am left with the question. Am I going to get a fair hearing? I want everyone to know I intend to win this and then I am going after that Olympic medal because the bottom line is that I never took any drugs, I am completely innocent.

Thank you all again, and keep the support coming.

SPENCER SMITH

Smith as the case had continued had started to become increasingly aware of the power wielded by the federations and their executives. Previously their power had been muted and to some degree impotent since he had been winning the races and indeed had a much higher profile than most if not all of the officials. The federations, the races and indeed the sport had needed him, but now that he found himself under attack quite publicly from the ITU he became more conscious of what he considered to be a vendetta against him and the power struggle that he now found himself in could have undoubtedly ended the career of some athletes with lesser profile and finance.

As if to demonstrate that fact, if Smith felt he was being treated unfairly by the ITU and then the WTC with regard to his exclusion from the 1999 event, then he was not alone. In fact at least he had the possibility of returning to Hawaii as long as he won his case. Such an option was not available however to Belgium's Rodolphe Von Berg who had place fortieth when Smith had placed fifth who found he had apparently no case for appeal.

Forty three year old Von Berg, a Havard graduate and closely associated with the Belgian Royal Family had long been engaging in triathlon. Having first raced there in 1986, Von Berg placed 17th over all making him the third European to cross the line, a significant achievement at a time when the Americans were dominating the sport. A well respected athlete in his own right he became friends with such distinguished athletes as Mark Allan and Scott Tinley among others, but the sale of the family's international banking conglomerate, marriage, and children soon put pay to his triathlon career. Despite his inability to continue to race seriously, Von Berg had clearly been bitten by the triathlon bug and vowed to return to Hawaii ten years later to beat his 1986 time of 9:35:52.

Good to his word, Von Berg qualified at Ironman Germany and confirmed his place in Hawaii 1996 as promised, and duly returned to the Big Island coming fifth in his 40-45 age group in a time of 9:26:58 and 87th overall thereby beating his target. Although Von Berg had promised his family he would only come back to Hawaii every ten years, "until I am a hundred," he had said, his success in 1996 coupled with the inevitable Hawaii bug had got the better of him and with his family's blessing he continued to race. Unfortunately for him however his success in the 1998 race was to potentially cost him the opportunity to ever race at Hawaii again when he found out what it is to be at the wrong end of a WTC decision.

On Sunday October 3rd 1998, when he crossed the line on Halui drive Von Berg achieved the highest pinnacle of his triathlon career. Having finished 41st overall, in a personal best time of 9:23:57, Von Berg had won his 40-45 age group. It was the crowning moment of his long triathlon career, but his excitement was soon to be severely dampened.

Upon completing the race Von Berg planned to celebrate his win the following day at the awards ceremony with his wife and three young children, aged eleven, eight and five. Unfortunately however Von Berg had originally expected to be accompanied to Hawaii by only his wife and their oldest child, and hence had only bought three tickets for the banquet.

At that time, Von Berg had been unsure as to whether his two youngest children would be able to make the trip since one was ill and the head of the school was making difficulties for the other one to miss classes, so when his wife brought all three children whilst pleased that the whole family would be in attendance, he had the problem that he was two tickets short for the awards. Aware that the tickets for the awards ceremony had all been sold, Von Berg and his family arrived early at the banquet on the evening of October the 4th, which ironically was his youngest boy's birthday, in the hope that they would be able to buy any spare tickets that were available from competitors. This however was about as likely as seeing a Monk Seal of the coast of Hawaii. (The Monk Seal is one of the many endangered species that's natural habitat had been the Hawaii coastline.)

Standing at the entrance with his children and finding no sellers, Von Berg requested a solution from the staff on the door, who were checking tickets. Unfortunately, Von Berg found no tickets and no sympathy from the Ironman staff and was told quite emphaticall. No tickets, no entry. "I had a $50 bill in my pocket to buy them but could not find any, and the race direction did not care and refused to let them even sit on our laps during the awards."

Von Berg remonstrated with the staff stating that the children would take up no room and would sit on their laps, a point that seemed unnecessary since there were plenty of empty seats due to a degree of non attendance, but the answer was still no. Clearly agitated at his inability to get his family into the presentation, Von Berg continued to protest in the hope they might give in, but as his protests continued, he was becoming increasingly aware that his requests fell on deaf ears. "I refused to get out of the line until a solution be found." Von Berg admitted later, but protested that at no time did he become violent or abusive, a point echoed by a number of witnesses.

Following his refusal to step out of the queue, the door staff called Ironman security who despite attending swiftly, were also unable to persuade Von Berg to move, and eventually the Kona Police department were called. "I was pulled out of the line, beaten on the legs and handcuffed," recalled Von Berg admitting it was an extremely distressing and frightening end to what had been expected to be a great family evening out. As his daughter ran away crying, he was led away to a small windowless storage room in the Kig Kam hotel before then being transported to the police station where he was photographed, fingerprinted, and charged with disorderly conduct only to be released on half an hour later on bail. "The $50 bill bailed me out so I could return, with a police escort, to get my award," recalled Von Berg ironically. Returning to the awards ceremony in search of his wife and children, he was surprised to find, his children and it would appear a number of other ticketless onlookers had been let in for free after he had been taken away by the police. Whilst Von Berg tried to celebrate it was clear that the whole Ironman win had been overshadowed somewhat by the awards experience and whilst at that point it could have perhaps been all forgotten, Von Berg was still clearly angered by the incident.

Believing the police actions to be totally unjustified nineteen days later, on October 23rd, after returning to France, Von Berg faxed a letter to the owners and directors of the World Triathlon Corp, threatening a lawsuit unless they agreed to a list of changes to their policy which included free entry to the awards ceremony for all children under age of ten, last minute ticket sales to all relatives and friends, the nomination of a new race director and the reimbursement of all Von Berg's arrest-related expenses, which stood at around $3000. Three weeks later on November 12th Von Berg received a faxed reply from a lawyer representing the WTC which described Von Berg's account of the case was, "wholly inaccurate," and deemed his demands as, "ridiculously unacceptable."

As Von Berg had time to reflect and calm down, so he began to realise that his initial fax had been a bit strong and sensing he had come on a little to heavy, Von Berg then mailed several conciliatory letters to the WTC President Lew Friedland suggesting that the whole unfortunate incident should be forgotten by all parties, but in March, Von Berg's letters were labeled, "harassment" by the WTC's lawyer, who requested that he stop them.

By then, to avoid making a trip to Kona in March, Von Berg decided to plead 'no contest' in the case against him and his charge was lessened from a misdemeanor to a violation, required him to give $500 to a local charity. If there were no problems in six months, all charges would be dismissed, at least that is by the Kona police department, but the WTC were not going to be so forgiving. In June 1999, having not received the application letter that is sent to all the previous years age-group winners, ironically the prize that he should have received at the awards ceremony, Von Berg attempted to contact Friedland's office by phone, but unable to contact Friedland himself, eventually the President contacted him.

Von Berg received a fax dated June 15th from Friedland stating that he had violated the WTC's rules regarding athlete conduct and that they were exercising their rights to decline him an invitation to the 1999 event and he would not be permitted to race. A few days after receiving the fax Von Berg managed to get through to WTC office where he spoke to Friedland in an attempt to both plead his case or at least ascertain how long the ban would remain in effect. "I called Kona's office in order to know where is my application booklet since I do not need to qualify. I am told to call Lew Friedland, the WTC President in Florida and there he tells me; I do not want to see you in Hawaii as long as I am in charge. Basically banning me for life."

According to Von Berg, Friedland, President of the WTC clarified what was meant by the term "for good" which had been in the fax. The WTC's President told him on the phone, "that means until you die." At the time Von Berg was flabbergasted, in a state of complete shock, and even now Von Berg struggles to find any justification in the excessive stance taken by the WTC officials who he believed in order to justify their actions, had undertaken to exaggerate his actions and words on the evening of the presentation. He now believes that they sincerely believe that what they were describing really occurred, with the brutal intervention of the police giving credence to their claims, but insists that he did not hurt, hit, or even touch anyone nor did he curse, use foul language, or insult anyone at any time. Looking back on the event it has still left a 'sour taste' as he so eloquently put it, in his mouth.

Despite the ban from Hawaii, Von Berg continued to race and race well at events away from Hawaii, first winning the ITU Worlds in Nice (40-44 age group), and then winning his age group again at Ironman Austria in July which should have automatically qualified him for Hawaii but the WTC stepped in again. From here Von Berg relayed the story. "The race direction refuses to give me one of the two slots for Hawaii. Why? They had received a fax three days before the race from Lew Friedland ordering them to deny me the qualifying slot. The race direction told me that they had to comply because they were at the end of a two or three year contract with the WTC and were going to Florida to negotiate a several years extension. Thus, if they were giving me the slot I had rightfully earned on the field, what every single principle of sportsmanship would demand, they would have no chance to be granted the extension. WTC Power!!"

Not one to be outdone Von Berg continued to fight his case but it took some considerable time and it was not until September 2000 that Von Berg found a lawyer in Florida and sued the WTC there, whilst the WTC sued Von Berg in Hawaii. If a positive was to come out of the problems Von Berg faced in 1998 and the following court case in 2000 then he was to find some solace in the modifications made by the WTC surrounding the ceremonies, which saw some significant adjustments. "During that year, the WTC decided to implement a new policy around the awards, seat capacity was increased and, most interestingly, children were offered tickets at discount prices. Obviously, it was a direct consequence of the problems I had in Kona." Von Berg reflected.

But it was not until Spring 2001 that Von Berg was given any personal reprieve, and after months of judicial procedures, both parties lawyers in Florida were talking about mediation and settlement and came to an agreement. "The WTC accepted to lift the ban, so the case was settled and all actions dismissed." Von Berg confided later, clearly pleased at the outcome. But he was still angry at their initial actions and asked the question. "Why did the WTC settle so soon? I believe the WTC was starting to lose too much money in that venture without getting anything in return except bad publicity. Either way Von Berg had at last received what he felt to be some kind of justice.

Whilst the actual events of that evening will undoubtedly continue to be argued by both sides, as will no doubt the severity of the sanction put in place by the WTC, which many will argue to be disproportionate with the offense, the concerns over the power of the WTC and their ability to affect the lives and livelihoods of athletes would undoubtedly have been of concern to Smith who was already having problems with the ITU.

The power of the WTC was summed up by Von Berg who had taken some considerable time and some considerable expense to force the WTC to back down. "It is important to understand that the WTC yields enormous power in the world of triathlon, particularly in Ironman triathlon, which besides the Olympics is the most important part of the sport. It has such power that triathlon magazines, journalists, professional athletes, sponsors, national body officials hesitate a great deal to criticize or even say anything negative about the WTC. In private, off the record, yes, but in the open, no way." Von Berg later commented. "It is of no bearing that it did not bother my racing that I was banned. It did not bother me only because I had the money to sue the WTC. If it would have happened to anyone else (most triathletes do not really have the financial means to go against the WTC), it would have wrecked their racing, their life as long as the Hawaii Ironman was one of their goals and dreams. A pro? It would have shattered his/her career."

One lesson that perhaps Smith would learn from this case, was that it is not a good idea to tangle with the WTC or criticize them too heavily, less he risk the possibility of also finding himself banned from Hawaii and facing yet another legal battle. He had after all already found himself excluded from the World Championships, which was the next major race on the calendar where both Smith's and the BTA's appeals for his inclusion in had fallen on deaf ears.

12th September 1999 World Championships, Montreal, Canada.

When it came to the race day at the World Championships, no less than twenty athletes on the elite male start line up were ranked below Smith on the ITU points system. But on the positive side, for the British however, Lessing, chasing a fourth title in five years looked fresh and comfortable in the singularly hot and breezeless day.

The swim played little part in the final outcomes and nor did the bike with an uninspiring but visually aesthetic cycle stage on the Gilles Villeneuve Grand Prix circuit and a big field making breakaways harder if not impossible and eventually the group ended up parading round the circuit with nobody willing to commit to a breakaway which after the event, had led the young British contender Tim Don, who Smith had beaten at Windsor earlier in the year, to go as far as to say he had been on harder training rides back home in south London. With the triathlon ending up as an inevitable foot race it looked likely that Lessing was going to take the honours.

Clearly one of the fastest runners in the pack he started to stretch out the field and had established a twenty second lead on the fourth and last lap of the 10km run. Amazingly however, and much to the horror of the British contingency of the extremely vocal supporters and age groupers who had raced earlier in the week, Lessing was caught and astonishingly passed by Dmitry Gaag of Kazakhstan with only around 400m to go. Gaag having put in a super human burst, had crossed the line just six seconds ahead of Lessing with Miles Stewart of Australia holding off Britain's Andrew Johns to take bronze.

To describe it as a shock win would be an understatement. Gaag was not only an unexpected winner but was so unfancied that the organisers had not even bothered to get a recording of the Kazakhstan national anthem, and strangely enough Gaag had almost withdrawn from the race when his bike was delayed on his journey over, but had fortunately for him arrived just in time for him to compete. For a man who had just lost a World Championship, Britain's Simon Lessing was surprisingly philosophical. "You can't win every time. Besides, I don't think that what happened in the race will have any bearing on next year. I beat everyone who I consider will be a threat in Sydney," he said. Second place nevertheless ensured Lessing's qualification for the Olympics.

The bike section of the event, which had been draft legal was without doubt one of the most obvious parades in the event. Whilst the running had been hotly contested, the criticisms aimed at the format as voiced by Smith, seemed to have unquestionably manifested themselves in this race with few if any real attempts by any athlete to get away on the bike. But unlike many of the pros, Spencer still felt that there were still big gains to be made on the bike in triathlon generally for not only himself but also for other triathletes he had however voiced his opinion that a significant proportion of athletes racing under this format, would get out of the swim at the front but would feel that the chasing bunch would soon descend on them and see no point in going as hard as they could, and would simply wait for the bunch to arrive, and when riding in the bunch nobody would bother to try to attack of the front. This was a point that had been backed up by Tim Don's comments.

Smith's strength on the bike became legendary.

TRANSITIONS THIRTEEN & FOURTEEN
Second Hearings & Triathlete to Cyclist

21st September 1999 The ITU Hearing

The ITU Appeals Panel, which heard Smith's case consisted of three people, Patrice Brunel, a Montreal lawyer and strangely enough a confidante of Les McDonald, who stepped in as Co-Race Director for Montreal Worlds. USAT's choice was Bill Hallet, Tri Canada President and the third member, Dr. Petra Frey of Switzerland, Director of the 1998 ITU World Cup in Zurich and member of the ITU Race Directors' Observers' Commission.

Throughout the period coming up to the hearing Burnell continued to play a major role in Smith's case, and would confer with Morton-Hooper and research more closely the possible failings in the procedures and practices that had resulted in Spencer's alleged positive test. Burnell was highly methodical when it came to the court case and it was decided that he was to help Morton-Hooper with the case, whilst Spencer would try to concentrate on his racing. Spencer had been finding it hard to concentrate on both the case and his racing, and given that he was still grieving for his dad it seemed the best move. It showed the sort of faith that Spencer placed on Bernie that he would allow him to deal with it all, it in some ways replaced the faith that Billy had placed in him a few years previous.

Even if those who claimed Smith's acquittal at the BTA enquiry had been as a result some misguided partisan support for the British athlete or fear of the financial implications of a guilty verdict, the ITU appeals hearing could in no way be accused of the same. The second hearing however took a completely different format and was held as a telephone conference. All the documentation had been made available to both sides including the chain of custody documentation that had miraculously now appeared, though its lack of appearance at the initial hearing led Burnell to doubt its validity. But the process that the case was to be held under conditions that appeared truly astonishing to not just Burnell but also to Morton-Hooper.

"Tony (Morton-Hooper) was told that he had two minutes to put Spencer's case," recalled Burnell. "Tony immediately objected to the two minute time limit placed on his defense and said he could not possibly do any fairness to his clients case in two minutes and requested that be logged on record." Irrespective of this he attempted to do it but he wasn't comfortable. Burnell to this day was astonished that this could be permitted, making the point that if athletes were aware that this was the so called legal process they would go through they would almost immediately give up any hope of a fair hearing.

Morton-Hooper had indicated to Burnell that at any time that he felt appropriate he could stop the proceedings, which he considered to be 'absolutely outrageous,' and contest the findings of the panel. But nonetheless, for the moment they continued with the process. The reason that they had continued with the case was because whilst Burnell believed that this was a set up and that there was little likelihood that Smith would get a fair hearing, he had in his preparation for the appeal noted a strange anomaly in the case for the prosecution. "I wanted to know what exactly Spencer was being charged with. I was going through the medical documentation and basically I couldn't see anything." Confused by the omission Burnell immediately contacted Hooper and discussed the point. A point that Morton-Hooper concurred with Burnell should mean that the case would be thrown out. There seemed to be no solid evidence that would stand up to legal scrutiny that a positive test had been given, the scientific evidence that was being used by USAT was clearly suspect and neither accurate nor legal.

"We knew they didn't have the right documents but we were wondering how much of a kangaroo court it would be. What we didn't consider that there might be some people up there who were honest. And there were." Burnell said later. Whilst Morton-Hooper believed that the lack of appropriate evidence meant that the case should automatically be thrown out, he was still concerned because the appeals panel were in a position to simply ignore the documentation and simply find in favour of the offence, in which case Smith would have to appeal the case and so the fight would have to continue. It seems a strange situation that any evidence for the defense could be simply ignored, but it appeared that this was a distinct possibility. Again a frightening thought for any prospective athlete attempting to prove their innocence.

"He (Morton-Hooper) let the other side have their two minutes," recalled Burnell, "and low and behold they brought the document up and even before Morton-Hooper could challenge the findings, one of the panel brought up the fact that it had clearly stated on it. Not to be used in litigation. Estimates only."

Morton-Hooper put thumbs up to Burnell as if to say, they're taking notice of it. The question came back from the board, so where is your evidence. At this point Mark Sissons butted in. This seemed a strange action for a representative of the ITU to take given that the prosecution was coming from USAT and all representatives outside of USAT should have been seen to be impartial, but Sissons according to Burnell, seemed clearly in favour of winning the prosecution on the part of the USAT. "Mark Sissons said. Oh no you can do it on that and they all turned round, all three of them and said. No you can't!" Burnell recalled. The panel had been on many of these types of hearings and knew quite clearly that the prosecution didn't have the proper documentation. The proper test had not been taken on Smith, and there was literally no accurately conducted scientific evidence to suggest that he had anything in his blood that shouldn't have been there. The proper test had never been carried out. Talking later about his concerns that one of the panel may be biased towards the ITU Burnell made the comment. "Apparently he was a friend of Mark Sissons but he wasn't that much of a friend of Mark Sissons."

The ITU panel, none of whom belonged to either the BTA, USAT, or the ITU's executive board, dismissed the charge in a hearing lasting about an hour. Nine hours less than it had taken the allegedly biased BTA to come to their decision. But unlike the BTA hearing where the majority of its focus appeared to be with regard to the chain of custody, in this second hearing, the panel did not even discuss the chain of custody issue. The panel could not find, from any of the evidence it considered, that Smith had been in any violation of the misuse of drugs in any way what so ever.

The belief that USAT felt they could prosecute on the basis of a test, which was only an estimate and had clearly stated on its accompanying documentation, "Not to be used in litigation" seemed ludicrous. Since they could not establish a specific level of nandrolone metabolites in the sample it clearly doomed their chances of succeeding in the hearing. It almost seemed inconceivable that they had attempted to base their case on something that was so flawed as to make it completely inadmissible even by their own admission.

In order to understand the decision given it was necessary to have some scientific knowledge on the use and testing of drugs. Whilst some banned substances, including stimulants like cocaine and artificial steroids, are relatively easy to deal with because they are not found naturally in the body. If these are detected at all, the athlete is immediately banned. And whilst nandrolone, a close chemical cousin of testosterone, was thought to be in this category until recently, recent scientific evidence had now challenged that initial thinking. Following in the wake of the Bernhard case, study had since shown that normal people can have a small but significant level in their bodies 0.6 nanograms per millilitre of urine and this new finding resulted in some serious misgivings over the results of tests for this drug. This coupled with the inaccuracy of estimates meant Smith was sure to win his case in any court of law that had up to date scientific knowledge.

Whilst some federations such as the United States Triathlon Association and International Amateur Athletics Federation were taking a strict and some would say misguided stance over the matter, in contrast some other federations who were some may claim to have been a little more knowledgeable about the drug testing procedure and analysis such as UK Athletics, had misgivings about the tests and started to look into the validity of all the positive findings. Uncovering more up to date scientific knowledge allowed them to identify some evident flaws in the so-called positive tests that had recently been manifesting themselves at an alarming rate. The ultimate conclusions drawn from this additional research was that even though a drug test may indicate that the subject had nandrolone present, it did not necessarily prove doping or any wrongdoing on the part of the athlete.

Further study had showed that it was possible for the body to naturally create a form of nandrolone, particularly if the subject has eaten large quantities of meat contaminated with steroids which was not unknown in the US, and it had also been shown as Smith had originally contested that it was possible that dietary supplements taken perfectly legally by some athletes could be broken down by the body to produce the same substances created when nandrolone is broken down. These were undoubtedly key findings.

Whilst it was obvious that some drug abuse takes place within sport, and that some athletes who take anabolic steroids escape detection because they stop taking the drugs prior to competition, giving the body time to break down the compounds. Many argued that nandrolone was such an unsophisticated drug and so easily detectable, that no athlete thinking seriously about cheating would be likely to use it. Coupled with this weakness in the argument against Smith was the case that the increased musculature that would result from its use would be positively detrimental to his performance in an ultra endurace event like the Ironman.

At this point in terms of both scientific evidence and a degree of common sense it seemed inconceivable that Smith had ever been banned in the first place. With one panel concluding that the chain of custody was not secure enough to ensure that the sample had been Smith's in the first place and now evidence from the hand of the UCLA themselves which stated clearly that the accuracy of their tests was open to question how on earth this type of fault ridden testing could be allowed to determine the fate of athletes around the world, was a question many started to have to ask.

Whilst the decision stuck in the throat of both the USAT and UCLA, it came as a great relief to both Smith and the BTA. It appeared at last that Smith's ordeal was over. Smith was now free to take part in the Hawaiian Ironman in October, and to continue his quest to compete in ITU World Cup and Olympic competition.

Smith thanked his fans and his family for the support he had received during the ordeal reaffirming his innocence. "The day that I feel I can't win under my own power is the day I quit," said Smith. "Triathlon may be important, but it is nowhere near as important as the love and trust of my family. I would never lie to them and drag their good name and integrity into this whole mess if I wasn't 100 percent innocent." Whilst his ordeal looked over Smith could not help but add fuel to the fire already burning in the USAT headquarters by criticizing the testing methodology and procedure and commenting on the increased number of nandrolone positives of athletes such as Linford Christie, Merlene Ottey and Olivier Bernhard.

There seemed little doubt that this sudden increase in positive tests indicated that there could be a problem with the testing standards. In Christie's case it seemed somewhat strange that an Olympic and World Champion who was retiring would take these substances, but if Christie was a strange situation then by far one of the most surprising cases in the media was that of the German distance runner Dieter Baumann, who had won the Olympic gold in Spain in the 5000 meters at the Barcelona Olympics and had now been tested positive for nandrolone at two training controls.

Like Smith, Bauman said that he didn't know where the nandrolone concentration had come from, but what made this case interesting was that Baumann was also well known for his fight against drugs in sport and together with the German track and field organisation had led the way in developing and promoting a number of high profile campaigns against misuse of drugs in sport. The case against Baumann was high profile in Germany and left the German Federation's President who had worked closely with Baumann against doping for some years, clearly shaken by the allegations and even led him to consider tendering his resignation. Whether Baumann was now somewhat embarrassed by his previously rather dogmatic stance in relation to alleged doping cases where he had once stated. "Everybody who shows high concentrations of drugs is doped, no matter which way the drugs came in," is open to question, but the once advocate of unannounced training controls and tough penalties was now facing a two-year suspension and was perhaps increasingly aware that doping in sport was not such a black and white issue as he had once thought.

On the plus side for research one of Germany's most experienced doping researchers Prof. Werner Franke was an advocate of the belief that some athletes could produce high nandrolone concentrations as a result of intensive training and was offering to do research on Bauman to prove that point, but once again it highlighted that with nandrolone at least there were some important issues that needed to be addressed. Smith stated "It seems a lot of good athletes are being tarred with this brush and it is time to look carefully at the brush." The problem of increased positive tests became so acute that it was getting front page news and the federations were clearly feeling the heat. Either sport was so full of nandrolone users that it was hard to believe that any of the athletes were not doped, or it was apparent that there were some problems with the testing for this drug. Either way the public concern was obvious as was the reputation of the federations.

For a considerable number of months, the accused athletes who had once been heroes for many youngsters now found themselves becoming synonymous with drug abuse and most notably the drug nandrolone. Whilst the no smoke without fire gossips pointed fingers and accused each and every one of them, the finger pointing started to change direction when it was increasingly argued and publicly acknowledged by many that nandrolone could occur naturally in the body as well as a variety of foodstuffs. At this point the problem for the authorities increased considerably.

In a pattern which was all too familiar to Spencer Smith, the European 200 metre Champion Dougie Walker was cleared by UK athletics, a decision not accepted by the IAAF, whilst Christie was next to go through the process of a positive test and subsequent clearance by UK Athletics, and Jamaican Merlene Ottey was cleared, by her own federation and eventually by the IAAF.

Smith as the accused had been joined by a rash of international athletes with recent positive tests for nandrolone, and court cases and tribunals seemed to be the story of the day on the sports pages. Apart from nandrolone other steroid based drugs cases came to the fore, which included the suspensions of U.S. middle distance running legend Mary Slaney and sprinter Dennis Greene for exceeding the testosterone to epitestosterone ratio limits.

Whilst US sprinter Dennis Greene and his lawyers argued that factors other than illegal steroids such as stress induced sleeplessness, a bout of drinking and lovemaking and amino acid supplements in his diet had caused his testosterone level to rise above normal just prior to an unannounced test on April 1st 1998, Slaney claimed that birth control pills and menopausal changes were responsible for her elevated levels of testosterone. In both cases, despite the American Federation appeals panel ruling in favour of both athletes, the IAAF overturned both rulings and let the bans stand.

Like many of the other athletes in the news, Smith claimed he had been tainted by the accusations made against him and said. "Because of all this, if I do get past this, people will still say, we always thought he was on something." He was aware of the proverb throw enough mud and some will stick.

Relating his position to that of Dougie Walker also cleared by his own federation Smith complained. "It's never quite enough." Smith continued. "It is strange, all these nandrolone charges. People must think we're on some special deal. two-for-one nandrolone at the corner shop? Something isn't right." In that statement Smith had summed up the feeling of many people in the sport, with the exception of perhaps the drug testers. Clearly there was a problem, even if the drug testers weren't admitting to it.

Whilst Smith confirmed that he had taken vitamin pills and had vitamin B12 injections in the last year he confirmed that they all checked out, perfectly legal. "I just cannot understand it. I have done everything in my power to find out where the nandrolone came from, and we can't find a single trace." In querying the number of high profile cases, it was a good question that Smith had rhetorically put to the press. If so many positive tests had come about, why now? For some, the answers seemed obvious. Either more athletes were taking nandrolone or alternatively the testers were getting better, but on looking deeper into the epidemic there appeared even more complicated reasons at the core of the problem.

Whilst the reason for the increased number of nandrolone cases was always going to be open to some subjective speculation the major factors that could definitely have a major impact on the number of urine samples showing signs of nandrolone metabolites needed to be considered and could in part be traced back to two possibilities. Firstly the drugs and secondly the testing.

In the first case the increase in availability of improved drugs was undeniable. Inevitable in the war against drug abuse the testers were always fighting a losing battle, since common sense says that it is not until a new drug becomes available that the testers have the opportunity to start to develop effective and accurate testing procedures. As such the cheats have often been one step ahead of the game, having moved on to a new drug by the time the test for the old drug had been sufficiently proven. In the case of steroids, the possible increase in nandrolone positives could have been put down in part to the development of and increasing availability of norandrostendione, one of the many so called supplements on the market that is claimed to have beneficial effects for athletes was increasingly available. Unlike its historical predecessor, Deca Durabolin, which was an injectable nandrolone and could stay in the body for a considerable time, norandrostendione, which is metabolized as 19 nortestosterone, is a pill and does not stay in the body for a prolonged period. For drug cheats there were clearly severe drawbacks to using Deca as it was commonly known.

The problem was that metabolites of the older Deca Durabolin were capable of finding their way into fat cells and could be maintained in the body for long periods sometimes being excreted even months after being injected. This clearly made nandrolone a very undesirable product for anyone being drug tested as they could never be sure when it was going to show up in a drug test. Norandrostendione however had overcome this problem at least to some extent, since timing one's "clearance times" for banned drugs has always been a dangerous game for those in sport who were doping, the new drug at least had made it easier.

For those more cynical of athletes the increased number of positive tests for nandrolone could be linked quite clearly to the prohibited use of norandrostendione. Those who failed the tests could be argued to be guilty not only of doping but also being unable to work out the time the drug would take to clear from their body. This argument was however a little shaky given the speed with which the drug could leave the system.

Whilst there is little doubt that, nandrolone in the form of norandrostendione had become increasingly available in some countries, especially the States. Since detection of the drug in urine samples would only be possible within a few days of its use, it would appear extremely unlikely that athletes would run the risk of taking these drugs so close to competition. It was possible however that some athletes intent on cheating would take them as part of preparation and hence the importance of out of competition was paramount in catching such athletes. But clearly in Smith's case the test had been done immediately after the race, so that argument did not hold water.

The other possible argument behind the increased number of positives was a lot less sinister and related more to the methods used to detect metabolites in the urine rather than placing the blame at the door of so called cheats. The increasing use of High Resolution Mass Spectrometers (HRMS), which had become standard equipment at all IOC drug testing labs was bound to have an effect on the findings of drug tests. Whilst years ago, the amounts of nandrolone detected in the positive samples was generally very high, later positive testing in some cases showed significantly lower levels Smith's being one in question. The fact was that the HRMS presently used in drug testing in the late 1990's could detect significantly smaller quantities of nandrolone metabolites than the mass spectrometers previously used would clearly have an effect on the number of cases picked up, but would not necessarily indicate doping on the part of the athlete.

The fact that the testing labs were now able to identify minute quantities of nandrolone metabolites from 2 to 5ng/ml, the argument goes that this evidence of nandrolone metabolites in an athletes urine did not signify that the athletes found with low nandrolone metabolites were cheating, but merely signified that nandrolone metabolites were more common in the human body than the scientists had previously realized.

When you consider that prior to the scientific investigations resulting from a number of recent court cases, it had not been believed by some scientists that it was possible for humans to metabolise any level of nandrolone metabolite, where as now the scientists were becoming increasingly skeptical of the original viewpoints held, it threw continual skepticism on the whole issue surrounding nandrolone. So whilst the reasons behind the possible existence of nandrolone metabolites became vast and various all with varying degrees of credibility, what had become increasingly apparent was that medical science and metabolite testing is not a pure subject, but one in which advances in medical study are continually resulting in the establishment of completely new scientific theories and the complete elimination of some traditionally held beliefs.

In the case of nandrolone, some of the positive findings pointed to 'tainted meat' consumed by those being tested. With a strong scientific case being put forward following studies of cattle injected with anabolic steroids, a practice which is prevalent in the United States, there seemed strong indications that the consumption of such meat could indeed result in the passing on of those substances to humans which then could result in a positive test.

Whilst some scientists remained skeptical of this argument the paradox remains similar to reports a number of years previous from a Jewish Hospital in New York that the human could 'naturally' create morphine and codeine. At that time it was not recognized that consumption of poppy seed food products could result in significant and detectable amounts of morphine and codeine in the human body, a point that is now commonly accepted. Further research also showed that pregnant women appear to excrete nandrolone metabolites in their urine, thus highlighting the fact that the potential does exist for higher than expected levels of nandrolone metabolites to be found in the urine of individuals who are not doping.

Whilst Smith could not claim to be pregnant, the point that scientific understanding is still developing and that the science regarding tests for nandrolone were not yet perfect is the fact that should be considered, and in his case, the former argument seemed entirely plausible given the extent to which Smith was renowned for eating large quantities of beefsteak.

Because of these types of scientific findings the IOC labs no longer declared a positive test on an athlete who had any amount of nandrolone metabolites in their urine but instead used a measure to determine guilt with a 'cut off' which consisted of 2 ng/ml for males and 5 ng/ml for females. Any Athletes falling under these thresholds were then not declared to have produced a positive test, whilst, those who were over the thresholds were reported as positive by the laboratories. Clearly by this time at least some federations were recognizing the presence of some higher levels of nandrolone as naturally occurring, but the question of the accuracy to which those thresholds can be deemed to be accurate for any given athlete, remained in question.

Since at this point scientific studies had not been done to clear up the seemingly unanswered questions about nandrolone levels, it would appear that a case could now be made by all athletes who had been deemed to have produced positive drug tests, that the specified levels were not proven and as such this argument would opened the floodgates for athletes accused to challenge the findings of the federations. This was something that clearly concerned the ITU and after the conclusion of the ITU panel, they posted a press release outlining their upset at the panel's decision. This release is transcribed in part below.

22nd September 1999 ITU Press Release:
ITU appeal results in dismissal of Spencer Smith case

An independent International Triathlon Union (ITU) appeals panel has dismissed the case brought by USA Triathlon (USAT) against Spencer Smith regarding his positive sample taken at the Hawaii Ironman Triathlon last October. USAT had appealed the case to the independent ITU Appeals Board after the British Triathlon Association dismissed the case in a preliminary hearing last March. In the current case, the ITU panel cited inconsistencies in international doping reporting procedures and believed it had insufficient evidence to conclude that a doping violation had occurred.

Both USAT and the ITU were clearly embarrassed at the findings of the panel which had led USAT Executive Director Steve Locke to, state that, "as of today, neither panel in these two hearings has yet addressed the fact that the laboratory analysis clearly demonstrates the presence of a significant amount of nandrolone." Either Locke was ignorant of the fact that the evidence had not been provided by his own organization, which was clearly unlikely or he felt that the term 'estimates only. Not to be used in litigation' still validated his case for what he deemed 'a significant amount' of nandrolone, which for an intelligent man, who must have by now at least have some understanding of the legal process, if not the scientific evidence, this really seemed an unusual stance to take. Irrespective of the obvious conclusions to any fair minded and unbiased onlooker, that the case on its merits had to be thrown out Locke confirmed that the USAT would appeal the findings, and take the case to the Court of Arbitration for Sport (CAS) in Lausanne, Switzerland.

In addition to Locke's determination to continue to fight the case, Mark Sissons in his role as the ITU's Anti-Doping Chairman also indicated that they would join USAT's appeal an effort to as he put it, "to finally have this case heard on its merits and not dismissed on technicalities." Clearly from Sissons point of view the inability for an organization to carry out the procedures required and the appropriate test on an athlete was merely a technicality.

From the content of the press release it was apparent that Smith's battle against both the USAT and the ITU was not going to end with his second acquittal. The decision grated on Sissons, the integrity of both the ITU and the American Triathlon Federation and the drug testing procedures had it would appear been irreparably damaged. Despite the findings of this clearly non partisan and highly qualified panel Sissons still felt he had a more than compelling argument in defense of both the chain of custody and in the test result itself. And although certain onlookers agreed with the sentiments behind the press release and believed Smith's second acquittal was based on a "technicality," where the panel judged, all be it, rightly or wrongly, that the amount of nandrolone, rather than its mere presence was significant to the decision of innocence or guilt, it must have been concerning for both the USAT and the ITU who both appeared to believe in Smith's guilt, that in two hearings both panels dismissed the same charge on different grounds.

Whilst many of those familiar with the case felt that Smith had done enough to prove his innocence, behind closed doors at USAT and the ITU offices this was not a viewpoint held by their senior staff, and it would soon appear that the threat to continue to take the case further was not an idle one, but in the mean time Smith having obtained his second acquittal now could at least return his focus to training and Hawaii which loomed ever nearer.

Away from the second court case, whilst his preparations for the 1999 Hawaii Ironman had undoubtedly been affected, Smith was still positive about his forthcoming race and believed he could still better his time by up to twenty minutes. Given that the USAT appeal was now concluded with Smith being acquitted once again, Smith looked forward to the race and the opportunity to put the second court case behind him despite the possible threat of a third one being on the horizon and called up Friedland to firm up the details of his entry for Hawaii.

Following the previous confirmation from Friedland that if he won the appeal, he would be eligible, he believed this confirmation to be a formality, but he was wrong. Friedland told Smith, he wanted to see the transcripts. He wanted to know how they came to their decision. Smith was surprised at the request having fully expected the original offer to stand, but he was told that he was still not in, and that Ironman had not yet made up their mind.

Whilst the WTC pondered over the findings of the enquiry, Smith just had to sit and wait both angry and disillusioned at the way he had been treated. It was a difficult time for him to train and he was struggling to focus. "It is very difficult to go out and do those miles with this hanging over your head. It has been a rough couple of years, what with my dad, and now this." Smith had said at the time.

The days dragged to weeks and in the end it was not until some time after his initial discussions with Friedland on the 29th September, that Smith was informed he would be permitted to race. This was eight or nine days after the hearing had cleared Smith and many felt that at best it should have been the day after the hearing.

Smith however by this time had already made his own decision not to race Hawaii, his training had been so much further delayed that he felt he would not perform to the standard he wanted to and withdrew his application. "I set a deadline for myself, where if the Ironman didn't come back with the answer I was looking for, I would just not be able to go on and do the race. Their answer just came too late."

Rumours ran wild and many argued that Friedland should have only needed to know the results of the appeal not the reason on the basis that either Smith was eligible or he wasn't. If he won the appeal they reasoned then he should have been immediately entitled to race. The request for the transcripts and the delay in the invitation just added fuel to the suspicion that the WTC made its promise to Smith just before the second hearing, because the USAT had convinced Friedland that there was no possibility that Smith was going to win his case against them.

It seemed a possibility, and given the WTC's need to protect the image of their race and not wanting it tarnished by the prospect of it being won by an athlete who would at a later date be banned for drug abuse, was understandable from a commercial and public relations perspective. But for Smith the outcome remained the same, and whilst not accusing the WTC, did confirm that their delay in extending an official invitation to the Hawaii race following his September 21st vindication was a contributing factor to his withdrawal. But given the power of the WTC to prevent him from racing any future events it had not been likely that he would.

Smith was never one to just take part and following all the red tape surrounding his participation wasn't making the progress he wanted to. "I could see I wasn't recovering fast enough after runs and my swimming and biking were down and then I realized I just didn't have enough time." According to Black, Spencer's former coach, Smith had always been an advocate of the philosophy. "If you are on the start line, there can be no excuses," and in this case that philosophy had led Smith to withdraw from the race. "Whenever I get to the line, I expect that I will be prepared to win." said Smith "but my training results have indicated that isn't possible now." A point that had perhaps come to him a few weeks previous whilst out training with a group led by Jurgen Zack and Greg Welch, when Smith had found himself unable to keep the pace, an indicator that all was not well and perhaps the catalyst in his decision which when added to further delays he had in being confirmed a place in the starting lineup just added strength to his resolution to withdraw.

He felt that if he performed badly in Hawaii, he would have undone everything he had accomplished the previous year, Smith summed up his feelings towards the race. "This is such a great race. It allows no weaknesses, I wanted to come and do the business. I wanted to deliver the goods. I wanted to do it justice." Smith had felt if he had performed badly people may have felt sorry for him and that was not an option that he felt comfortable with, so his decision was final and his season was over. He could now take time to reflect on his options.

For Spencer since his father's death in August 1998 his life had been like a rollercoaster ride with things moving so rapidly and changing so significantly, that he was finding the pressure of being under constant scrutiny increasingly intrusive and significantly more than he wanted for either himself or his family. After the alleged positive test in November 1998 Smith had spent more time back in the UK and whilst the test findings weren't public knowledge at that time Spencer was acutely aware of the possible consequences of a doping conviction.

When Spencer returned to the UK he would often join the guys at Sigma on a Sunday ride and that was where he had occasion to meet Julian Clarke who was to set up the Linda McCartney Professional Cycling team and who back in 1998 just after Hawaii had given Smith an option of turning to Professional Cycling prior to being aware of the ensuing doping accusation.

"Spencer suggested there was going to be a problem in the future," Ian Whittingham recollected with regard to his conversations with Smith shortly after his Ironman debut in November 1998, "but he didn't tell us what it was. Nobody knew any more than that." So whilst Smith had met Clarke the year previous, his subsequent meetings with him in the autumn of 1999 would result in another twist in the Smith saga. "He came out for a ride with us, and by the end of the ride I think (Spencer) had agreed he would be riding for the team the following year...a couple of more rides and I guess the deal was virtually done," Whittingham recalled. And true to his commitment, Smith spent the autumn and winter training ferociously in preparation for the move to cycling. In an attempt to ensure he could adjust to the longer races in the pro scene Smith upped his biking to six hour rides at a time when much of the European peleton was winding down its training.

At that time the Linda McCartney Team was in its early stages and was an English based team preparing to launch into Europe the following year. By coincidence, the team was on the lookout for some fresh talent and Smith had at the same time become so increasingly angry at the politics in triathlon and his constant hounding by some of its senior officials after he won his second appeal and subsequently not been able to race in Hawaii, that when was offered a contract to take up cycling, and race for McCartney in the 2000 season of European road racing he agreed to it. It appeared he was leaving the sport that he once so loved.

The Linda McCartney Team, which was sponsored by the

vegetarian food company founded by the late singer, and wife to Sir Paul McCartney, was managed by Sean Yates, and had the image of the clean team. An all vegetarian, strictly anti drugs outfit, which seemed to fit with what Spencer wanted to show himself as, and all be it a difficult transformation for an athlete who was known to like his meat, Smith believed this offered him a further opportunity to get away from the politics that had been turning his life upside down. Whilst USAT and the ITU had continued their war against Smith, the young Londoner had been secretly entering into negotiations with the McCartney Team, and as a team with a squeaky clean image and a vegetarian sponsor the team could not afford and would not tolerate bad publicity associated with any of their riders, but were convinced sufficiently of Smith's innocence to offer him a contract.

In addition to the team image, Smith had for some time considered a career in cycling and with a Team Manager like Sean Yates who was an icon in British cycling, and had himself ridden not just the Italian Giro but had worn the Yellow Jersey and won stages in the Tour de France and the Tour of Spain, Smith was acutely aware that if his career was to be professional cycle racing then he could learn a lot from Yates. Spencer was not the healthiest of eaters at the best of times having a liking for chocolate, (but not those shitty penguins) fish and chips and steak, but through nutrition and keeping the training going and going and going Smith had managed to turn himself into the world class triathlete over all distances. Now he had the chance to do it all again in a different sport and on a vegetarian diet of tofu and nut cutlets.

Apart from the clear excitement manifest from Smith's demeanor, Yates, a former Motorola teammate of Lance Armstrong, could see potential in Smith and some wondered if he saw the emergence and single mindedness of former triathletes like Armstrong as a characteristic that could make a good pro biker. If the deal was done, Smith would be set to join the team at its new Toulouse base in the south of France in early November. News of the potential move away from triathlon spread like wildfire throughout the community and whilst many respected the reasons for Smith's decision to switch from triathlon to cycling and wished him well in his new venture, others were clearly less supportive, the USA elite triathlete James Bonney being one who even went as far as to post a message on the internet triathletes web that read. "Good luck to him. I hear there's an opening on Festina. I'm sure he'll fit right in." Clearly a reference to the scandal at the Tour de France and their alleged drug taking.

Whilst Smith had tried to play down the move until a contract had been tied up, following the various rumours in the cycling and triathlon press that Smith had already joined the Linda McCartney team and had given up triathlon for good. It was decided by John Deering who dealt with all the team's press, that it was about time the official story was given and so a press release was issued which in part read as follows.

20th December 1999 McCartney Cycling Team Press Release: Spencer Switches Sports

One of the world's best known triathletes has turned his back on the sport to become a professional cyclist. In a fantastic coup for Britain's top cycling squad, Spencer Smith has signed for the Linda McCartney Pro Cycling Team.

The release quoted Smith as saying ever since he was a junior he had regarded cycling as his, "long term career," stating. "I'm still only twenty six, so this is the time to do it now or never." Whilst Yates confirmed that they had been trailing Spencer for a year saying. "We first spoke to him in 1998, because I'd heard of his ambition to make it in cycling, and I wanted to make sure that if that happened, Linda McCartney would be his destination." The release then went on to give an account of the situation leading up to his signing for the team making reference to the alleged positive test for what they termed. 'notorious nandrolone,' the focus of so many dubious tests in recent times.

With regard to his move into a sport that had a very negative association with doping, both historically and more recently with the 1998 Tour de France and the ongoing court cases that continued to haunt the cycling press Smith stated. "If I had something to hide, I certainly wouldn't become a cyclist. The testing in cycling is the most stringent in any sport in the world. They lead the way. Linda McCartney are known as the 'Clean Machine,' and I want people to know that I'm part of that." There was little doubt that triathlon had given Smith a great lifestyle and made him a wealthy sportsman, but in turning to cycling he was going to find the riches and the successes much harder to come by, but Smith was confident that he could achieve it. "I know that I can do it. It's going to be really hard, I'm putting my reputation and career on the line, but I have no fear, because I know I can do it."

The move to professional cycle racing made by Smith, looked strangely reminiscent of the course taken by Tour de France winner Lance Armstrong, who had also been a triathlete but had converted to road racing. Whilst Armstrong had not reached the heights that Smith had achieved in his triathlon career, few really expected Smith to reach the dizzy heights that Armstrong had achieved in cycle racing. Interestingly, Smith's new team manager, Sean Yates, one of the few British riders to wear the Yellow Jersey, was one of Armstrong's closest friends and exerted a big influence on the Texan's transformation from brawny endurance athlete to slimmed-down road-racing champion, who had subsequently gone on to win the Tour de France in 1999 a year after the Festina affair.

Whilst Smith's withdrawal from triathlon and subsequent conversion to cycling was similar to that of Armstrong the reasons behind the change were very different and in Smith's case it had been clearly hastened by the stress of the past twelve months. As if to prove the point that they were drugs free, Julian Clarke, the McCartney team's general manager, confirmed that they had a clause in their contract with all the riders, making it clear that any positive test would result in their dismissal and Smith would be treated in the same way as all the other riders. In truth Smith was not as important to the team as the team was to him. In short he had yet to prove himself as a cyclist.

In terms of the development of a new team, Yates had released all but three of his 1999 team having been unhappy about his team's lack of staying power in the bigger European events. Apart from Smith, other riders who would be joining the Linda McCartney 'Clean Team' would include the Anglo-Italian Max Sciandri Olympic medal winner and Tour de France stage-winner, and the very accomplished and high profile figure of Pascal Richard, a Swiss rider who had notched up an array of major profile stage wins and overall victories in the major races, including the Olympic Road Championships, the Tour de France, Liège-Bastogne-Liège, the Tour of Lombardy and the Tour of Italy. The only other Briton that Yates had retained in his team was the former British National Champion Mathew Stephens who ironically had been contracted in the previous season just to make up the numbers but had performed admirably despite having to hold down a full-time job at Marks & Spencer in Chester. To consider the two contrasting lifestyles between Smith and Stephens was almost laughable.

Alongside Sciandri, Richard and Stephens, language didn't look like it would be a major problem even if the majority of races were to be based in Europe. For the first time in many years Smith would now find himself to be a small fish in a big pond. Clearly the contracting of Richard and Sciandri, both renowned one-day riders, was a great boost for the team and increased their chances of them getting the team into the bigger races with events such as the Tour of Flanders, Het Volk, Tirreno-Adriatico, Criterium International and ultimately the Giro d'Italia, and whilst there was pressure on the team to perform well Yates was not keen to put that pressure on the Neo-Pro Smith. "I've no idea how Spencer will perform," Yates had said. " Spencer is clearly a great athlete and will follow the same programme as the rest of the team, but how he will convert to road racing is an unknown quantity."

The all-vegetarian squad, had a strict policy that its members, would not eat meat while on squad duty and whilst for a consummate meat eater like Smith, it would be difficult for him to abstain from the carnivorous delights offered by a beefsteak wholesale, it was sure to prove an interesting experiment. More importantly for Smith the clean image of the team in a sport that had suffered countless accusations of drug abuse was something that both Smith and his manager Burnell recognized as sending out the right signals and if he could cope with the diet it was a bonus.

As to whether Smith could perform well on a meat free diet Team Manager Sean Yates had little doubt that he would. Having been a vegetarian until he was twenty, Yates only began to eat meat when he went to live in France and fell into what he called the 'Gallic ways', because "everyone ate steak," but had reduced his meat intake over the years and had his best Tour de France in 1988, when he ate no meat at all. Yates did however admit that being vegetarians created other problems for the team. Primarily the fact that they were unable to transport vast quantities of vegetarian food around with them on the races throughout Europe and hence they had to rely upon the cooperation of the hotels where race organisers book them rooms, and the capability of their catering staff.

Apart from the change to cycling from triathlon, and the adjustment from meat eater to vegetarian, the move into professional cycling would bring with it some significant lifestyle changes to both Spencer and his wife Melissa, and as a result of the swap, Smith had been training in Spain in the expectation of making his European road-racing debut early in 2000 and would now have to relocate from his home in San Diego to Toulouse, where the McCartney team and its new European headquarters were based. Which if nothing else would be a significant culture shock.

Ian Whittingham met up with Smith when he was out there visiting the team. "I went to stay with Julian for a few days, Spencer seemed really, really motivated and as always the consummate professional, you wouldn't ultimately realise anything was wrong but one day we pulled up outside Spencer's flat, it was a little flat in a little village square in the middle of nowhere, absolutely deserted on a Sunday afternoon and I'll always remember, Melissa and Spencer came down and I asked where they were going and Melissa said they were off to the circus. She said we wouldn't ordinarily get excited about that but life's quiet around here. You could tell that it wasn't so great the situation there."

Apart from having to move to Europe the nature of racing on the European circuit involves weeks of living out of a suitcase in hotel rooms and events that result in day after day of racing rather than a one day race, that leaves the rest of the week to recover and prepare for the next one and whilst this was something else Smith would have to get used to, he was eased into the squad attending the Tour down Under with the team, just in order to observe and get a chance to get to know the riders better. But in January Smith's long awaited move into the world of the professional cycling tours arrived.

And so it was that in January 2000 Smith found himself on the start line at the commencement of the 5th edition of the Malaysian, Tour of Langkawi. Whilst not expected to feature at the front of the race his job was to be that of a domsestique for the leaders in his team, a water carrier. For the first time in a very long and accomplished sporting career, the eyes were not looking at Smith in reference to any podium expectations. His job was not to be in there sprinting at the finish, but to be riding back through the peleton to bring up water bidons for some of the other riders in the team, to chase down the attacks when it was needed and to pace his team leader on the climbs and in the straights giving up his own chances of glory for the good of the team. This was a serious transition from the, it doesn't matter if you win or lose, it only matters if I win or lose' ethic, that the world of triathlon had come to expect from Smith.

Whilst not exactly a European race, with a significantly eastern nature the race was still well respected amongst the riders and given its location there was a strong relationship between the Malaysia's multi-racial and multicultural make-up and its history. Whilst colonial rule by the Portuguese, Dutch and the British had an impact on Malaysia it was still strictly Asian having achieved its independence on in 1957 and with the country's large Muslim population not permitted to drink alcohol celebrations and a couple of beers after the stage, or a glass of wine with your meal, whilst not strictly frowned upon, were at best the limit to the festivities and the nightlife. Still Smith was there to race and not sightsee.

Besides the local Malays and the native groups, Malaysia is made up from immigrants from China, India, Indonesia and other parts of the world who have all contributed to the multiracial composition of its population and the cultural melting pot evident in the unique blend of religions, socio-cultural activities, traditions, dressing, languages and food, with food playing a major part in the riders concerns, given that they would normally need to consume in excess of 7000 calories per day just to maintain an calorific equilibrium and steady weight. So clearly diet was to be a major concern for all.

The race had been put in place to promote Malaysia as a tourist attraction in a country that saw over eight and a half million tourists visiting it in 2000, an increase of nearly thirty three percent on the previous year, though to what degree this was a result of the increased international coverage the country had received as a result of the tour is open to speculation. Nevertheless, the race that consisted of a number of professional European and American teams, the Linda McCartney squad and a number of more local teams had managed to gain increased coverage and recognition within the cycling fraternity.

As coincidence would have it Malaysia's Tour de Langkawi, was promoted and managed by Sport for Television, who had staged the Manchester Triathlon World Championships in 1993 with Alan Rushton and Mick Bennett at the helm, so Smith would find himself amongst old friends.

Spencer was one of two Brits in the six man team to be wearing the Linda McCartney colors, Matt Stephens being the other the other, whilst his four other teammates included the Aussie Duo, Benjamin Brooks and David McKenzie, with the Norwegian Björnar Vestöl and Ciarán Power the Irish prodigy, making up the six. Although the race was only a UCI category 2.4 event, the Tour of Langkawi carried one of the largest purses in world cycling, standing at around $US 400,000 and so was sure to prove a good pay day to those who performed well.

Singularly different from the events he had been used to, the race was sure to test Smith's resilience over a protracted period where rather than a one off all out effort of one day's racing that he had been used to, Smith would now have to survive a twelve stage event that would involve him covering 1605.8 km, between the 26th January and the 6th February with a dozen consecutive days of racing over terrain consisting of both flat stages and stages that required considerable climbing.

26th January 2000 The Tour of Langkawi, Malaysia.

With the first stage a 9.2 km time trial around Langkawi Island Smith wearing number 86, (a far cry from the number one that he had been accustomed to wearing at most of the events he was racing as a triathlete), was able to get into his typical head down and go mode with no peleton to think about. In the end Smith fared well, finishing in 54th place, out of the starting field of a hundred and forty nine riders, one minute and nine seconds behind the American Mercury Cycling team winner Floyd Landis who crossed the line in 12:20:88 averaging a speed of 44.7 kilometres an hour. But perhaps more importantly for Smith was the fact that he was the third of the McCartney team to cross the line with only Vestöl making a McCartney impact on the race taking 15th spot whilst Ciarán Power took 52nd place with only hundredths of a second splitting him from Smith as Matt Stephens took 55th just two seconds adrift. For Smith the tour then set out on its long arduous stretch, which would see him working hard to holding his own in the peleton whilst learning the ropes from the pros.

Cycle racing was a far cry from triathlon for the young Londoner who was used to finding himself in the top three at the end of a days racing, and he knew he would have to satisfy himself with a place mid pack, at least for the majority of the stages, but apart from experience gained from the racing Smith was also soon to learn a lot about what it was to be a professional cyclist outside of the tactics and strategy in the peleton.

The heat and the humidity in Malaysia was a constant concern to the riders making dehydration a serious problem for many of the peleton who were using anything up to twelve bidons (water bottles) a day each. Understandably in such conditions, intestinal troubles, which lead to diarrhea, and issues relating to the heat were a factor in the racing with a number of European riders also taking some time to adjust to the Eastern diet.

On several stages throughout the tour, it would be fair to say, that a number of riders found themselves in dire need of what could be termed 'emergency sanitary stops,' which whilst not pleasant for the riders, in some cases were a much less pleasing sight for the startled onlookers and spectators, but fortunately for Smith who had a strong constitution no such major issues manifested themselves.

On his second stage in the race Smith found the going tough and was the last in the McCartney team to finish, some nine minutes and seventeen seconds down on the winner, which was both a shock to the system and the ego of the regular podium taker, but the following day with the whole peleton staying together he comfortably held the pace and cruised in with the bunch to take 70th place.

Despite not setting the race alight, a prospect that had never been expected of him, Yates confirmed that he was generally pleased with the rookies performance so far, but Smith, who was not used to being off the podium at the end of a race, was determined to do better than what was perhaps possible for him to achieve as a novice.

By way of proving that point, the fourth stage which according to the promoters, featured the 'world's longest climb in a bike race', a forty nine kilometer ascent between Lumut and Tanah Rata, finishing in the Cameron Highlands, was sure to test the new boy's resilience and whilst undoubtedly a stage that many would be pleased to just finish, Smith was determined to do well on it.

It had always been anticipated that the climb would create havoc in the peleton even among the experienced riders, but after nearly four and a half hours of racing Smith had stuck to his plan and proven that he could hold tough even in such punishing conditions, by finishing in 40th place a mere one minute and fifty three seconds down on the wisp like Telecom Malaysian All Star climb specialist Kam-Po Wong who led the field.

Smith's time made him impressively the third rider across the line in Linda McCartney colours, which given his stature had surprised not only his team but some of the other more accomplished climbers in the peleton who started to nickname him, 'Tri Hard.'

But if Smith was to prove his climbing prowess a second time in the tour as he had done some years earlier when racing Jurgen Zack up Palamo Hill, he would soon get another chance to prove his abilities, since whilst this had been the longest climb, the hardest climb of the race was yet to come, and was waiting for them in stage ten from Kuala Lumpur to Genting.

Stage five saw yet another tough race, and Smith found himself learning a lesson about saving some for the next day's racing, paying dearly for the effort he had put in the previous day and arriving at the finish a further six minutes down on his teammates picking up 74th spot, but he was not the only one suffering.

As the race progressed through the Malaysian countryside the heat had become so prolific in the tour that the organisers had taken the initiative to hose the peleton down with fire hoses at the finish of the stages, again not a normal procedure in a major tour, but then this was not a normal tour.

It had however been something that had been done once before on a race promoted by Rushton and Bennett under the Sport for Television banner, most notably one year on the Nissan International Classic in Ireland, at a time when Sean Kelly and Stephen Roche were at the peak of their careers and Britain and Ireland were awash with major cycling events including the Kellogg's Tour of Britain, The Scottish Provident League and the McEwan's City Center series.

Despite the Nissan Classic being held in Ireland where it would seem to invariably be raining, in one year the heat had been quite astonishing which had led the helicopter pilot who was employed to help the Irish television production team to come upon the brainwave of flying close to one of the giant spray hoses that the farmers used to water and irrigate the fields and position himself so that the rotor blades blew the spouting water over the peleton, thereby cooling them off.

The instant cool down was more than welcomed by most if not all the riders and later that evening in the hotel restaurant, many of the riders thanked the pilot praising him on his quick wittedness, patting him on the back, and asking him to do it again the following day if the opportunity arose. The pilot was the hero of the hour and lapped up the praise graciously supping many a Guinness at the expense of others. Unfortunately for the pilot his status was to be as short lived as his pint.

The following day, the sweltering heat remained, and as instructed, the pilot whilst going about his duties in covering the race for television was determined to find an opportunity to refresh and cool down the riders once again and as the day progressed went off in search of yet another irrigation hose, eventually finding one some way into the race.

Positioning himself once again so that the downdraft blew the spouting water into the peleton, he was unable under the noise of the helicopter engine to hear the screams and curses of the riders as they waved their arms frantically in the direction of the pilot in their attempts to make him stop. Unfortunately for the pilot, and perhaps more importantly for the riders, the spray that was jettisoning from the irrigation hose was not indeed water but slurry! That evening the pilot who had the day before been a hero, was silently ignored with looks of malice and malcontent, to the silent smirking satisfaction of the officials who had been nicely protected in their brand new Nissans, with windows tightly shut and sunroofs secured. But such is the world of professional cycling.

Back in Langkawi however, no such silage problem occurred on the road, but in a race that could be safely described as a learning curve for Smith the young Londoner found himself often rolling across the line in the peleton in positions well down on what he would normally be accustomed to taking 133rd place, 116th place and 110th place over the next three stages and not coming into his own again until the treat of the toughest climb emerged on the tenth stage held from Kuala Lumpur tower to the Genting Highlands.

For many of the riders, having ridden some of the steepest climbs in the European races, whilst the climb up to the Genting Highlands clearly promised to be tough one, few had little idea of exactly what was entailed, having not had a chance to ride it prior to the race start, and a standard 39/23 or 39/25 was for the majority the sort of gearing ratio selected.

Given the average ascent of the climb, there is little doubt that this was an appropriate choice for the first twenty kilometres of the climb which rose steadily, but the last five kilometres was a killer, almost vertical in some parts, which led some riders who hadn't set up their bikes with bigger gears more akin to 39/27 to hurt themselves seriously in an attempt to reach the summit without stopping, whilst their knees screamed for a smaller gear.

Unquestionably this was the best day of the tour so far for the McCartney Team and for Spencer Smith, since whilst Matt Stephens who had been riding impressively throughout the tour and was holding 4th spot on General Classification managed take second place falling prey to Julio Alberto Perez, who had attacked with three kilometres to go, Vestol, Power and Smith managed to take 16th, 23rd and 28th spots respectively which made it a good day to celebrate for the vegetarians.

Whilst a good performance had been put in on the climb, once again the exertions of a tough stage would be paid for by Smith in the following days and over the final two stages Smith in his domestique role would do well to secure 75th place for the second and third time in the tour. The McCartney Team had done well by the end of the race and whilst the final podium places would evade them, Matt Stephens, their team leader had secured fourth place over all, just one minute and five seconds behind the eventual winner Chris Horner of Mercury Cycling Team who had finished the tour in 38 hours, 34 minutes and 39 seconds averaging 41.72 kilometres per hour.

Smith had done a good job as a domestique and had impressed both his teammates and his manager, and whilst placings don't count for much in professional cycling with the exception of first second or third, his performance throughout the days of racing had been more than anticipated of him. Having finished 41st for Smith was still however a far cry from the firsts that he had begun to expect in triathlon. It was to be a tough apprenticeship before he would be allowed to lead a team, and this had perhaps become more apparent throughout the tour.

Shortly after Langkawi Smith admitted to how much it had taken out of him. "I knew that I would struggle, and I knew how much I would be hurting, but I'm also only human. Cycling hurt a lot. It's a completely different lifestyle, a different feel, a different mental attitude. You go to races, you race to get fit, you do a hundred races a year. It's a continuous cycle of racing and travelling."

But a statistical look at Smith's first tour had shown he potentially had what it took to make the grade in the peleton. Of the hundred and forty nine riders who started the race only a hundred and twenty six would finish with 126th place going to Suryo Agung Joni of Indonesia who would finish nearly two and a half hours down. The Linda McCartney team would fair much better with Vestol in 13th place at two minutes and fifty six seconds down on the winner, Power 23rd at 8.21, McKenzie 30th at 11.25 and rookie ex triathlete Spencer Smith finishing only twenty two minutes and fifty seconds behind Horner. Not a bad start to a cycling career. But now it was time to go home.

After eating rice for two weeks, which whilst a great source of carbohydrate there is little doubt that the riders Smith included, would be glad to get back to some good home cooking, but the other thing that had been cooking up whilst Smith had been racing was the nandrolone controversy.

On a wider scale, the nandrolone scandals had continued to grow in the UK media and at a level much closer to the concerns of Smith, USAT had also continued to prepare their case against him, becoming more vociferously confident of the outcome, with Locke continuing to claim that the levels allegedly produced by Smith could not possibly be produced naturally by humans despite the fact that the evidence they had presented confirmed that they had no accurate readings.

Away from the specifics of Smith's case the contoversy related to the levels set by the IOC which had previously received considerable criticism from at least one leading expert, Dr Mike Wheeler, at St Thomas' Hospital, continued to rage following Wheeler's coment to the BBC News that the International Olympic Committee's nandrolone limit of two nanograms per millilitre was, "awfully close," to the level at which an, "unacceptable number of innocent athletes might produce positive tests."

The fact that Dr. Wheeler had also gone on to explain a number of reasons as to how these 'false positives' might occur, relating his conclusions closely to the stresses athletes place on their bodies in training and competing could raise the natural levels of these banned substances in their bodies had not gone unnoticed especially after he stated. "There is some evidence that after an event, an athlete's testosterone goes up, therefore if nandrolone is produced from testosterone, it could be that the nandrolone goes over the detection limit." This reasoned and qualified argument now meant the testers were now suffering at the hands of the scientists.

Wheeler also interestingly made criticism of the tests that tried to establish the limits for athletes who by the nature of their training are physiologically different to the ordinary person on the street noting. "We have to remember that the nandrolone studies used very few individuals and, crucially, not athletes." He continued his criticism of present testing methodology arguing. "The nandrolone tests were (or appeared) correct when they were introduced but they have to be reassessed in the light of new knowledge." Clearly the scientists still remained divided but USAT's Steve Locke remained unconvinced and reconfirmed that they would appeal to the Court of Arbitration for Sport in Lausanne, and were in the throws of preparing their case.

Whilst Smith, Burnell, Morton-Hooper and the BTA looked on helplessly, it appeared there was no doubt that Smith would have to wager yet another battle against the USAT to clear his name, and as if adding fuel to the fire, Locke had outlined to the press that if the USA Triathlon hearings validated the earlier alleged positive Smith was to face a further problem with regard to a ban.

Locke noted that since Smith, had subsequently given up triathlon and was now riding in the ranks of professional cycle racing he would now potentially come under UCI regulations governing the sport of cycling which differed significantly from the ITU's.

In accordance with to USA Triathlon rules, his suspension, should he be found guilty at the third attempt, would have started from the date of the original positive test, which meant he might be eligible for competition as early as April. As a cyclist, however, Locke pointed out that Smith faced a potential two year ban from the time of the conviction, therefore highlighting the possibility of the drugs nightmare hanging over Smith for even longer.

Some believed that Locke's continued attempt to discredit Smith was more than was good for the sport. Locke's official stance on the subject however remained one of technicalities and science. When Locke had argued that neither panel in either of the hearings had addressed the fact that the laboratory analysis demonstrated the existence of nandrolone, he made it clear that once again the natural versus unnatural nandrolone argument was at the core of the USAT's case.

Even from the start of the CAS appeal, it seemed inconceivable that Smith would be found guilty. The previous appeals panels had cited so many inconsistencies in international doping reporting procedures and the ITU Panel had concluded it has insufficient evidence to conclude a doping violation had even occurred since the laboratory reports contained nothing about the concentrations of the levels of nandrolone that were consistent with an offence. Even if the ITU still believed, despite much evidence to the contrary that nandrolone could not be produced naturally and therefore any evidence of nandrolone in Smith's sample made him a cheat, there was significant scientific evidence to have proved otherwise, and there was nothing to lead to the belief that USAT would be able to discredit this scientific evidence which they themselves had submitted.

Whilst the ITU had stated initially that they supported USAT's case, many believed that the ITU would back down given the overwhelming evidence against them and having already lost considerable respect in their previous encounter but in the end they continued to support USAT. Locke had suggested that in the ITU hearing, the panel either did not understand or misinterpreted the information, but for the first time he did accept that if that were the case then USAT were in part to blame in that they had not flown in scientific experts to interpret the information for the panel. At that time USA Triathlon had spent somewhere in the region of $45,000 in legal fees but it seemed they were willing to spend more if needed. Locke contested that it was his job to uphold USAT's anti-drugs laws which he referred to as the cornerstone of the sport and argued that whilst it was undoubtedly a very expensive process it was nevertheless one he felt was necessary for the sport. At the same time Locke protested that there was, "no vendetta against Smith," but some in the British camp were not so sure.

When informed that the third appeal by USAT would go ahead, Smith was clearly angry. "Now I've won my case on two separate occasions and before different panels," he said. "Even those who have doubted me before would agree I've done enough now to show I'm innocent." Smith continued. "I find it a bit odd that USA Triathlon's Steve Locke would say he didn't believe the ITU appeals panel understood the evidence," added Smith. "They are intelligent people. Now Steve Locke says I have not addressed why that substance was in my sample. I think we addressed that. Why do you think they threw that out of court? I immediately had myself tested, at my expense, to see if there was any substance in me or any long term residue of that substance and they found nothing." Smith who had clearly been suffering under the pressure of the two previous hearings and had found the ITU appeals panel ruling to be a large emotional relief, clearly believed there was a vendetta against him. His second acquittal had opened the door for him to attack his second Hawaii and then concentrate on his build up to Sydney Olympics, but then the first door had been clearly slammed in his face and the second one was only just ajar.

Eventually the date for the final appeal to the court for Arbitration for Sport was set for the end of March, with the venue to be New York. An unusual location for CAS hearings, which are usually conducted in Lausanne, Switzerland, but Smith just wanted to get on with it. He wanted the nightmare behind him.

Eventually all parties would make their way to the hearing, for Sissons and Locke it was about credibility and reputation, for Smith it was much, much more. On this occasion both Smith, Burnell and his lawyer Tony Morton-Hooper flew in from London for personal appearances before the Court of Arbitration for Sport. Whilst the previous hearing at the ITU level in September took the form of a teleconference at which Smith had not been present, but had left it in the hands of Burnell, in this case Smith wanted to be there to clear his name for the last time.

Going into the hearing, both Burnell and Morton-Hooper stopped short of providing any details of a settlement that the USAT had apparently offered a few days in advance of the CAS hearing leaving Morton-Hooper to state that. "It would be inappropriate to comment on that," although he did not deny it happened and Burnell would later admit that Sissons had contacted him to try to arrange a deal.

According to Burnell, two days before they flew to New York, Sissons phoned him and tried to make a deal. In this conversation Burnell recalled that Sissons actually admitted that he didn't feel Smith had intentionally taken a banned substance but made the point clear that he had to do his job. On the one hand Burnell respected Sissons standpoint but on the other he felt that they had been over zealous in their attempts to prove him guilty, but nonetheless in order to prevent Spencer from having to go through yet another case Burnell was willing to hear what Sissons was willing to offer.

According to Burnell, Sissons made it clear that from his standpoint they had to have a ban, a years retrospective ban which meant he could continue to race and his only penalty would be the loss of winnings from Hawaii for fifth place which would work out at $5,000. Burnell knowing that if justice prevailed in the final hearing Smith would be found not guilty anyway, immediately refused to even consider the possibility ban, but agreed that if the case was dropped, and Smith was formally cleared of any intentional wrong doing Spencer would accept a warning telling him to be more careful of what he took in the future but would be entitled to keep the prize money he was owed from Hawaii. Sissons refused, they had to have a ban. They had a stalemate.

Sissons in dealing with Burnell after the second hearing must have been acutely aware that he was on a losing team. Two cases and twice

Smith had won, in both cases on different grounds. In fact, the case was so flawed that it was becoming an embarrassment, a highly publicized embarrassment which one could assume would have been the reason that Sissons had made the call, but now there seemed no way out. Burnell confirmed his stance as far as any deal was concerned. "I gave him a time limit, I said if you don't get back to me by eight o'clock on Thursday night, you can forget it....They never got back to me."

Both Smith and Morton-Hooper were confident going into the hearing to the point that Morton-Hooper had actually stated he was looking forward to the hearing, though whether Smith was looking forward to it as much is a matter of conjecture.

The USA Triathlon Federation and the ITU were represented by attorney Howard Jacobs and were well supported with an array of expert witnesses which included Dr. Elmo Alexander, a USOC physician who was in charge of the doping tests conducted at the race, Dr. Don Caitlin, Director of the UCLA lab that handled the sample and of course Mark Sissons, the Chair of ITU's Doping Committee was also present.

Having spent $45,000 in prosecuting Smith, USAT and would now incur further costs estimated to be in excess of $10,000 for expenses for the CAS hearing, but they would not make the same mistakes as they felt they made in the ITU hearing. They would have all the back up they felt they needed. On Smith's side his support was sparse by comparison, with just himself, his manager, Robert Burnell and his brief, Anthony Morton-Hooper, and whilst the outcome was not definite, one thing was known and that was that this hearing at least would be the last.

During arduous and drawn out hearing USAT and the ITU called three of their four planned expert witnesses. Unfortunately for USAT Dr. Larry Bowers, from the Indianapolis drug testing lab was unable to attend the hearing because of flight problems, nevertheless, the panel agreed that it would receive the declaration of Dr. Bowers as evidence, which it duly received. Strangely however, Steven Locke, USAT's Executive Director, had chosen not to attend the hearing, which led Burnell to conclude that Locke had been, "Sissons' puppet all the time," a viewpoint that Burnell had held since the outset.

Argument and counter argument were put forward by both parties to a panel of three, which comprised of US attorney Carolyn Witherspoon, a German lawyer Dr Christian Krahe and was chaired by

Canadian Judge, the Hon. Hugh Fraser. Burnell recalled being concerned at the conduct of one of the panel who in his opinion seemed to be taking little interest in the proceedings, but instead seemed more intent on looking out the window and tapping their pencil. Burnell a good judge of both character and situation felt this was not a good omen.

Of the most interesting of the cases put forward and by far the most revealing was the testimony given by Caitlin. "Caitlin was an honest guy," according to Burnell but at the same time Burnell felt him to be, "very arrogant." Caitlin put forward the scientific case according to the UCLA, which sounded credible until he admitted that there had been a mistake in terms of one of the calculations made by his laboratory.

Caitlin admitted that he checked the figures a week before the hearing and found the mistake, According to Burnell, Morton-Hooper asked Caitlin, 'Well why did you check the figures? What possessed you to check?' to which Caitlin claimed that this would be his normal procedure. But to Burnell checking through these calculations seemed a little unlikely given the magnitude of the task. It appeared in calculating the level of nandrolone in Smith's urine, one of the team in the laboratory had mistakenly put in the figure 8 when the correct figure should have been a 3. Caitlin confirmed this and testified that his lab mistakenly written the level of the nandrolone metabolite found in Smith's sample as 8 nanograms per milliliter when the actual level present was 3 nanograms per milliliter.

"He said in producing those figures there were two thousand calculations that none of the panel would understand," said Burnell later, " but we got him down to, why did someone mistake a three for an eight. Morton-Hooper said that surely this miscalculation would make other figures wrong and when Caitlin answered not necessarily Morton-Hooper looked astonished and said rather drolly. "Well when I was at school normally that would have made a tremendous difference."

Morton-Hooper blasted the overall credibility of the testing procedures and highlighted the typographical error that Dr. Caitlin testified that he had not found until the week prior to the CAS hearing, during his preparation for testimony. In addition he also challenged the chain of custody and the way in which the samples had been stored noting that the individual in charge of the test sample, the USOC's Dr. Elmore Alexander, had stored the sample bottles in his hotel room at room temperature in Kona from Saturday night to Monday morning when a courier took the sample from the Kona airport to the lab at UCLA. "We felt there was no immediate documentation verifying the whereabouts of the sample for a significant amount of time," said Morton-Hooper. "We felt it was unsatisfactory given the length of time that passed before he testified. Based on his recollection of events in October of 1998 we feel the documentation of the events of the chain of custody should be contemporaneous and complete."

In contrast to Morton-Hooper's approach, the case put by USAT continued to be based upon the argument that there was no threshold, or at least one did not exist at the time of the infraction for metabolites of nandrolone and hence they continued to argue that a positive remained a positive test under any circumstances. Irrespective of the fact that CAS had more recently used in its rulings a 2.5 ng/ml threshold, underneath which a positive test is not considered worthy of a penalty, Locke continued with their protest that the IOC does not specify a ratio, and that USAT and ITU are not only allowed, but obligated, to prosecute positives.

"They listened to all the evidence and when Caitlin admitted that mistake. It was basically it," Burnell recalled. Whether they really found the mistake then or whether they actually found the mistake earlier is open to conjecture. "Eighteen months later we found out Caitlin admitted to a mistake, now did they know that at the beginning?" Asked Burnell after the case. "Not only couldn't they afford to lose face but what about the court action afterwards for damaging Spencer's reputation. It might have been someone decided to bully that through and get it against him. Who knows?" In the end only those who decided to continue with the prosecutions would know the answer to that question.

Six days after the CAS hearing the news officially broke. Smith had been finally cleared of doping allegations by the Court of Arbitration for Sport, this for Smith was the final phase of the eighteen month battle to clear his name.

At this point in time, the CAS panel only revealed the result, and not the reasons behind its decision, which left those involved time to speculate as to the reasons behind the split decision, which went two to one in favour of Smith, but Burnell had his own opinions on that one, and all that mattered now to Smith was that for the third and final time he had proved himself innocent. "I've had to do that now at three separate hearings so it's been a difficult time for me and my family," Smith said immediately after the result.

On being informed of the verdict, Smith sent a simple e-mail to sponsor Met-Rx with two words. "We won!" News of Smith's win travelled faster than a T2 transition, with faxes, e-mails and phone calls congratulating Smith flooding in. The cloud had lifted, and those who had supported him throughout felt vindicated.

Whilst the Linda McCartney Pro Cycling Team who were still his current sponsor were the first to issue an official statement, the ITU and USAT were somewhat slower to respond with both Sissons and Locke declining to comment until they had seen a written report from CAS and could investigate the reasons behind the decision. But Burnell was not so shy and lambasted both the ITU and USAT stating that they wanted all the evidence to be heard when all the evidence was produced it just underlined all the errors and mistakes in the whole testing process.

Smith was understandably elated. "It's a fantastic feeling to have proved my innocence," he said in a statement from his training base in Denia, Spain. "Now I can get on with my life without carrying this huge burden on my shoulders. It's difficult to shake off the stigma of such an allegation but I've won all three rounds of my fight so I feel totally vindicated."

The final reasons for the findings of the panel were eventually issued and related to not just one of the issues raised on behalf of Smith but a multitude of problems relating to the prosecution and the procedures which had led to the alleged violation including the reliability of the tests, the appropriateness of a set allowable limit, clerical error and chain of custody.

The panel concluded that whilst the drug standards of the IOC only require proof of the presence of one metabolite beyond the 2 nanogram limit to ban an athlete for up to two years upon first offense there was little doubt that the testing procedures undertaken at the UCLA laboratory were not of sufficient standard to ensure the validity of their findings or why else would they themselves noted on their own documents, 'estimates only not to be used in litigation.'

The unreliability of the findings of the tests led the panel to state. "The Panel finds that the new information concerning the concentration levels calls into question the reliability of the tests. It is trite law to state that findings of doping infractions must be made or confirmed with the highest possible degree of certainty. Where doubt has been created with regard to the test procedure, such doubt must go to the benefit of the athlete. The Panel finds therefore, that a definitive case of doping has not been established against Spencer Smith. It is also apparent that Dr. Bowers followed the erroneous calculations contained in the UCLA testing analysis report to arrive at his conclusions."

Whilst the allowable limit determined by the IOC at that time remained at 2 nanograms per milliliter. The scientific 'gray zone' in which guilt was not clear-cut meant that until improved scientific evidence was forthcoming it would be not only inappropriate but immoral for an organization to take away the livelihood of an athlete on the grounds of such. To this point Morton-Hooper stated that he felt, "there was also a pressing need for further work in the science related to drug testing. There is too little known at the moment," and cited the lack of consistency between the Olympic laboratories and determinations as to what they regard as sufficient evidence to be in need of tightening up.

Whilst the credibility of testing procedures ultimately lay in the hands of individuals who can with all good intentions make mistakes, it undoubtedly had to throw into question the whole validity of such procedures and it should not be forgotten that according to Morton-Hooper. "Caitlin made a sworn affirmation of the accuracy of the test results long ago, and only corrected his testimony very late in the game."

Caitlin had revealed during questioning that he had recorded one of Smith's sample as containing 8ng of nandrolone, rather than the correct figure, which was 3ng. This was a simple clerical error, which nearly cost Smith not only his reputation but almost his entire career. One had to ask why it had not come to light in any of the other hearings. Whether it had been an honest oversight on the part of USAT or a deliberate attempt to try and cover up a mistake was a question that only they would ever know, either way it was a terrible and unforgivable mistake, which had turned Smith's world upside down for eighteen months.

"Caitlin knows his job, but he made a mistake," Smith said. "It's scary to think that these people think they are above making mistakes. He shrugged it off as if it was nothing, that it didn't matter, but it did matter. I don't give a damn how good he is in his field, this was my career, my reputation, at stake, of course it mattered."

Whilst the panel also broached the subject of chain of custody, which had been the focus of the BTA hearing in which custody protocols were argued to be totally inadequate to ensure the validity or the security of an athlete's sample. The CAS panel stopped short in issuing a ruling on chain of custody, stating only that, "given our finding that a definitive case of doping cannot be made out against the respondent, the panel need not rule on this aspect of the respondent's argument."

Away from the protocol and the science of the events surrounding the dismissal of the case, a major concern that manifested itself throughout Smith's ordeal was that whilst officials who have little scientific knowledge continue to try to base their arguments on their own subjective views irrespective of how politically led or scientifically misinformed they may be there are always going to be serious problems.

In Smith's case, Burnell, said Smith had been the subject of, "a witch-hunt by powerful government bodies," and went on to state that it was always going to be difficult for an athlete to prove their innocence when they're up against what he referred to as "powerful and politically motivated bodies who run the sport." ...The sport needed to be run he said by people who were, "above personal grudges," he concluded clearly unconvinced that this had been the case, "Whilst the rules are tough and rightly so, everybody should be entitled to a fair treatment when accused of something as serious as Spencer had."

Locke in response to the criticisms targeted at both him and the federation stated that the Smith case pointed to structural problems in enforcing drug cases in sport and argued that, "right now drug testing is being operated by the USOC under the auspices of the IOC, and their national governing body is given the responsibility of enforcing the verdicts of these tests by other agencies. If these agencies made an error in the protocols and weren't precise enough for CAS, we are left holding the bag and expected to proceed with due process on behalf of all the athletes who expect us to do our best to keep the playing field level and keep drugs out of the sport."

Locke made it clear that he was in favour of handing all drug testing over to an independent agency, as the IOC recently has done, "to handle all aspects of anti-doping enforcement," and added that if the CAS panel exonerated Smith because of protocol violations, "we need to sit down with the USOC and straighten out the procedures and protocols. We can't be having agencies like USA Triathlon or USA Boxing taking the brunt of the finger pointing. We are now placed in a position where we can't win. We are perceived as adverse to athletes, but if we don't pursue those who have showed positive on doping tests, then we are perceived as too easy on the offenders and lax in trying to preserve a level playing field. I think Mark Sissons and I did the right thing. They can call it a witch hunt, but we were simply trying to pursue the truth."

Bemoaning the spending of $55,000 to prosecute the case, Locke once again expressed frustration with the old process and looked forward to turning over testing and prosecution of doping offenses to an independent agency. "I am feeling a little bit handcuffed by a system that apparently makes it virtually impossible to prove positive tests."

If USAT and the ITU were to feel aggrieved at the result and the amount of money spent on prosecuting the case then the costs to them at that time would appear little in terms of the costs that they could incur should Smith consider further legal action against them. Whilst it was not the job of the CAS tribunal to award costs to either side, there was little doubt that the eighteen month saga had cost Smith dearly, not only in legal fees but also in lost earnings. Having lost the opportunity to compete for seven months at the beginning of the case and then losing the opportunity to compete in the 1999 ITU World Championships, the 1999 Ironman, and ultimately being forced to abandon the sport for cycling, Smith's earnings had significantly suffered. Whether Smith could resist the possibility of suing USAT for loss of earnings was something that at this point he would not be drawn on, though Morton-Hooper did comment that they would, "consider the consequences of this final decision."

"There were times before we won all three hearings that I almost forgot I was innocent," said Smith. "I'm out $100,000 (£65,000) in lawyer's fees but it was money well spent. Before the weight was lifted, I never realised how wearing it was. I might have been saying I wasn't thinking about it, but just by the act of saying that, you know you were." Smith had seen his annual income drop from £130,000 to a pittance, whilst he had continued to have to pay out significant sums to defend himself. One had to ask the question as Von Berg had asked earlier. If it had been a case against a less successful athlete with less money available to spend defending themselves, would they have been able to afford to prove their innocence?

Whilst little by way of comparison to his lost earnings over the eighteen months, Smith was at least now finally eligible to receive a cheque for his fifth place finish at the 1998 Ironman Triathlon World Championship and more importantly able to resume racing and training without the concerns of a further court case looming over his head, but now there was another question that was being asked. Would he return to triathlon or stay in professional cycling.

On hearing of the acquittal the non-triathlon press were quick to report on the possibility of Smith challenging for an Olympic place. David Powell of the Times suggested the likelihood of this outcome whilst the Independent carried a similar story in which Mike Rowbottom quoted from Burnell, who argued. "There's no good reason to keep him out of the Olympics and that's been part of the problem because he's a real contender, I'm sure there were plenty of people who wanted him out of the way."

Despite not racing for some considerable time, Smith was still ranked 88th in the ITU points table which meant he was in a good position to race off against the other GB hopefuls to get a place should he so wish, so the story seemed to have substance, which was then reinforced when the BTA confirmed that they would welcome him back with open arms. They had after all supported him throughout his cases and had cleared him once in their own tribunal, so when Greg Millet, the BTA's Performance Director, commented on Smith's case personally and opened the door for him to qualify, the pro Smith quarter looked hopefully towards the possibility of him racing triathlon again, in the three selection races which were already on the calendar.

Whilst Simon Lessing and Andrew Johns were already automatic qualifiers with their top twenty five rankings, Smith was entitled to fight it out for the third slot along with any of the other British athletes who were ranked in the top ten, who at this time it potentially included Tim Don, Marc Jenkins, Richard Allen, Richard Stannard and Craig Ball.

All that Smith had to do was remain in the top 100 and take up a BTA membership, which he had declined to do earlier in the season due to his change to cycling. "It is obviously of major importance for the GB Olympic squad ... I still need to speak with the British Olympic Association to ensure few details, but Spencer is more than welcomed in the trials." Millett confirmed.

Whilst it hadn't taken long for the rumours linking Smith to the

Olympics to start, nor did it take long for Smith to squash those rumours, with him quickly refuting the claims that he would be challenging for a place in Sydney. Despite the hopes that Smith would return to triathlon, Smith confirmed that he still had a few things to sort out before he would decide on any course of action, and being that he was presently contracted to race for the Linda McCartney Cycling Team, Smith was by no means sure that he would return to triathlon, at least not in the short term.

He made it clear that a return to triathlon was not an immediate objective, stating. "I am focused on cycling and if I go to the Olympics, it will be for cycling," but at the same time was careful to not dismiss any possible options and went on to establish that he had still retained his love for triathlon stating. "I am not closing the door to triathlon. I still have my demons that need to be put rest with the Big Island."

Hawaii 1998. Celebrations followed by heartache.

Spencer Smith is Number One! World Championships 1994

TRANSITIONS FIFTEEN & SIXTEEN
Return to Triathlon and Return to the Big Island

Spencer now had had time to think about his future with the last of the court cases over. His career was his own rather than left in the hands of the lawyers and the federations and by mid April almost a month to the day after his final hearing Smith confirmed that he had decided he would after all be returning to triathlon, and in a press release issued by the Linda McCartney Pro Cycling Team his return to triathlon was formally confirmed. The press release read in part as follows:

21st April 2000 Lynda McCartney Press Release:
Smith quits cycling for triathlon return

Spencer Smith of the Linda McCartney Pro Cycling Team is retracing his steps to focus his career on the Ironman Triathlon discipline. Staying within the Linda McCartney umbrella, Spencer will cut short his road-racing programme and build toward a new big target, the Hawaii Ironman.

"The racing has been excellent so far this year," said Spencer. "I had a really good start in Malaysia at the Tour of Langkawi, then it was back to Europe. To be honest, I've found the racing in Europe unbelievably hard, and I've struggled at times, which I fully expected. I still think I can make it to the top, but it's going to take a year or maybe even two before I'm at the sort of level I need to reach to compete."

A move back to triathlon gave the Linda McCartney foods brand an opportunity to broaden their sponsorship platform with them being represented at the peak of two international sports.

In support of the faith that the team had put in him Smith went on the praise those who had stood by him saying, "I can't stress enough how brilliant the team and the whole McCartney organization have been to me, Julian Clarke and Sean Yates stuck their necks out for me, and I'm desperate to repay their faith. I'm so pleased that they want me to stay within the Linda McCartney setup. Also, the overwhelming support I received from family, friends, athletes and followers within the triathlon world was astounding and had an immeasurable impact on my decision to return to triathlon."

Yates having got to know Smith throughout the season praised his professionalism stating, "Spencer is one of the best trainers I've ever seen in the sport. His technique and his endurance and recovery are all excellent. His motivation and focus can't fail to impress anybody who meets him, and in some ways, that's where this change of plan has come about, Spencer is used to being the best in the world, and he's impatient to get to the top. He knows it's going to take a long while to do that in cycling, and he knows that success in triathlon is well within his grasp."

Apart from the McCartney release Smith also personally confirmed his return from his second home in Spain, the prodigal son was definitely returning primarily because it seemed that the lure of the Big Island was too much to bear, but a return to Hawaii gave him only six months of preparation.

Some time later Smith would admit that he had perhaps expected too much of himself when he first started with the team stating. "I knew that cycling is a very, very difficult sport. I knew it would take at least a couple of years for me to reach the top, and I'm not even sure that I would have achieved that. The guys in cycling are champions for a reason. Not just because they are strong and know the tactics, but they have experience. I knew it would have taken a good two seasons for me to find my feet and feel confident."

Whilst his change of direction was to some degree a disappointment to his cycling teammates, Smith clearly had the full support of the Linda McCartney Cycling Team management, which had signed him only four months earlier and they confirmed that they too were pleased to have him on board.

For the McCartney Team, Smith was working out to be just another domestique on its ten man squad and despite a successful pro cycling debut in Langkawi, once the team and the season turned to the European events, Smith had in truth found himself struggling to keep up, and whilst Smith had stated, "It's not that cycling wasn't working for me. The team has been good to me there are absolutely no problems there," there was little doubt that cycling hadn't brought him the kind of results that he was accustomed to, a point demonstrated when he admitted. "When you've been winning races as I was doing in triathlon, you become impatient when you don't win. That's what makes a champion, I suppose the patience." Smith clearly hadn't got the patience and wanted to go back to being a winner not just a competitor.

Smith claimed that he felt that he had needed to, "step away," from triathlon for a few months to fully appreciate it how much he loved the sport. In a sport which is as tough as professional cycle racing Smith could not have been expected to make his mark in a short period of time and perhaps felt that he was in cycling terms a small fish in a big pond, especially when it came to racing on the continent, but he felt more at home in the world of triathlon.

One of the areas he admitted to missing was the supporters and the people who had been with him throughout his career. "The people are amazing." Smith had said. "I missed that. I needed the time away to realize that. Nearly every day since the CAS ruling, I'd get some e-mails from triathletes I don't even know, saying we miss you and the things you did in triathlon. It was a super feeling to realize the number of people who are actually interested in what and how I am doing. That's what's bringing me back."

Smith however had learnt a great deal in the professional ranks, not least, the importance of being able to race on smaller gears. "I think it has helped me to become a little less prone to push big gears all the time, which will be helpful when I start the run, especially at Ironman," he admitted, which was something Bill Black was pleased to hear, all be it nine years later than he wanted.

But since he had concentrated solely on the bike for the last few months, some problems were sure to arise in returning to swimming and running training, but Smith did not seem overly concerned, stating. "I don't think it has done any harm, let's put it that way. It would be nice to stay at the level of fitness on the bike that I have achieved through my cycling, but I have to be realistic. I believe it will drop due to the fact that I have two other disciplines to work on again, and as we all know, the race does not end on the bike."

Whilst many may have thought the return to triathlon as being an obvious move for Smith, Smith had been far from convinced about his return. Only a year earlier Smith had felt betrayed by the politics of the sport, despite the supporters who had stuck by him, but he had not been aware of the extent of the feeling towards him. The subsequent manifest demonstration of support following his acquittal had however prompted him to reevaluate his situation. "The decision did take some time. It was not something I could take lightly, but the amount of e-mails and faxes I received was incredible. It made me realize how many people actually enjoyed watching me race. That for me was one of the major issues that made me return. I think with everything that has happened to me over the past year and a half, taking a rest from the sport has allowed me to regain my passion. I believe that a lot of that had been drained away from me."

Smith was obviously feeling able to put it all behind him and start afresh with a positivism, which he had not felt for some time. "I am a guy who doesn't have a lot of talent compared to some people. But when I race, I race with two things, firstly heart and secondly passion. If either of these ingredients are missing, I am not being true to myself or the people I support. I feel I have both of these ingredients back."

At the time Smith confirmed that his return to triathlon would be solely Ironman orientated, and that he had no real interest in pursuing the Olympic triathlon and whilst officially he was in a position to statistically secure a place, he now felt that in practical terms his world ranking had fallen too far for him to be eligible, given the British Triathlon Association's guidelines for qualifying. "I'd be kidding to say I was never interested, but I certainly have lost more interest. The sport, for me is not about the Olympics, it's about the three disciplines. I hope the British team wins gold in Sydney, but it's not really my target," explained Spencer. "I'm aiming for Ironman that's the true test of who is the best all-round athlete in the world in my book."

But for Smith the return to triathlon was going to be a long slog, he hadn't ran or swam since January and the muscles in his upper body had deteriorated significantly. "I'm excited to get back on the road and in the pool," he said. "I'll just pick up and improve from where I left off."

Since turning from triathlon to cycling Smith had found himself spending more time in Europe, but his return to triathlon meant that he could return to his adopted American home in California where he could reunite with both his coach Paul Huddle who had replaced Mick Gillingham's short reign and the host of triathletes who had stood by him since the 1998 Hawaii Ironman.

Hawaii was definitely back on the cards if he could secure a wildcard, and generously Smith stated that he hoped the WTC could give him one. For an athlete who had been falsely accused in a year when he came 5th it seemed the least the WTC could do.

"In the future, I will be doing an Ironman schedule, two or three a year, though three may be a lot." Smith admitted clearly excited about returning to the sport.

Whilst three Ironman events would be a heavy load in terms of Ironman distance, as a professional athlete it was obvious that he would need to earn a living and as such would be forced to race some shorter events if only to bring in some money in terms of appearance money and winnings. This was a point that Smith recognized, but despite the contrast in training needs Smith clearly felt that he could still find enough speed in his legs to do well in the shorter Olympic distance races as well, confirming however that such races would only act as preparation for a mostly Ironman oriented schedule.

Despite the transfer back to triathlon, Burnell and Smith were happy with Julian Clarke's proposition to remain on the McCartney books and bearing in mind what Spencer had just been through, their image which was squeaky clean, was an image that they both thought would help Spencer recoup some credibility among those who still doubted his innocence over the drugs accusations.

To this end, Clarke had informed Burnell that they would talk sponsorship and sort out an appropriate contract, and initially Burnell was willing to take him at his word, but despite continued efforts on the part of Burnell to come to some arrangement the discussions never materialized and he became increasingly concerned at the allusiveness of Clarke when it came to money, especially as there remained an unresolved issue regarding the money that Clarke already owed Smith as a result of him racing for the cycling team, which included, wages and expenses and came to about four thousand pounds.

"It was murder getting it out of him," recalled Burnell who as a manager was a bit sharper than the average Joe. Years of being involved in the second hand car business, not only made Burnell a good negotiator but also made him a good judge of people, "you know when they're buying and you know when they're lying," Burnell later said, and he wasn't convinced by the patter. "I told Spencer this sponsorship deal ain't gonna come off with this guy, in my honest opinion I thought it was all bollocks. If I can't get four grand out of him how the hell am I gonna get more. I went along with it for a while but it got increasingly clear that he wasn't going to pay us this four grand that he owed, so I started legal proceedings and threatened to go to the papers. To someone like Julian that must have had bigger problems that he was trying to keep under I think he must have decided it was easier to pay three or four grand than what he owed the others. That we now know. In the end I said. Fuck me Julian I think you're a nokker. I had him sussed. My job was to get this money off him and I got it off him. It's a shame. It would have been a nice partnership. Linda McCartney and us."

So despite the money eventually being paid, all the talk of Linda McCartney continuing with their sponsorship did not work out in the end. "It was obvious that he (Spencer) wasn't happy with cycling, and I think really truly Julian knew what was coming up," said Burnell, "The break up was mutual."

Referring to Julian Clarke, Burnell said. "He wanted to ride on the coat tails of Spencer. Use him. The PR bit and get in the paper, but he didn't want to pay for it." But despite being unwilling or unable to pay for it the Linda McCartney Team continued to race the European circuit and one month later on Saturday 13th May, Smith who had always wanted to ride one of the major tours, must have had at least some misgivings about not continuing to ride for the McCartney team as his former teammates from the Linda McCartney squad paraded themselves to the cycling fanatics of Italy at the start of the millennium Giro d'Italia.

13th May 2000 Tour of Italy

This was definitely a case of the vegetarian message being taken to the heart of the land of the Italian unbelievers in terms of the vegetarians venturing in to the carnivore's den, and was as much of a coup for their vegetarian food sponsors as it was for the team themselves. While the Gazzetta dello Sport ran the headlines, 'Niente carne, siamo Inglesi' 'No meat, we're English.' The real news was that the Linda McCartney Team, had become the first ever British based team to start the Giro, since it was launched in 1909.

The Beatle connection and the vegetarian eating habits of the riders were things that the Italian media couldn't help but get its teeth into with this strange British eccentricity a major talking point in a velo passionate and carnivorous country, so much so that a breakdown of what the riders would eat was actually profiled in La Gazetta.

Whilst the team had generated a lot of publicity, Yates was keenly aware that this was just based on novelty value and he was determined to see his team go on to justify their invitation to the race in place of some other extremely capable teams that had been overlooked by the promoters. At the same time he also recognized that six of his riders were, "going into the unknown," with only three of them ever having ridden the Giro before and had made it clear that one of his major objectives was to get as many of his team to the finish. With Richard and Sciandri providing the bulk of experience having won six stages in the Giro between them over their careers the responsibility weighed heavily on their shoulders.

Having met the Pope the day before, along with all the other riders, the McCartney team then found themselves racing against the major players in the cycling world including teams such as Mapei who had budgets over five times the size of McCartney's alleged paltry £1million and a squad of over thirty five riders to select from as opposed to their squad of only nine which was the number needed to even get to the start line in the Giro.

Whilst the fact of being limited to a vegetarian diet as such drew no major concerns for the team, Yates did stress his concerns over the ability of the Italian chefs to prepare anything that resembled a decent vegetarian meal, arguing that in his opinion 99.9% of chefs didn't know how to make a decent veggie meal, with the carnivorous French being the worst.

But if Yates was to be concerned over their performance and the possible problems of getting a proper diet on the tour, Such worries vanished in a matter of days when their the young twenty five year old Australian rider David McKenzie decked out in the McCartney colours made a heroic lone escape after only eleven miles of a hundred and thirteen mile course and headed for victory on the seventh stage whilst the peleton who had allowed him at one point more than twelve minute lead, were left to fight it out for the minor placings a mere fifty one seconds later. To add to the vegetarian's celebrations, McKenzie's win was followed the next day by Sciandri taking second in the longest stage of the race, finishing a mere six seconds behind Axel Merckx, son of the great Eddy Merckx.

For Smith who would have undoubtedly found himself on the starting lineup for the team had he remained with the McCartney team as opposed to returning to triathlon, the success in the Giro unquestionably would have brought the mixed emotions of pleasure at seeing his former teammates doing so well and the feeling of, what if? Relating to what he may have achieved had he remained in the sport of cycling.

The McCartney team in those two stages alone had justified their invitation and marked major step towards the teams ultimate goal of securing a place in the Tour de France in the next two years, which had once been a lifelong dream of Smith, a dream that he had now clearly put behind him.

Whilst the euphoria of the successes of the team reverberated through the British cycling media and dreams and plans were being hatched as to the future goals of the team, unfortunately the seeds of failure had already been sewn within the team some time earlier and this would be acknowledged as the highest point in the teams' short life when Burnell's concerns over the Linda McCartney Team's financial standing would soon be proven.

Whilst the McCartney team had been racing the Giro, Smith had been getting back into the running and the swimming, but having only started training in early May he was finding it tough. With Hawaii on his mind he knew he could not and he knew he must not ease up. "Believe me, it is very, very hard at the moment," Smith had said, "but time is on my side."

He had moved back to Carlsbad, and had a number of races planned none of which would take him too far away from home. His programme would start with the San Diego International Triathlon, and would include Carlsbad Triathlon on July 8th, Mrs. T's Chicago Triathlon on August 27th and the Los Angeles Triathlon on September 10th. His season would then conclude on October 14th in the only one that really mattered. The Hawaii Ironman.

With the McCartney deal not working out Smith's sponsors returned to him quickly with nearly all the same sponsors that he had before he quit triathlon for cycling. Speedo (apparel), Saucony (shoes), Met-Rx (nutrition), Zipp (wheels) and Rudy Project (helmet and shades) all stuck by him with the exception of a bike sponsor, but it didn't take long before that one was sorted out courtesy of Ian Whittingham at Sigma.

The next contact Whittingham had with Smith was when he'd finished with McCartney and was staying in England for a few days before he was heading back to America. "Spencer popped into the shop because Duncan Rolley (of Speedo) had arranged that he come in and pick up some bike clothing from us, because he didn't want to wear his McCartney gear any more," recalled Whittingham.

As it happened, while he was there, Sigma were in the throws of building their own triathlon team for the forthcoming season, a team that in the previous year had included Tim Don, Andrew Johns and Richard Allen among others and it looked like they were angling for a pretty strong squad for 2000 as well. "One of the team bikes was sat at the front of the shop and Spencer seemed quite keen on it as he looked it over. I just said to him, what are you going to do, ride Principia for the rest of the year? I was a bit surprised when he said had no deal and he had to sort himself out a bike sponsor and just before he left I said hey Spence I'd be really keen to work with you if you don't find anything else."

Whilst Whittingham at the time was the first to admit that he didn't think for one minute that they would be in a position to compete with the likes of the major bike manufacturers like Specialized, Cannondale, Principia and Quintana Roo he thought he may as well throw his hat in the ring. As Smith walked out the door he reiterated his offer. "If you are interested we are too," to which Smith replied that he would call him.

A couple of days later, before he returned to the States Smith duly made the call as promised and told them he was interested, and would contact them to sort out a deal when he got back to the US, and within a week, Smith and Whittingham had agreed a package for the last six months of 2000, which would take into account the Hawaii Ironman, so long as he was given permission to race by the WTC. Amazingly, Sigma Sports, the London bike shop that had sponsored him back in 1993 would now return as his bike sponsor.

Sigma had sole distribution rights in the UK for an Italian frame builder who in the past had built frames for Chris Boardman, Fondriest, Jallabert, Credit Agricole and the Lampre Team among others, and whilst normally they would have built a frame especially to fit Smith, given the time available to them the option of building a frame specific to his measurements was not possible and he would end up riding an off the peg bike.

Having spent most of that year racing in the cycling peleton, Smith had decided he would ride a standard road bike with a 74 degree angle, nothing flash, nothing steep angled which would only be modified for Hawaii by the adding of some tri bars. "We were delighted and had the whole thing done and shipped over to America within two or three weeks," recalled Whittingham, noting that Smith also appeared to be happy with the deal.

There had been the question of whether he would have to qualify for the 2000 Hawaii, as he hadn't raced in 1999 given the cloud of the doping hearings, but on June 5th, the World Triathlon Corp.'s Media Liaison officer confirmed Smith as an official competitor, having had his application accepted on the grounds that anyone finishing in the top fifteen automatically qualifies for the next year's race, and whilst he had not raced in 1999 his fifth-place finish in 1998 which would have qualified him for last year's race, was rolled over to 2000.

Some triathlon observers thought that, once vindicated of any doping charges, that Smith might have a good case to sue the WTC for essentially keeping him from racing Hawaii in 1999. However, Smith said that he has always felt kindly toward the Hawaiian Ironman, and that suing for damages was never an option. "I was feeling unfulfilled because I haven't yet become the complete and utter champion without winning the Hawaii Ironman. For me, personally, that was always there." Smith had said. "I was never going to sue Hawaii, and that was never our intention at all, we never wanted to close any doors in triathlon, that's for sure. I never hated this sport. I never felt this sport was terrible for the way I was treated."

Given that the only people who had been threatened with legal action following the final CAS hearing had been Julian Clarke at Linda McCartney it would seem strange that one of the organizations who had been supportive of him came closest to being sued by his manager for such a small sum of money, but Burnell was to eventually be proved a good judge of character when some months later the whole team would collapse owing thousands of pounds to its staff.

Whilst for Smith it may have been a disappointment in some ways that he was no longer racing for the team unfortunately the celebrations of the team in May 2000 would turn to anguish and tears almost exactly eight months later to the day at the end of January 2001, when on returning from the Tour Down Under in Australia, the riders arrived in London for the team presentation, scheduled to take place in Trafalgar Square, only to be told that Britain's only professional team was going to fold.

Whilst the founder of the team, Julian Clarke was conspicuous by his absence, Sciandri and Yates issued a statement of intention to form a new management structure in an attempt to save the thirty plus jobs at stake and the careers of the riders but with no money in the pot, some of the riders held out little hope and were already undertaking negotiations with other teams.

It seemed that Clarke had been hoping that new sponsors would be attracted by the McCartney name, but apparently the sponsors' names that appeared on the team jersey (apart from the McCartney sponsor) which included the wine maker Jacob's Creek and the British car company Jaguar, either paid little in the way of sponsorship to the team, or in the case of Jaguar, knew nothing about the team what so ever. It seemed that the team were facing debts of £1 million after funds anticipated by Clarke failed to materialize. In the end telephone call from Yates and Sciandri to ex Beatle, Sir Paul McCartney ended any remaining hopes of survival for the team.

Of all the riders, Sciandri was hit the hardest financially stating that he was owed £175,000 in wages from last year by OC Racing, run by the team's former proprietor Julian Clarke and whilst Clarke blamed the termination of the team on what he called, "the low level of support by the team's main named sponsor," rumours were that the money had never been there in the first place. It later came out that the deal, with Jaguar Cars, had never been finalised even though their name and logo had featured prominently on the team jersey, whilst the deal with Jacob's Creek, was evidently only made on the basis that money might be paid if the sponsor was happy with the team. Together, the two sponsors were expected to supply the majority of the £2.5million budget needed for the year but only a fraction of that income ever materialized so it appeared that Spencer's manager Burnell had been right all along about the financial standing of the team.

A matter of weeks later Sciandri was still training for six hours a day in a plain jersey, (highly reminiscent of Smith's return to a plane jersey when he left the team previously) in the vain hope of picking up a new contract. Despite scratching around for a team Sciandri knew that at the start of the season most teams would have already contracted a full complement of riders and that his chances of getting a contract that justified his talents was slim. And at thirty three years old he was concerned as to whether he would ever compete again. At the same time, the former British champion Mathew Stephens who had won the stage in Langkawi when Smith had been racing with him, was selling his house and probably considering a return to stacking shelves in

Marks and Spencer. Whilst the iconic cycling legend Sean Yates had found work on a building site.

The collapse of the team had been devastating leaving thirteen of the nineteen team mates out of work. Sciandri was bitter about what had happened to them and felt that Clarke had let them down by not being honest about the problems. It was a sad end to a dream that Smith had fortunately got out of before the rot set in.

But all this was not to happen until three months after Smith's second Hawaii and in the mean time Smith had a job on his hands getting ready for the big one with all races prior to Hawaii designated just for preparation. Acutely aware that whilst his cycling fitness was at an optimum, his swimming and running were still way behind what he knew he would have to achieve if he was going to perform well on the Big Island. He had made it clear that he would not be putting any pressure on himself to get any good results on the way, he stated if he did then great, but all other events would be a means to an end, but at least now Smith was beginning to feel good mentally which as he put it, was the one thing that had, "not been right for some time."

By way of getting himself back into the fray Smith returned to triathlon quietly in San Diego on the 24th June, but there was little doubt that most people, spectators and athletes were pleased to see Spencer back on the triathlon circuit. The slightly unusual distance of one kilometer swim, thirty kilometer bike and ten kilometer run, which involved around 1,200 competitors, gave Smith the opportunity to race in front of an adopted San Diego home crowd who were keen to see his return. With a strong field the likelihood of Smith picking up the win was slim and whilst Smith was valiant in his efforts the time out of the sport head left him rusty, and instead of a triumphant return, the crowd saw twenty seven year old, Chris McCormack take the honors and the first prize, but it was undoubtedly Smith who got the biggest standing ovation of the race when he crossed the line in third just behind Greg Bennett.

Whilst Smith had a lot to prove with Hawaii not so far away, McCormack also had a lot to prove having been left off the Australian Olympic team and having been unbeatable ever since. Making this win his fifth in a row McCormack admitted he was racing on anger, but despite his feelings towards his non selection he was pleased to be racing up against Smith again. "It was a pretty historic race, having Spencer back," McCormack said. "I was looking forward to racing him." Unfortunately for both of them, the opportunity to race against each other in Sydney would never materialize.

For Smith, who admitted he had found the race tough, it was his first race since August and his transitions were a little slower than his customary frenetic pace, and whilst finishing third behind McCormack and Bennett would have to do for now it was seen by others as a significant accomplishment given the fact that he had only had five weeks of training under his belt having been out of triathlon for nearly a year.

The result didn't seem to hold much concern with Smith who made it clear about his objectives after the race saying. "It's important to be realistic and use this as a preparation for the Ironman," and as his mum Barb looked on as he crossed the line, with total faith that he would come back stronger than ever, Smith grinned as if to say he would make it in the end, and Spencer had never been one to let his family down.

Whilst Smith continued his Hawaii preparation in the States, on July 13th 2000, the British Triathlon Association announced the final three athletes to make up the six strong team who would be competing for Great Britain in the Olympics. Spencer was already destined to not be among them, but many a supporter dwelled on how different things could have been.

Following successes at both Windsor and the European Championships Andrew Johns and now Tim Don were set to join Simon Lessing on the starting line in Sydney. Greg Millet Performance Director of the BTA who had previously discussed the possibility of Smith working towards the Olympics following the final CAS acquittal stated that he was, "confident that Great Britain is taking the best team for the first appearance on the Olympic scene," and emphasized that all of the athletes selected were capable of, "an outstanding achievement." For the supporters of Smith and perhaps for Smith himself, it was a disappointment that he would not be racing. Smith however was solid in his support for the British squad and if it was inevitable that he would be excluded from the final lineup, he made it clear he bore no ill will towards them, stating, "I hope the team wins gold."

27th August 2000 Mrs. T's Triathlon, Chicago, USA

Two weeks before Olympic Triathlon would be staged as the opening event for the 2000 Sydney Olympics, Smith would be racing again in Chicago in Mrs. T's and even if not for a gold medal then at least the pay packet looked good. Chicago, which had hosted this major US triathlon event for seventeen years had for the second year in a row been selected to host the USA Triathlon Pro National Championship and with a $38,000 prize purse for the top ten finishers, offering $5,000 as the first prize, $3,700 for second place and $2,900 for third it was sure to be hotly contested.

Smith remained resolute that the result in this race was not his major concern but given the size and the quality of the field coupled with the prize purse and the USAT National Title it was clearly a good scalp for Spencer to take and would help him to compare his progress with some of the other major pro's.

Involved right from the outset, Smith performed well throughout the three disciplines and seemed comfortable in his performance and at the end of the day, involving the standard 1.5km swim, 40km bike and 10km run, he seemed happy to accept third place with Australian Chris McCormack, taking the first prize yet again in a time of 1:49:21 followed closely by Conrad Stoltz in 1:50:05. Smith's third place saw him pick up a $2,900 pay packet for his 1:50:19 finish, and interestingly, saw him pip Richard Allen who was the reserve for the GB Olympic squad, to the line, when he came home just behind Smith in a time of 1:50:58 to take fourth place. If nothing else this signified to Smith that he was definitely on his way back to form.

Whilst the American triathlon circuit continued and Smith was still preparing for Hawaii, the eyes of the rest of the world were looking towards Sydney and the 2000 Olympics. Under other circumstances Smith may have been there but now the possibility of bringing home medals to Great Britain was left in the hands of three others. His old adversary, Simon Lessing being the favourite to bring home the gold, Andrew Johns, who remained a good medal contender and Tim Don, who was the outside chance.

Unfortunately for Don, early preparation had not gone too well in the long term, when in March, he had incurred a loss of six weeks of training following a fall from his bike during a training ride in South Africa which had necessitated the insertion of a titanium pin in his hand, making it hard for him to regain the sort of flexibility in his wrists that is vital to a swimmer, but now he was there to give it his all.

As the media got more exited about the race so the stories began to flood in with new angles being used to gain column inches and television time. One interesting story covered by a number of journalists was the danger of shark attack. With the race taking place in Sydney Harbour a number of concerns had been raised with regard to the safety of the athletes, this was Australia after all and according to many of the less informed British and European journalists it was muted that there was a distinct possibility of a shark attack on the swimming leg. In fact the last fatal shark attack had been in middle harbour in 1963 and there had not been a shark attack in the inner harbour during the cooler periods in the last two hundred and eight years, and it was now September, and with the water temperature said to be 16C (61F) the only damage that was likely to occur to the athletes appeared to be the danger of the cold taking their breath away when they dived off the pontoon. Still better the breath than a leg.

Nevertheless following a rare attack in February 1998 the Sydney organising committee's programme manager for environment had arranged for a report to be compiled if only to allay the fears of the federations. The report produced by biologists and shark experts concluded the chance of an attack in Sydney Harbour was, "infinitesimally small." A more realistic concern however was jellyfish, a point that US triathlete Hunter Kemper was able to attest to having been stung on the neck during a practice swim though it was so mild he had thought it was simply that his wetsuit was chafing his skin. Fears of sharks and jelly fish duly dispelled the real concerns that the British trio had were those of their own personal performances, with the most pressure undoubtedly focused on Lessing who some already had down as being the outright winner come what ever.

When Lessing took his place on the pontoon at Sydney, he would become the first South African Olympian to represent Britain since Zola Budd in 1984, and if all went to form, he would end the day as Britain's first gold medallist of the millennium. Despite his background Britain would have every right to celebrate the win even if Lessing had originated from South Africa, since unlike Budd, his allegiance to Great Britain had been long term and over time he had proved his racing under the Union Jack to be much more than an allegiance of convenience. Having claimed a record five ITU World Titles under the British flag, four at Olympic distance in 1992, 1995, 1996 and 1998 and one at long distance in 1995, Lessing had now regained the option to race under South African colours given the political changes in his birthplace, but had steadfastly remained with his adopted country. "I feel British, I have never considered going back to South Africa," he said when asked about his allegiances just before the Sydney games unfolded.

In fact over the previous few months Lessing had begun to spend more time in the UK, partly due to his attempt to fine tune his Olympic preparations with the elite performance coaches put in place by the BTA. A decision that had resulted in a full scale move from France to the UK, which had seen him residing in Bath which enabled him to train at the centre of excellence based at the University where some of the best triathlon support and facilities in the country could be found.

Whilst he may have felt British, the pressure on his shoulders due to the British public's expectations was immense and undoubtedly something that he could do without, but nonetheless, Lessing, an intensely self assured, private and some would argue isolated individual claimed that he was not permitting the pressure of the nation to compound the stress he was already feeling. The twenty nine year old had been there seen it and got the t-shirt to prove it. Well almost but the Olympics was surely different. "I've been in the sport for a long time and my main motivation is to myself," he said. "In the past I've felt I've been racing for sponsors, for other people, but now I'm just trying to satisfy my own expectations."

Also flying an adopted British flag was Andrew Johns, the overall winner of the 1999 ITU World Cup series, who though born in Peterborough spent most of his life in Australia. Unlike Lessing, Johns had switched allegiance to Britain only three years previous after failing to get the support of Australian triathlon authorities and whilst still strongly supported by the British public, this acceptance of Johns probably had more to do with his openness and friendliness to them, and the fact that he raced in the UK considerably more than Lessing. Whilst Lessing was admired and acknowledged, Johns for many was actually more acutely part and parcel of the British feeling.

Johns at the time perhaps recognised his position within the GB squad was more of convenience than through a heart felt want to be considered British, a point that seemed to be demonstrated when he stated. "I'm incredibly grateful for the opportunity and support I've been given. It would be great if I could give something back to the sport in Britain by winning a medal," There was a very strong likelihood that Johns would do just that and whilst the abundance of media attention was focused on Lessing, he was keenly aware that he was also one of the outstanding favourites for the gold medal.

Apart from Johns acknowledging his own capabilities he was also a keen supporter and teammate of the third member of the squad, the only born and bred British athlete of the three, Tim Don. Johns and Don were very close friends and Johns was highly complementary about the youngest member of the team. "Tim, is a young guy who is probably the most outstanding talent to come through the junior ranks in triathlon ever. He is improving rapidly and could very well be right up there in Sydney," Johns had said a week out from the race, and whilst the sentiments were honest, in truth Don would be considered to have done well if he achieved top ten.

A well loved British athlete who come up through the same west London club as Smith had, Don raced in the UK constantly through the season with a gregarious nature and a fun loving outlook that was contagious, and since Smith's departure to San Diego, Don was rapidly becoming the new Spencer Smith, in that he was becoming the nation's favourite and given his unreserved nature, Don was sure to enjoy the event irrespective of the outcome all be it that he was arguably too inexperienced to cause a major upset. Whilst Johns had claimed there was a definite possibility that the team could come away with all the medals, it was probably said as more of a motivational and supportive boost to Don's preparation than any form of realistic prediction.

Away from the specifics of triathlon, as if the normal pressures of competing in an Olympics weren't enough, Britain's top contenders were not only competing for medals but also aware in many cases that they were also fighting to secure the financial future of their sports. UK Sport, which has responsibility for distributing funds to the sports federations in the UK, had warned that upon the conclusion of the 2000 Olympics, the amount of money it had to distribute would be expected to fall by nearly a third before the 2004 Games in Athens, and that only the most successful sports would continue to receive funding after Sydney. Whilst a total of £18.6m had been awarded to twenty four Olympic sports for 2000-2001, because of the lottery's falling ticket sales that normally filled up the coffers, that figure was predicted to fall to £16.4m for 2001 and £14m by the period 2004-2005.

With the whole programme of funding based upon performance, the biggest losers would be the sports that did not win Olympic medals and after Sydney, UK sport explained that they would be left no choice but to prioritise which sports would continue to receive funding. This course of action meant that the pressure on athletes like Lessing, who was the favourite to win the triathlon gold medal in Sydney, was increased. If he failed to live up to his the expectations of getting gold the consequences could be catastrophic for the BTA, a federation reliant almost totally on their annual Lottery hand-out of £500,000 to fund their development and administration programmes.

The Lottery had made enormous strides in bringing Great Britain on to a level playing field with other countries who were better funded and even though they did not want to add to the pressures on their athletes even Greg Millet, the BTA's performance director admitted they were, "quite scared how this could affect us."

With the BTA only starting to receive funding two years previously, it was argued that this had not been long enough to ensure they got things right at the first attempt and the concerns that a loss of funding would affect the long-term success of its athletes remained paramount in the minds of the BTA executive and officials. Even if Lessing had broad shoulders to carry the weight of the Olympic hopes on, they would surely have to grow to take on a little more pressure.

But if the future funding was initially of the topic of conversation at the squad's training camp on the east coast of Australia, this soon changed with the news that Johns had contracted a cold. Final preparations had gone well for both Lessing and Don but for Johns it was quite a different story. Whether it was the change of climate or just bad luck Johns had picked up a cold, which was sure to hamper his performance and the finals were now only a matter of days away.

17th September 2000 Olympic Games, Sydney, Australia

As the fifty two competitors plunged together into the water of the pontoon beside the Opera House there was little doubt that the eyes of the world were seeking out Lessing. Lessing began the race exactly as he had intended, taking a good early position in the swim to eventually emerge from the water in second place in a time of seventeen minutes and eighteen seconds, a mere six seconds behind Hamish Carter, the Kiwi who was determined to play a major role on what was so nearly home soil, whilst Tim Don's exit from the water in seventh place amongst a throng of other swimmers, just twenty seconds down on Lessing, demonstrated that the injury to his wrist incurred in South Africa was standing up to the Olympic test.

As Lessing, Carter, Craig Walton and the Swedish born Joachim Willen exited the swim to the transition and onto the bike, so Carter signaled to the others to come through and share the workload in an attempt to maintain and extend upon their slender lead and instigate a break away from the bunch, but the other riders were unwilling to commit so early in the race and instead sat in, waiting for the following twenty strong bunch to make contact with them. Even Walton, a swim, bike specialist looked unwilling at this stage to go it alone, especially when, the considered greatest challenge in the guise Lessing also refused to comply with Carter's request.

The bike section consisted of six laps of an awe-inspiring circuit that only Sydney could offer in the middle of their capital city, and the thoughts now were about as far away from Manchester as they could possibly be. The course rose up from the waterfront, up through the botanical gardens, past the New South Wales art gallery and St Mark's Cathedral, before plunging beside the skyscrapers of the financial district back to the start-finish area where it crossed a carpeted section of the course that slowed the riders considerably in contrast to the sheer, smooth black tarmac that offered an almost perfect surface on the rest of the circuit.

At the end of the first circuit Walton attacked hard but was eventually tracked down by the main group who were unwilling to let anyone get too far out of sight, then the smaller chasing groups eventually caught the main pack and the whole race came together. As small half hearted breakaways continued reign, it seemed that the only rider willing to be aggressive enough to go with them was Walton who knew if he was to have a chance at the title it would mean he would have to lead off the bike, whilst Lessing maintained his position near the front of the pack in an attempt to both maintain the pace and to neutralise any attempted breaks that would offer him any concern.

On the penultimate lap Olivier Marceau, the reigning World Champion, attacked hard in what was to be the last attempt to break away on the bike but was followed by only one other rider in the guise of South African born Conrad Stoltz, with the unfortunate Walton too spent to be able to respond for what would have been his umpteenth attack. At this point no one in the main bunch seemed willing to commit to the chase and so for the first time in the race a break away succeeded as Marceau and Stoltz led the field by nearly sixty seconds as they entered and rapidly exited the second transition.

For the first lap so the shape of the race remained, with Marceau and Stoltz holding on to their lead resolutely, but some challenges from the faster runners in the pack were sure to emerge and as the final lap evolved and the pace quickened those who had done too much too soon started to drift to the back.

With the race far from over the pursuing pack chased the tails of the leading duo with the crowd expecting Lessing to lead the charge, but the long rangy figure of Lessing was not the runner who would mount the challenge and instead it was left to the German, Stephan Vuckovic to catch and pass the early leaders, in the first section of the second and final lap. As the shaven-headed German rounded the leaders, so the slim Canadian figure of Simon Whitfield came onto his shoulder, whilst much to the horror of the British supporters, there continued to be there was no sight of Lessing, who following his work on the bike could not find the legs to put in a challenge, a point that he reiterated when he and admitted later that he had found he had, "nothing left for the run."

So it was that instead of Lessing sprinting across the line with the Union Jack on his chest and arms held high, It was the Canadian Simon Whitfield, a renowned sprinter, who kicked on the final descent past Government House to overtake Vuckovic as they entered the short finishing straight to claim an historic Olympic victory whilst Vuckovic just held off Jan Rehula of the Czech Republic who took third.

As Lessing crossed the line in ninth place exactly a minute down on the winner, the British public sighed for the would-be hero, who just couldn't achieve what so many had expected of him on the day, only to be roused again when four seconds behind Lessing, in 10th place, came his team mate, Tim Don, the 1998 World Youth Champion who having run a thirty one minute, fifty seven second final ten kilometers had outperformed what many had expected of him, leaving many to consider that perhaps in Athens it would be Don that the British public would be looking to, to bring home the medals.

When Lessing crossed the finish line, he had stopped dead, with the backdrop of Sydney's Opera House and Sydney Harbour Bridge, he bowed his head slowly and retched. Struggling to sit down just past the finish line he poured a bottle of ice water, over his burning thighs looking despondently at the ground. Whilst all eyes were on Whitfield, who was understandably celebrating winning what was unquestionably the most widely publicised triathlon ever held, Lessing sat in a trance.

He had finished in ninth place, sixty seconds behind the winner, with seven other competitors between them who he had proven he could beat, time and time again. This was not at all what he, or the British spectators had been led to expect. After eleven years as a triathlete and with four Olympic distance World Championships behind him, Lessing tried hard not to show the disappointment he was feeling at finishing ninth in the most prestigious triathlon race he had ever taken part in, a race that had redefined the event's standing in the world of sport.

A short while after the race, as Lessing began to recover his composure he began to analyse the experience, and with an assured and detached clarity, and perhaps a shade of resentment in his tone Lessing complained that he had been a marked man throughout the race. "People are always focusing their race around what I'm doing, and if I don't do anything then nobody else does." Whilst that was undoubtedly the case Lessing had known it would be like that from day one and had been a marked man for most of his professional career yet he had remained at the top of the sport for some years. This time however it was just not to be.

As Lessing had worked at the front of the bike keeping the pace high, attempting to prevent the breakaways, others had sat in and let the hard work go on ahead of them in an attempt to save their legs for the run. Whilst this was a risky strategy with the danger of missing the break if it goes, on this occasion it had worked for a number of the other athletes. Lessing was unfamiliarly critical of some of those who had finished in front of him. "It's very easy just to sit at the back of the pack," he said. "The guys who did well, we never saw in front." But the Olympics was always going to be a different tactical race to qualifying events where a change in position from ninth to tenth made a difference to the points achieved.

In the Olympics places meant nothing with the exception of podium places and so many of the contenders had nothing to lose and gave it their all when it was least expected. It appeared Lessing had simply made a tactical choice that had not worked out on the day. Lessing outlined that his tactics had been, "just a question of trying to play it carefully." In the end it had been the risk takers who had prevailed. "Maybe in 2004 the pressure will be off and I can be one of those guys who can take a risk." Lessing said.

In contrast Tim Don's delight in the day, in the crowd, in the setting, and in his own performance made a poignant contrast with Lessing's measured dejection. "I was coming here hoping for a top ten place," Don said, "but I wasn't expecting it. In triathlon you can't come to a race expecting something. That would be arrogant. I just saw top ten as a realistic goal." Don had been trained to race in negative splits, i.e. to run the last kilometer quicker than he runs the first one, and later Steve Freestone confirmed the success of yet another of the boys that had come up through the Thames Turbo Club. "I think he was the only athlete in Sydney to negative split the 10k run, doing the last 5k quicker than the first 5k which is what he was asked to do by his coach Graham Fletcher, you can't ask more than that."

Whilst Don was pleased about his own performance, he was also the first to offer his support for Lessing. "I'm only twenty two and most of the guys are twenty seven or twenty eight. It's my first Olympics and I hope I've got two more ahead of me, but don't write Simon off, this is only one race and you don't always get what you deserve. Given the amount of pressure on him, he handles it so well." Johns alternatively had not handled it so well when the affects of the cold he had caught only a few days later led him to pull up in the middle of the race, upon realizing all his efforts were in vain.

Whilst the result of the triathlon could not help but be a disappointment to both the British squad and the British public, it was soon to be forgotten amongst all the other events that were to take place over the next couple of weeks and if Lessing had failed to do the expected, then track cyclist, Jason Queally managed to do the opposite and stole the thunder from what was considered by many to be an unsuccessful triathlon outing.

Born in Great Heywood near Stafford, Queally who now lived in Preston had once made his own foray into the world of triathlon but had been drawn to track racing after an induction course at Manchester Velodrome. In Sydney, he delivered Britain's first cycling gold since Chris Boardman in 1992, defying the odds in a manner to which the cycling press had become accustomed with Queally whose rise to the top had been truly meteoric.

Even Queally couldn't believe his own success. "I came here thinking of a potential medal maybe a bronze, but it all depends on what happens on the day and something strange happened."

Having only started racing bikes seriously in 1995, at the age of twenty five, twelve months after his first 1km time trial, he found himself included in the National squad's training programme. Now five year later he was Britain's first gold medallist of the Sydney Olympics. It hadn't been all smooth riding for Queally though and following his early successes he came close to not only ending his cycling career but also his life, when whilst leading a race at Meadowbank in Edinburgh he crashed at a speed in excess of forty miles per hour. The Meadowbank track was not as good as it could be and some of the wooden boards at the track were rotten which resulted in two giant splinters over eighteen inches long and one inch thick to rearing up from the track surface and lodging in his back extremely close to his chest cavity. The wounds which required seventy stitches and were so close to penetrating his chest cavity that he had been informed by doctors that the accident could have been fatal. But despite almost dying in the accident, Queally's resolve was unperturbed and he had now succeeded in giving Great Britain their first gold medal in his first Olympic Games and in so doing had stolen triathlon's thunder.

With the cycling success still fresh in the public's mind, there was more success to come from the other British squads for some of the other minority sports and if cycling had stolen triathlon's thunder then it was rowing that surely stole its anticipated lightning as Steve Redgrave went on to win his fifth gold medal in five Olympic Games in what was described by one journalist as "the greatest six-and-a-bit minutes of sport any of us will ever see." The British coxless four came home in a finish that stretched the nerves of the spectators to breaking point. With 1500 metres to go it seemed that the Brits had it in the bag, but as the coxless four consisting of Redgrave, Mathew Pinsent, James Cracknell and Tim Foster all decked out in red, white and blue looked set to coast home, a finishing flourish from the Italians, resulted in a finish of quite appalling tension, as the British crew made it home by a mere 0.38 seconds and thirty eight year old Redgrave was hailed a the new British hero a man of stern deeds and a trait of character that was the prerequisite of sporting champions. Determination, intensity, and the will to win.

Having won his fifth gold Redgrave looked enigmatic almost embarrassed by all he fuss being made, his almost mythical silences, which were as well known to the press along with his generously understated reflection of his achievements gave him a likable British aura. Whether it was his nature, unreadable and unknowable or whether it was a result of the training and the intensive pressures that had been inflicted upon him by the British public and the British media,

Redgrave seemed almost under-joyed by his achievement and almost struggling to hold back a smile was the nearest to letting his feelings show. Redgrave himself had once said that sometimes things got robotic. "Passion and flair get drained out of you with training." Whatever the reason tiredness or his nature, Great Britain had its hero, and it couldn't have had one that was more British.... Other than perhaps Spencer Smith one triathlete supporter bemoaned, stating that if Smith had been there, perhaps Britain would have had another hero.

But back in the world of Ironman triathlon Smith had little time for watching the Olympics, he instead was focusing on his preparation for Hawaii. Smith had returned to the UK for a short while prior to Hawaii and as usual had popped into the Sigma shop for a chat and a coffee. Whilst in there, there was much discussion about the Olympics and in particular Tim Don's "pose" method of running. The American triathlon federation, USAT, had taken on board the pose method of running around 1997, so all of the US athletes were running this pose method based around stride frequency rather than stride length and it was the major topic of conversation among many coaches in both triathlon and running circles.

"I had just done a coaching weekend with Graham (Fletcher) and Nick (Romanov) with a group of Sigma juniors," recounted Freestone, "and Spencer just overheard as we were talking in the shop, and asked us, what's that all about then?" Freestone explained briefly what the new method entailed and outlined its purported benefits. Spencer's response was typically Spencer.... "What a lot of old bollocks that is." Freestone laughed as he recounted the story, "You just run don't ya!" Spencer had said. "You just get off your bike and you run as fast as you can! He said I agree with all the heart rate stuff, and all that he said but apart from that you just run don't ya!" Freestone couldn't help but love the simplicity of Smith's approach, a blood and guts runner who could race on pure adrenalin and determination. Spencer was just from the old school, just hard and fast, and that remained his method of training as he prepared for October 10th.

As Smith continued to prepare for Hawaii so did USAT. The high profile loss of face in the Smith case had forced them to review their drugs procedure and in mid October 2000 it was confirmed by Steve Locke that an independent drug-testing agency would be taking over responsibility for all drug testing of athletes for the United States Olympic Committee and for USA Triathlon. "This is a very significant step forward in the fight against drugs, since in the past the national governing bodies have had to adjudicate tests that they conducted and the results have been expensive, controversial and fostered mistrust," Locke had said of the move. Either way Locke believed that this new procedure would eliminate the appearance of a conflict of interest, and went on to confirm that the new testing agency would debut at Hawaii and the athletes would be informed of the new testing protocol.

One of the major differences with the new protocols was that once both A and B samples were found positive by the independent lab, the results would be made public during the appeals process. In the recent past, American track and field and triathlon officials had been criticized for withholding announcement of results until all appeals had been concluded. Given the no smoke without fire argument it would appear that now athletes had even more to fear from positive tests even if they were innocent, but the IOC Vice President Dick Pound had ridiculed the United States sports drug policy, pointing out that charges against murderers were made public and trials with accusations and defenses given equal exposure. Whilst the USOC sided with Pound, whether that was out of belief that the policy was right or whether it was out of not wanting to go against the IOC was open to debate but given the problems that Smith had faced following the accusations aimed at him, it was undoubtedly a policy that would be to the detriment of athletes whether they were innocent or not. Nonetheless the decision stood. but for Smith his mind was on Hawaii.

14th October 2000, Ironman World Championships, Hawaii, USA

The day before the Hawaii Whittingham whose company Sigma were still providing the bike briefly visited Smith to wish him good luck. In order to avoid placing undue pressure on him, Whittingham had decided to stay in a different part of the island, but having visited him he was surprised how relaxed Smith seemed to be, noting that, if anything he felt "Melissa was more uptight about the whole thing than Spencer." For Spencer however, it was the calm before the storm.

The toughest thing about Hawaii is its length, but Smith had been through a pretty long battle of his own over the last eighteen months and had experience of the course as well. The swim all 3.8 kilometres of it is just the smallest part of a momentous journey whilst the 112-mile bike and the 26.2 mile run through the foreboding lava fields offered not respite at all.

Nonetheless Smith was clearly looking forward to it. "Having been away from it, I find I still have a passion for that race," said Smith. "There may still be demons for me there, but I am a purist about the Ironman and am still attracted to that distance because I believe there the best man and the best prepared man will win."

Smith not only loved the race for the competition that it provided, but the fact it was the same for everyone. A true run race he most of all loved the fairness about it. "I love the idea of the Ironman," he had stated previously, "I love that the age-groupers start with the pros, can race the same course, same rules. Ironically my dad never wanted me to do the Ironman because he saw how hard it was on people. He always said, 'That race is not for you.' And he never let me do it, but I always knew I would do it. I think I came to it sooner because he died. Maybe he saw me and wasn't happy about it. But no one could have kept me away forever."

Often, individuals who watch athletes racing, competing winning, can be fooled to think that they are there for the history making, or the myth making of it all, but nothing could be further from the truth for Smith. for him, the myth and the history was the job of the media, the press officers, the journalists and the spectators, it's was the role of those who watched. At his second attempt, Spencer Smith was at Hawaii for precisely the same reason that he was here the first time, a desperate, wearisome, unabridged need for victory. It was almost an affliction, and just before the race when asked how he felt about the Ironman, after all that had happened, Smith stated in his usual direct manner that he didn't like all the politics of sport which he referred to as, "bullshit" but he still, "loved the Ironman." He was just there to race.

Four years earlier Smith had said of Hawaii. "I'd trade in all the World Championship and even Olympic medals for Hawaii." Well he had traded in a lot since his last appearance. He had lost his chance to race at the Olympics. He had been stopped from racing at the Worlds, he had lost eighteen months of his career, which is a long time for an athlete, and all for Hawaii. Along the way he had also lost his father Bill, a much more painful loss than all the races in the world, but now as he stood in front of the world's media again for the second time in his life, he had something to prove.

When the cannon sounded at seven in the morning, the sea, which had resembled a mirror in conditions that were near perfect with no swell and barely a ripple began to froth and bubble as the athletes headed out into what was going to be a very long day's racing.

Smith in his usual manner remained never far from the front but it was an unknown age grouper from south Australia by the name of Michael Pietsch who grabbed his opportunity to make a name for himself in the early part of the swim and led the pack round the boat that signaled the halfway point, but as is often the case so his swim and moment of fame as the early leader of the most prestigious triathlon race in the world was to be short lived.

By the time the swim had made its way towards the exit the usual suspects had started to emerge at the head of the field with the exception to the rule a forty four year old American age grouper by the name of John Weston who was the first to exit the water in 49:44 with American professional James Bonney who had previously been so accusatory of Smith, exiting a close second in 49:51. As the pro field started to exit thick and fast, it was the Russian contender Alec Rukosuev who emerged in third spot, whilst brothers Tony and Tim DeBoom left the water almost side by side with Ralf Eggert along for company some forty seconds later. Next out of the water was Christophe Mauch in a time of 51:40 with Yves Cordier and Smith on his tail in 50:47 and 50:48 respectively, less than a minute behind the soon to be overtaken leaders.

By the time transition was over which had seen Smith enter and then exit T1 in just under one minute, the chase was already on for the lead while Lothar Leder, then Peter Reid, then Norman Stadler materialized from the Kona surf in unison a minute further down on Smith to take up the chase. As is often the case the placings when leaving the swim mean for nothing when it comes to the overall race and by mile ten into the bike leg it was Cordier, leading the field with, Eggert and the unfortunate Rukosuev who had already received a time penalty for a bike infringement who were leading from Peter Reid and Christoph Mauch all with a mere thirty seconds separating them.

Smith who despite a good start on the swim was not having a great start to his bike section and had drifted back slightly down the field whilst in the meantime Peter Sandvang who had exited the water just a few seconds behind Smith had achieved just the opposite and soon found himself moving up the field to take up the challenge in the top three. But it was to be a day of changes and despite the somewhat slower start to the bike than Smith may have wanted, in the end he would fare better than both Legh, Ruukosuev and Cordier who would all eventually pull out of the race.

With the tempo on the bike set early, the conditions looked to be in their favour for some good times, but suddenly from nowhere the winds started to pick up building up to twenty five miles per hour gusts by the time the riders hit mile twenty and by the time they hit the turnaround on the Queen K, thirty mile per hour gusts of wind were being reported with the addition of rain thrown in just for good measure. With the conditions undoubtedly suited to the stronger riders, it was not surprising that by that point in the race it was Norman Stadler who was leading the men's race by three minutes despite having been more than a two minutes down on Tim DeBoom when leaving the Kona surf and over a minute down on Peter Reid. But now having reached the turnaround point he was heading back into town using the tail wind to accelerate himself to speeds of over forty five mile per hour.

All the usual suspects had now come to the front with Tim DeBoom, Peter Reid, Christoph Mauch, Peter Sandvang, Ken Glah and Smith all determined to not let the conditions prevent them from making it to the finish. But in conditions that were referred to by one Ironman official as, "really brutal," accidents caused by athletes literally being blown from their bikes nearly put pay to both Peter Reid's and Tim DeBoom's race when after the turnaround and as they began the race back to Kona, an age-group racer headed in the other direction was blown over the road crashing between them and narrowly missing putting the duo out of the race entirely. Apart from the problems of staying upright, the race consequently encountered problems with a number of athletes suffering from dehydration as winds prevented aid-station volunteers from getting bottles of liquid into the hands of the riders as they passed.

By the time Stadler had made it to the second transition, his lead had been reduced to two minutes but he was still looking strong as the run proceeded and maintained his two minute lead through the first four miles of the run. His bike split of 4:35:15, had shown just how strong he had been on the bike with his closest bike rival being Hellriegel who had still dropped over three minutes in the discipline whilst Reid had lost over four minutes, Tim DeBoom over five minutes and Smith had forfeited over six minutes despite having completed the hundred and twelve mile bike segment at an average of 23.9 miles per hour.

So it was that with Stadler out front, Peter Reid and Tim DeBoom running side-by-side went off in pursuit, with Mauch, Hellriegel, Glah, Smith, Neidrig and Eggert all well spaced out behind, but Reid's pedigree as a runner was eventually to show through and with a pace that was visibly faster than the American's, Reid eventually wrestled the lead away from Stadler leaving him to try and hold out against Hellriegel whose early part of the run had move up to third and Tim DeBoom who was holding fourth.

Apart from Hellriegel who was clearly demonstrating he could run as well as bike, Smith was also showing excellent form on the first part of the run, moving up to fifth place with an astounding 59:19 split over the first nine miles which calculated down to an incredible average of six minutes and thirty five seconds per mile, though whether he could maintain that speed was open to question.

By the time the leaders had reached the 'Natural Energy Lab' Reid and Stadler had retained their positions, while as Tim DeBoom had regained his third spot as Hellriegel began to drop back leaving him to battle it out with Smith for fourth place before they too dropped into the heat furnace of the 'Lab.'

After about sixteen miles Peter Reid had extended his lead to nearly three minutes while DeBoom in second place had succeeded in opening a small gap on Stadler. Smith however was beginning to really suffer for the speed he had put in over the first nine miles and now and had been overtaken by the German pair of Lothar Leder and Thomas Hellriegel as well as Swiss star Christoph Mauch. Having put in an average of just over six and a half minute miles in the first nine miles of the run, Smith now saw his average pace for the next 8.2 miles fall to a still respectable 7:03 minute miles, but was looking increasingly uncomfortable with every step.

In contrast Reid looked like he was just coming into his own and DeBoom was still looking strong. So strong in fact that Reid later admitted to becoming increasingly concerned that his lead could be whittled away from him that was until the line came in sight, stating. "I've never had to dig as deep as I did today ever." But in a repeat performance of the 1998, the thirty one year old Canadian reclaimed the World Championship title once again by putting in one of the most awesome running displays in what was considered some of the most difficult race conditions since the race's inception in 1978.

Reid's run split of 2:48:11 had given him a winning time of 8:21:01 leaving DeBoom in second, just over two minutes behind in 8:23:10, whilst Stadler held onto finish third in 8:26:44 just managing to stay clear of the fast finishing Lothar Leder who actually posted the third fastest run split.

Hellriegel too seemed to have got a second wind somewhere out there on the course and whilst for some time he and Smith had been fighting it out for fourth Smith who was having an agonizing and dismal finish to his run saw Switzerland's Christoph Mauch and Hungary's Peter Kropko overtake him as he struggled to maintain a sub eight minute mile pace for the last nine miles of the run. But on crossing the line in a time of 8:43:06 to take eighth place over all, it was clear from the look on Smith's face that he had given it everything he had as was always the way with the young Londoner. Did it hurt? Of course it did! Would he be back? Of course he would! Only next time he would be fitter, faster and more experienced and he wouldn't with luck have to face all the problems he had endured over the previous two years to get there.

Smith linked up with Sigma again in 2000.

EPILOGUE

If Smith's reputation had started to wane somewhat in 2000 with his prolonged absence from the sport, then Smith would look back on the majority of the 2001 season as the lowest point in his triathlon career in terms of actual racing achievements, with little in the way of success at either Olympic distance or Ironman distance. In fact Smith would become highly disappointed in his overall outcome for the year altogether that was until his season drew to an end.

Intending initially to race in the Ironman South Africa on the 31st March, Smith instead he found himself recovering from blood poisoning in a Gordon's Bay hospital, while Lothar Leder was on his way to his fourth Ironman win in four years, decimating the previous Ironman South Africa record.

Having sustained a cut in his foot a couple of days before the event while walking barefoot on the beach to a pre-race swim, Smith thought little of it, but the night before the race, Smith started to get chills and suffer with flu-like symptoms and noticed that both his ankle and his groin area had started to swell. Under escort from the Race Director, Gerhard Mynhardt, Smith was taken to the hospital where doctors diagnosed him as suffering from blood poisoning attached an IV to insert antibiotics directly into his bloodstream. "Once there, things improved quickly and I was released Sunday morning," Smith recalled, but it was too late for him to compete and his first chance at the Ironman in 2001 was gone.

Smith was clearly disappointed at not being able to race especially having stated that he was feeling really strong prior to the race, but the inability to race was not only a loss of that specific race but also undoubtedly confused his planned schedule for the rest of the season.

Whilst many then expected Smith to attempt another Ironman race to replace the lost opportunity in South Africa, following discussions with his coach Paul Huddle, Smith surprised many by announcing that he would not be attempting to schedule another Ironman race before Hawaii and would instead concentrate on some of the shorter distance races whilst preparing for the Big Island.

Trying to juggle both Ironman and Olympic distance races and training was considered by many an impossible task and had led Smith to limit the number of Ironman distance races attempted but if South Africa was a bad omen for the season then throughout the majority of the season Smith's luck was not to significantly change despite reverting back to the shorter distance. Despite a win in the Big Rock Triathlon at Lake Perris, California, being a good second start to his season at the end of April, the competition was sparse and whilst the win brought in a few coffers Smith was not overawed by the achievement. It would however be the only first place he would manage for another three months.

A few weeks after the Big Rock, Smith faced somewhat stiffer competition at the Funchial triathlon in Portugal, which billed as an ITU points race had also brought in a few accomplished international competitors, but in achieving a somewhat surprising and exceedingly disappointing ninth, rumours started that Smith was not what he used to be, especially having been beaten by three other British athletes namely Richard Stannard, Stuart Hayes and Andy Tarry, who despite being highly talented athletes, would not have been normally considered to place above Smith. If that was to be the first warning to Smith as to the improvements being made by the British athletes and his corresponding decline in form, then, when a month later he was to lose for the first time at Windsor where a home crowd saw Andrew Johns take the honours with Smith following in his wake it was clear that things were not right for him even racing at a national level let alone on the international stage.

A month later on the 23rd June an 11th place at the European Championships in the Czech Republic, seemed to verify the rumours and when on the 22nd July at the World Championships in Edmonton, Canada, Smith trudged home in 36th spot it seemed that the critics were beginning to put the final nails in the career of Smith's triathlon career coffin. In Smith's defence however, Smith did later admit that he had not known he was going to the Worlds until two weeks prior to the event claiming, "that was a bit offputting because you're not mentally prepared." It was nonetheless an uncharacteristically poor performance.

Smith however had been keen to reconfirm his goals as being the Ironman distance and appeared at least to pay little heed to the doomsayers. And if he was to regain any respect it was only a week later when Smith picked up his second win of the season in his adopted home town of Carlsbad putting on a display that saw him take the Olympic distance event comfortably from many of the competitors who nevertheless had focused on the shorter distance, and more than a minute ahead of his Ironman associates Tim DeBoom who took fifth and three minutes ahead of Christophe Legh who placed sixth, both of whom he would be meeting up with again when it came to Hawaii.

Despite the win, having tried to train for the Ironman and race Olympic distances in the mean time, Smith had now begun to realise the incompatibility of the two objectives and the results in the Olympic distance races had not been what he wanted. Now he had to see if he could perform at the Ironman distance.

6th October 2001 Ironman World Championships, Hawaii, USA

This was now his third visit to the Big Island as a competitor and whilst it was the key race of Smith's season, his failing performances and bad luck didn't bode well for his chances of a podium place, but Smith remained resolute from the outset and put in a good swim coming out with the leaders, which in his words was, "exactly to plan," but the plan was not going to run so smoothly by the end of the day despite his hopes of third time lucky.

Throughout the first half of the ride Smith and the rest of the leaders had stayed close to each other none of them wanting to lose sight of their major challengers. Unfortunately for Smith however, one of the race officials had felt that some of his shadowing was a little too close to be considered acceptable, and issued him a drafting penalty which he would have to suffer at the end of the bike discipline.

Smith clearly felt the penalty to be a little unjust in the conditions and circumstances especially as he had been the only one to receive it amongst the lead group, but made no real fuss about it at the end of his race, which was to demonstrate a time penalty to be the least of his concerns. "It wasn't a big deal. It was ridiculous really," Smith said. "A group of us were riding at similar speeds, trying to keep to ourselves and this guy singled me out. Anyway, I lost a bit of time, but caught up with the leaders again." As the ride progressed, however, just before halfway, Smith lost touch with Peter Reid, as the reigning World Champion picked up the pace, "I went through a bad spell and the legs went a bit. I lost contact with Peter at an important spot," but more problems were to come.

Smith claimed that when he got off the bike he, "felt reasonable" believing himself to be in a pretty good position holding ninth place overall, but after sitting in the sin bin for three minutes for the drafting call, Smith went from feeling reasonable to feeling miserable. Three miles into the marathon his hamstring started tightening up, with the pain eventually becoming so severe that when repeated attempts to stretch the muscle out failed, he feared that he had pulled or even torn the muscle. "I came out to run and the hamstring locked up. I stopped and the pain continued so that was it. Looking at it now, I made a judgment call at that moment. I have never had that sort of pain, so I thought it may have caused a worse injury if I had continued. I was dealing with the unknown." Aware that a torn hamstring could sideline him for months. Smith had quit.

For Smith who had planned his whole season around Hawaii it was a harsh blow. "This is the first time anything like that has happened to me," he later stated. "The whole season was built towards Hawaii, and now it's gone. It's changed the shape of the year for me, that's for sure."

With a season of misadventure and bad luck plaguing his Ironman attempts the mental strain had started to show on him and Smith admitted that at one point he had contemplated abandoning his Ironman dreams and considered a return to the Olympic distance where he had dominated for so long, with the option to go in search of Olympic gold for 2004 in Athens if things didn't go well. But with the discovery within the week that his injury from Hawaii was not as serious as he first believed Smith was determined to not dwell on the emotional downside of not performing to the high standards that he had set himself over the Ironman distance.

The question however was what would he do now? The answer was in truth that he would have to race again and soon if he was to recoup anything from what had been a disastrous season. Recognising that fact, Smith almost immediately confirmed that he would race again if the hamstring recovered in time and with the only major Ironman left on the calendar being the Florida event scheduled for November 10th only a matter of a few weeks away, it was clear that this would have to be the new target.

With Florida the new season goal, Smith knew that a place on the podium would not be enough to either silence his doubters or meet his own high expectations and he would have to hit the bullseye if he was to achieve what he felt he had to, and so he added to the already immense pressure on himself by making it clear that he had to win this one, not only from a professional level and a personal one but also for those that had supported him over the bad times too. "I need a win in Ironman," he stated, continuing. "I so badly want to do something for all the people who've helped me, give them something to repay the faith they've shown in me all along."

Smith admitted that he was due a break from racing, but countered that admission by stating that he was so fired up now that he was determined to make amends for the season that had appeared to beat him. "I want to get something tangible back for all the training and hardship," he had said. "I know I have good form and the legs are fine for a win."

10th November 2001 Ironman, Florida, USA.

More than a month after Hawaii, Smith still didn't know why the hamstring tightened up. "It's a mystery," he had said, but now Panama City Beach, Florida was giving Smith his third chance at an Ironman title in 2001 with the hope of no more mysteries or surprises putting pay to his endeavors. A relatively new Ironman option with 2001 being only the third year in which it was staged, the Ironman Florida, came just five weeks after Hawaii and offered those who like Smith had not made their stamp on the triathlon world that season a chance to redeem themselves with the last Ironman of the season.

The event was clearly no pushover and had been fast gaining a reputation as the quality of the field improved and so did the racing. Apart from the last chance to make up for what Smith considered to be a poor season overall the $50,000 prize purse with a guaranteed $10,000 prize for first place would also mean that Smith could recoup some of the financial losses that are inherent to an athlete who has under performed on the circuit.

The 2.4 mile swim course in the Gulf of Mexico has a personality all of its own that was known to change quickly from a mirror glass flat and serene environment to a harsh curling mass waves that whilst if not impossible to break through then at least had the ability to sap the energy of even the most capable swimmer. On the morning of the race however the water remained exceedingly calm much to the relief of the 1,850 competitors.

With the swim starting on the beach behind the Boardwalk Beach Resort the first part of the race went pretty much as many had expected with Tony DeBoom, Alec Rukosuev and Smith leading the pack out as they dolphined their way through the Gulf waters. The swim took the unusual format of a two loop circuit which at the end of the first loop, saw the athletes run onto the beach before having to dive back into the water and follow the same course for the second loop, and it was DeBoom who took the lead on the first lap completing the first loop and running up the beach, a matter of yards ahead of Smith and Rukosuev. His early exertions however would eventually see him fall back behind the two chasers by the end of the second loop and drop in with the chasing group.

As the leaders exited the water for the second time it was evident that the course record of 48:33 set by Californian Mike Schaffer, in 1999 who had just piped Wolfgang Dittrich to the swim title wasn't under threat. However, Rukosuev, had put in a good time holding the top spot in 49:23, with Smith a mere three seconds down in 49:26. DeBoom's swim however had gone a little against what was expected of the well respected American when he uncharacteristically faltered over the second lap and not only managed to lose his initial lead but also dropped more than a minute off the leaders, posting a time of 50:38. Whether the run up and down the beach between loops had affected DeBoom was hard to tell, but on heading out to the transition, neither Smith nor Rukosuev were looking back. Olivier Bernhard's 55-minute swim left him with a lot to do, but the two time Swiss Ironman Champion's uncompromising and formidable abilities on the bike meant that it was clear that it wouldn't be long before he was forcing himself through the field.

Once through the swim, the competitors ran across the beach and into the transition area, which was located in the parking lot of the Boardwalk Beach Resort. And with Smith initiating his characteristic quickfire change, he headed off on the 112 mile one-loop bike course which after heading through the main strip and a number of typically Floridian resorts then headed north through some very desolate and barren Florida countryside. Smith was already starting to race the way he had always loved to, that was from the front, and on a course that some felt suited his racing style, he was apparently keen to build up a lead from the moment he had left T2.

The bike course had been one of the major topics of conversation in the build up to the race with the consensus by many that the deadpan flat one loop circuit would make the ride difficult irrespective of whether their was a wind or not. Smith, himself had stated that the lack of incline or decline meant that there would be no chance to take a break on a downhill, or adjust the riding positions on an uphill section which meant the riders would remain in the same position throughout the bike discipline which they would have to endure for somewhere in the region of four and a half hours. Whilst some had felt that the flatness of the course would make it difficult for anyone to make a break from the rest of the field during the bike section, Smith was clearly confident that on a course as flat, and fast, as this one, the ability to turn over a big gear and maintain a high bottom-end speed could be the deciding factor on who was able to make the break on the bike. And Smith just loved the thought of being able to hammer away on the flat.

Sure to the belief that if anyone was going to find a way to pull clear on this pretty much flat bike course, it was going to be him, Smith struck out early literally dominating the first half of the bike, so much so that by the halfway point he had already established a five minute lead over Tony DeBoom, who himself remained two minutes ahead of a chase group of five which included Rukosuev, Olivier Bernhard, Dave Harju of Canada, Belgium's Marino Van Hoenacker, and Eric Burgan.

Whilst Smith was looking strong, he was undoubtedly aware that both Alec Rukosuev and Olivier Bernhard had the potential to put in a more than creditable run, which could knock him back if the run didn't go to plan. Keen not to give up any of the time gained, Smith continued to push even harder during the second half of the bike, eventually stretching the gap even wider, so that by the time there was little more than fifteen miles of the ride left he was leading DeBoom who remained his closest challenger, by six minutes.

DeBoom by this point was however looking extremely tired having tried desperately to maintain a pace that would keep him in touch with Smith and was now himself only just hanging on to a slim thirty second lead over Bernhard and Harju who had pulled away from Rukosuev, Burgan, Van Hoenacker

As Smith headed into the transition area he looked to still be in good shape despite having covered the 2.4 miles of swimming and 112-miles of biking in five hours and twenty eight minutes, and finished the bike in four hours thirty six minutes and twenty eight seconds which had seen him hold an average of 24.31 miles per hour. But whilst Smith was surging so DeBoom had been suffering which had seen him given way to Bernhard and Harju who were now riding in each others shadow.

Once a again Smith put in a rapid transition, and literally sprinted out on the run course, clearly desperate to not let the chasers take any time out of him and determined to start the run in the same way he had finished the ride. At top speed.

Much like the bike course, the run course was also flat and fast starting with a mile along the beachfront before winding its way through a series of residential neighborhoods and whilst the term fast had been used to describe it, the term had undoubtedly been used in a relative sense, Smith however appeared to have taken the description in a literal sense, a point manifestly demonstrated when his first mile was timed at under just six minutes. Smith had previously admitted to going off too fast in Hawaii 2000 and there was undoubtedly a concern that at sub six minute mile pace, he once again was in danger of blowing up later on in the run if he did too much too soon, but he seemed undeterred.

Whilst one of the great aspects of the first part of the run on the Florida course was that the route taken meant that the athletes enjoyed almost non-stop support as it went through a well populated residential area where the locals mass outside their houses to support them, the danger of getting carried away with the atmosphere meant any enthusiasm had to be tempered with conscious consideration to the physiological changes taking place in the body, but Smith aparently remained unconcerned. So much so that by the time Bernhard and Harju had got through transition Smith was more than a mile down the road and they were more than seven minutes behind him!

If the first half of the day's bike ride had been the Spencer Smith show then the first part of the run, that saw Smith averaging a blazing 5:52 per mile through the first six miles, meant the run show clearly remained his too. The out-and-back, two-loop, run course which was situated in St. Andrew's State Park was a picturesque setting but Smith was not there to sightsee and despite the fact that Bernhard and the newly recovered DeBoom who had re-overtaken Harju early into the third discipline were running well, they were not even managing to hold the gap.

Whilst Smith remained out in front in what appeared to be an unassailable lead having completed the first 13.1 miles in 1:19:07

which had seen him average 6:02 minute miles, it looked clear that the minor podium placings would be left to a fight between DeBoom and Bernhard a view that became increasingly evident when at the halfway point only thirty seconds separated them whilst Harju was a fully eighteen minutes back with Eric Burgan another minute behind. Whilst DeBoom was holding a thirty second lead over Bernhard by the start of the second 13.1 mile loop he was undoubtedly conscious of the heat of the Florida sun having suffered, dehydration and nutrition problems in Hawaii only a few weeks previous which had forced him out of the race 16-miles into the run and was determined to make amends and not make the same mistakes.

But it would be Smith who would make the biggest amends to what had been a disappointing season when with a smile as wide as the Thames, the young Londoner secured his first-ever Ironman victory, crossing the line arms aloft with a look of both relief and ecstasy.

Smith had not only won it but he had won it in style having raced from the front all day but in the process shattering Lothar Leder's 1999 course record by four minutes and fifty seven seconds whilst beating the second place finisher by a six-and-a-half minute margin.

Smith was clearly delighted, not just with the win but also with the way he had won it. He had taken control of the race by five miles into the bike when he passed last year's runner-up Alec Rukosuev for the lead and had never looked back. Smith rode a race-best 4:36:28 on a grindingly tough windy day, then closed the deal with a an awesome display of running posting a 2:52:07 on the marathon that was second best only to DeBoom's 2:50:26 record breaking final discipline.

How did he feel about the long awaited Ironman win, after all the ups and downs, the irretrievable losses, the accusations and battles, after all the transitions that had happened in his life that had seen him reach the peaks and suffer the troughs, there was only one thing he had to say and it said more about him than any cliché or prepared speech could ever say. "My dad would have loved it today." He said thoughtfully. "It's the way he saw me race....from the front. He loved that, you know."

END

THE FUTURE

In 2002, Smith planned to limit the number of non Ironman races he would enter, but of course Hawaii was already written in and underlined. "My passion is to win Hawaii."

"I guess it's all experience," Smith had said after one of the lower periods in the season. "They say that's what wins races like Hawaii, and maybe they're right. I'll be back." There seemed little doubt that he would be.

"Everyone likes victories."
Spencer Smith

The Author

Mark Shaw was born in London England in 1964. Following a period managing the Metropolitan Club gymnasium in London he moved to Nottingham where he completed a degree in Sport Science at Nottingham Trent University before moving to Australia to work with Channel Ten on a number of televised cycle races and to race his bike in the middle of nowhere. On returning to the UK he worked for Sport for Television both as an employee and a consultant, staging major professional cycling and athletics events throughout Britain and Ireland including the Nissan International Classic, the Kellogg's Tour of Britain, the Scottish Provident League and the Tour de France, and later went on to set up his own sports consultancy company where he moved into promotion of other televised sports including International and National athletics, swimming, basketball and volleyball. He now resides in Nottingham with his girlfriend Sibyl where he runs Transition Sport, his own sports promotions company, and is now primarily involved in the promotion of triathlon events. He has also written a number of academic books and lectures in marketing and sports marketing.

Bill Black continues to train both elite and age group
athletes both in the UK and throughout the
rest of the world.

Athletes interested in contacting Bill Black with
respect to training programmes can contact Bill Black
through Transition Sport by either e-mail or by using the
Transition Sport Website.

www.transitionsport.com
transitionsport@totalise.co.uk

Greek Gods and Triathlon Mortals
...a quick visit to the Olympics
A novel by Mark Shaw

Coupling Greek mythology with the trials and tribulations of an array of would be Olympians, 'Greek Gods and Triathlon Mortals' tracks the passage of those athletes from a spectrum of backgrounds and a multitude of culturally and geographically diverse beginnings to the gates of the 2004 Olympics, where untold riches and fame beckon with the successful pursuit of the gold medal.

Irreverently witty and uncompromisingly, if somewhat confusingly multiculturally jingoistic, the story ties together the heritage of the Olympics, the culture of the participating countries and the idiosyncrasies of those individuals that would be foolhardy enough to spend their entire lives devoted to the hope that they could swim, bike and run faster than everybody else on one summer day in the sweltering heat of Athens 2004.

An unforgiving and telling look at what makes us what we are, not only as athletes but also as British, American, French, German, Japanese, Chinese and Irish citizens, to name but a few. The book satirically caricatures the outlooks and actions of the main players within a framework of their past as well as their countries' histories.

Following the tracks made by the athletes in their quest, the story tells of the unwanted and often unwelcome intrusions by the Greek gods, ranging from Zeus to Adonis in the everyday plans and actions of the competitors who remain unaware of the intrusions of their overseers. As if getting to the Olympics wasn't hard enough without having to endure the wrath and the favour of Gods who themselves had chosen their favourites, and would stop at nothing to see them win.

A mixture of myth, history and individual achievement. Let the battle commence!

Photographs

Pages 8, 34, 64, 112, 160, 190, 236, 276, 318
courtesy of Bill Black

Page 276
Hawaii 1998courtesy of Delly Carr
PHOTOSHOOT

Page 306, 316
courtesy of Sigma Sport